Other Books and Series by Jeff Bowen

Applications for Enrollment of Chickasaw Newborn Act of 1905
Volumes I thru VII

Cherokee Intermarried White 1906 Volume I thru X

Visit our website at **www.nativestudy.com** to learn more about these
and other books and series by Jeff Bowen

I0222613

APPLICATIONS FOR ENROLLMENT OF CREEK NEWBORN ACT OF 1905

VOLUME I

TRANSCRIBED BY
JEFF BOWEN

NATIVE STUDY
Gallipolis, Ohio
USA

Other Books and Series by Jeff Bowen

1901-1907 Native American Census Seneca, Eastern Shawnee, Miami, Modoc, Ottawa, Peoria, Quapaw, and Wyandotte Indians (Under Seneca School, Indian Territory)

1932 Census of The Standing Rock Sioux Reservation with Births And Deaths 1924-1932

Census of The Blackfeet, Montana, 1897- 1901 Expanded Edition

Eastern Cherokee by Blood, 1906-1910, Volumes I thru XIII

Choctaw of Mississippi Indian Census 1929-1932 with Births and Deaths 1924-1931   Volume I
Choctaw of Mississippi Indian Census 1933, 1934 & 1937, Supplemental Rolls to 1934 & 1935 with Births and Deaths 1932-1938, and Marriages 1936-1938 Volume II

Eastern Cherokee Census Cherokee, North Carolina 1930-1939
Census 1930-1931 with Births And Deaths 1924-1931 Taken By Agent L. W. Page Volume I
Eastern Cherokee Census Cherokee, North Carolina 1930-1939
Census 1932-1933 with Births And Deaths 1930-1932 Taken By Agent R. L. Spalsbury   Volume II
Eastern Cherokee Census Cherokee, North Carolina 1930-1939
Census 1934-1937 with Births and Deaths 1925-1938 and Marriages 1936 & 1938 Taken by Agents R. L. Spalsbury And Harold W. Foght Volume III

Seminole of Florida Indian Census, 1930-1940 with Birth and Death Records, 1930-1938

Texas Cherokees 1820-1839 A Document For Litigation 1921

Choctaw By Blood Enrollment Cards 1898-1914 Volumes I thru XVII

Starr Roll 1894   (Cherokee Payment Rolls) Districts: Canadian, Cooweescoowee, and Delaware Volume One
Starr Roll 1894 (Cherokee Payment Rolls) Districts: Flint, Going Snake, and Illinois   Volume Two
Starr Roll 1894 (Cherokee Payment Rolls) Districts: Saline, Sequoyah, and Tahlequah; Including Orphan Roll   Volume Three

Cherokee Intruder Cases Dockets of Hearings 1901-1909 Volumes I & II

Indian Wills, 1911-1921 Records of the Bureau of Indian Affairs
Books One thru Seven;
Native American Wills & Probate Records 1911-1921

Other Books and Series by Jeff Bowen

Turtle Mountain Reservation Chippewa Indians 1932 Census with Births & Deaths, 1924-1932

Chickasaw By Blood Enrollment Cards 1898-1914 Volume I thru V

Cherokee Descendants East An Index to the Guion Miller Applications Volume I
Cherokee Descendants West An Index to the Guion Miller Applications Volume II (A-M)
Cherokee Descendants West An Index to the Guion Miller Applications Volume III (N-Z)

Applications for Enrollment of Seminole Newborn Freedmen, Act of 1905

Eastern Cherokee Census, Cherokee, North Carolina, 1915-1922, Taken by Agent James E. Henderson　　　　*Volume I (1915-1916)*
　　　　　　　　　　　　Volume II (1917-1918)
　　　　　　　　　　　　Volume III (1919-1920)
　　　　　　　　　　　　Volume IV (1921-1922)

Complete Delaware Roll of 1898

Eastern Cherokee Census, Cherokee, North Carolina, 1923-1929, Taken by Agent James E. Henderson　　　　*Volume I (1923-1924)*
　　　　　　　　　　　　Volume II (1925-1926)
　　　　　　　　　　　　Volume III (1927-1929)

Applications for Enrollment of Seminole Newborn Act of 1905 Volumes I & II

North Carolina Eastern Cherokee Indian Census 1898-1899, 1904, 1906, 1909-1912, 1914 Revised and Expanded Edition

1932 Hopi and Navajo Native American Census with Birth & Death Rolls (1925-1931) Volume 1 - Hopi
1932 Hopi and Navajo Native American Census with Birth & Death Rolls (1930-1932) Volume 2 - Navajo

Western Navajo Reservation Navajo, Hopi and Paiute 1933 Census with Birth & Death Rolls 1925-1933

Cherokee Citizenship Commission Dockets 1880-1884 and 1887-1889 Volumes I thru V

Originally published:
Baltimore, Maryland
2011

Reprinted by:

Native Study LLC
Gallipolis, OH
www.nativestudy.com
2020

Library of Congress Control Number: 2020917992

ISBN: 978-1-64968-080-8

Made in the United States of America.

DEPARTMENT OF THE INTERIOR,
COMMISSIONER TO THE FIVE CIVILIZED TRIBES.

REFER IN REPLY TO THE FOLLOWING:
N.C. -1.

Muskogee, Indian Territory, **August 3, 1905.**

Jesse McDermott,
Muskogee, Indian Territory.

Dear Sir:

You are hereby advised that on **July 28, 1905**, the Secretary of the Interior approved the enrollment of your minor child, **Helen McDermott**, as a citizen by blood of the **Creek** Nation, and that the name of said child appears upon the roll of new born citizens of the **Creek** Nation as Number **1**.

The child is now entitled to an allotment, and application therefor should be made without delay at the Land Office for the Nation in which the prospective allotment is located.

An entire allotment for said child must be selected at the time of the original application.

Respectively,

Commissioner.

BIRTH AFFIDAVIT.

DEPARTMENT OF THE INTERIOR,
COMMISSION TO THE FIVE CIVILIZED TRIBES.

IN RE APPLICATION FOR ENROLLMENT, as a citizen of the Creek Nation, of Helen McDermott, born on the 22 day of June, 1904

Name of Father: Jesse McDermott   a citizen of the   Creek   Nation.
Name of Mother: Allie   "   a citizen of the   Creek U.S. Nation.

Postoffice   Muskogee

AFFIDAVIT OF MOTHER.

UNITED STATES OF AMERICA, Indian Territory, ⎫
       Western   DISTRICT. ⎰   Child Present.

I, Allie McDermott, on oath state that I am 25 years of age and a citizen by -----, of the U.S. Nation, that I am the lawful wife of Jesse McDermott , who is a citizen, by blood of the Creek Nation; that a female child was born to me on 22 day of June, 1904; that said child has been named Helen McDermott, and is now living.

Allie McDermott

Witnesses To Mark:

{

Subscribed and sworn to before me this 12 day of April, 1905.

(Seal)   Edw C Griesel
                            Notary Public.

BIRTH AFFIDAVIT.

DEPARTMENT OF THE INTERIOR,
COMMISSION TO THE FIVE CIVILIZED TRIBES.

IN RE APPLICATION FOR ENROLLMENT, as a citizen of the Creek Nation, of Helen McDermott, born on the 22 day of June, 1904

Name of Father:	Jesse McDermott	a citizen of the Creek	Nation.
Name of Mother:	Allie "	a citizen of the U.S.	Nation.

Postoffice   Muskogee, I.T.

AFFIDAVIT OF MOTHER.

UNITED STATES OF AMERICA, Indian Territory, }
        Western   **DISTRICT.** }

I, Jesse McDermott, on oath state that I am 25 years of age and a citizen by blood, of the Creek Nation, that I am the lawful ~~wife~~ husband of Allie McDermott , who is a citizen, by ----- of the U.S. Nation; that a female child was born to ~~me~~ her on 22" day of June, 1904; that said child has been named Helen McDermott, and is now living.

                 Jesse McDermott

Witnesses To Mark:

{

Subscribed and sworn to before me this 4" day of March, 1905.

                 Edw C Griesel
                     Notary Public.

Applications for Enrollment of Creek Newborn
Act of 1905 Volume I

AFFIDAVIT OF ATTENDING PHYSICIAN OR MID-WIFE.

UNITED STATES OF AMERICA, Indian Territory, ⎱
        Western   DISTRICT. ⎰

I, J.W. Board, a physician, on oath state that I attended on Mrs. Allie McDermott, wife of Jesse McDermott on the 22" day of June, 1904; that there was born to her on said date a female child; that said child was living March 4, 1905, and is said to have been named Helen McDermott

J.W. Board

Witnesses To Mark:

{

Subscribed and sworn to before me this 28 day of March, 1905.

A.B. Allen

Com Ex   Notary Public.
June 24th 1906   (*Illegible*)

DEPARTMENT OF THE INTERIOR,
COMMISSIONER TO THE FIVE CIVILIZED TRIBES.

| REFER IN REPLY TO THE FOLLOWING: |
| N.C. -2. |

Muskogee, Indian Territory, **August 3, 1905.**

Geo. W. Stidham, Sr.
      Checotah, Indian Territory.

Dear Sir:

You are hereby advised that on **July 28. 1905**, the Secretary of the Interior approved the enrollment of your minor child, **Thomas Edward Stidham** , as a citizen by blood of the **Creek** Nation, and that the name of said child appears upon the roll of new born citizens of the **Creek** Nation as Number **2**.

The child is now entitled to an allotment, and application therefor should be made without delay at the Land Office for the Nation in which the prospective allotment is located.

An entire allotment for said child must be selected at the time of the original application.

Respectively,

Commissioner.

3

<table>
<tr><td>

DEPARTMENT OF THE INTERIOR,
COMMISSIONER TO THE FIVE CIVILIZED TRIBES.

</td><td>

REFER IN REPLY TO THE FOLLOWING:
N.C. -2.

</td></tr>
</table>

Muskogee, Indian Territory, **August 3, 1905.**

Geo. W. Stidham, Sr.,
    Checotah, Indian Territory.

Dear Sir:

You are hereby advised that on **July 28. 1905,** the Secretary of the Interior approved the enrollment of your minor child, **Cleo Stidham** , as a citizen by blood of the **Creek** Nation, and that the name of said child appears upon the roll of new born citizens of the **Creek** Nation as Number **2.**

The child is now entitled to an allotment, and application therefor should be made without delay at the Land Office for the Nation in which the prospective allotment is located.

An entire allotment for said child must be selected at the time of the original application.

Respectively,

Commissioner.

BIRTH AFFIDAVIT.

DEPARTMENT OF THE INTERIOR,
COMMISSION TO THE FIVE CIVILIZED TRIBES.

IN RE APPLICATION FOR ENROLLMENT, as a citizen of the   Creek Nation, of Thomas Edward Stidham, born on the 25 day of March , 1904

Name of Father:	**Geo W. Stidham**	a citizen of the	Creek	Nation.
Name of Mother:	**Jennie "**	a citizen of the	U.S.	Nation.

Postoffice   Checotah

AFFIDAVIT OF MOTHER.

UNITED STATES OF AMERICA, Indian Territory, ⎫
    Western   DISTRICT. ⎬

I, Geo. W. Stidham, on oath state that I am 26 years of age and a citizen by blood, of the Creek Nation, that I am the lawful ~~wife~~ hus of Jennie Stidham, who is a citizen, by ----- of the U.S. Nation; that a male child was born to me on 25 day of March, 1904; that said child has been named Thomas Edward Stidham, and is now living.

4

Geo W Stidham

Witnesses To Mark:

{

Subscribed and sworn to before me this 14 day of March, 1905.

Edw C Griesel
Notary Public.

BIRTH AFFIDAVIT.

DEPARTMENT OF THE INTERIOR,
COMMISSION TO THE FIVE CIVILIZED TRIBES.

IN RE APPLICATION FOR ENROLLMENT, as a citizen of the CREEK   Nation, of Cleo Stidham, born on the 26 day of Aug, 1902

Name of Father: **Geo W Stidham**   a citizen of the Creek   Nation.
Name of Mother: **Jennie   "**   a citizen of the   U.S.   Nation.

Postoffice   Checotah

AFFIDAVIT OF MOTHER.

UNITED STATES OF AMERICA, Indian Territory, ⎫
    WESTERN   DISTRICT. ⎰

I, Geo W Stidham, on oath state that I am 46 years of age and a citizen by blood, of the Creek Nation, that I am the lawful ~~wife~~ hus of Jennie Stidham, who is a citizen, by ----- of the U.S. Nation; that a female child was born to me on 26 day of Aug, 1902; that said child has been named Cleo Stidham, and is now living.

Geo W. Stidham

Witnesses To Mark:

{

Subscribed and sworn to before me this 14 day of March, 1905.

Edw C Griesel
Notary Public.

Applications for Enrollment of Creek Newborn
Act of 1905 Volume I

UNITED STATES OF AMERICA,)
    Indian TERRITORY,   ) SS.
    Western   District.   )

On this 13th day of March, A.D., 1905, personally appeared before me the undersigned, Charles Buford, a Notary Public, in and for the Western District of the Indian Territory, duly commissioned and acting in such, Jennie Stidham, who being by me first duly sworn, on her oath deposes and says: My name is Jennie Stidham, I am 31 years old, I am the lawful wife of George W. Stidham. My husband is a Citizen by blood of the Creek Nation, I live with my husband on his farm about 10 miles North West of Checotah, I.T. I am the mother of Thomas Edward Stidham, a son born to my husband and me on the 25th day of March, A.D., 1904.

The said child is now living with George W. Stidham and myself, his parents, at the farm of his father, 10 miles North West of Checotah, Creek Nation, Indian Territory.

Jennie Stidham

Subscribed and sworn to before me this 13th day of March, 1905.

Charles Buford
Notary Public.

My commission expires July 3rd 1906.

UNITED STATES OF AMERICA,)
    Indian TERRITORY,   ) SS.
    Western   District.   )

On this 13th day of March, A.D., 1905, personally appeared before me the undersigned, Charles Buford, a Notary Public, in and for the Western District of the Indian Territory, duly commissioned and acting in such, Jennie Stidham, who being by me first duly sworn, on her oath deposes and says: My name is Jennie Stidham, I am 31 years old, I am the lawful wife of George W. Stidham. My husband is a Citizen by blood of the Creek Nation, I live with my husband on his farm about 10 miles North West of Checotah, I.T. I am the mother of Cleo Stidham, a daughter born to my husband and me on the 26th day of August, A.D., 1902.

The said child is now living with George W. Stidham and myself, their parents, at the farm of her father, 10 miles North West of Checotah, Creek Nation, Indian Territory.

Jennie Stidham

Subscribed and sworn to before me this 13th day of March, 1905.

Charles Buford
Notary Public.

Applications for Enrollment of Creek Newborn
Act of 1905   Volume I

My commission expires July 3rd 1906.
United States of America
   Western District   ss
   Indian Territory

     T.C. Randall, being first duly sworn, on his oath deposes and says: My name is T.C. Randall, my age is 57 years, my residence is in the Town of Checotah, I.T. I am a practicing physician and surgeon. I attended Mrs. Jennie Stidham, wife of George W. Stidham, before, during and after the birth of their youngest child, this child, a boy, was born March 25th at his father's farm about 10 miles North West of Checotah, I.T. I have left a record of the birth of this child; this child has been given the name of Thomas Edward Stidham and is now living; I am well acquainted with the parents of this child and have known this child since its birth.

T.C. Randall

Subscribed and sworn to before me this 13th day of March, 1905.

Charles Buford

My commission expires July 3rd 1906.   Notary Public

United States of America
   Western District   ss
   Indian Territory

     Geo. W. McGuire, being first duly sworn on his oath deposes and says: My name is Geo. W. McGuire, I am 44 years old, I reside at Checotah, Creek Nation, Indian Territory, I am engaged in the Practice of Medicine, my profession. I am well acquainted with George W. Stidham and Jennie Stidham, his wife. George W Stidham is a citizen by blood of the Creek Nation. I attended as family physician Mrs Jennie Stidham at during and after the birth of their second youngest child, a girl, born August 26th 1902 on her father's farm about 10 miles North West of Checotah, I.T. This girl has been given the name of Cleo Stidham and is living on the date of this affidavit. I have kept a record of the date of the birth of this child and have known the child since its birth, having *(illegible illegible)* it to-day.

Geo W. McGuire

Subscribed and sworn to before me this 13th day of March 1905.

My commission expires July 3rd 1906.   Charles Buford
                                             Notary Public

DEPARTMENT OF THE INTERIOR,
COMMISSIONER TO THE FIVE CIVILIZED TRIBES.

REFER IN REPLY TO THE FOLLOWING:
N.C. 3.

Muskogee, Indian Territory, **August 3, 1905.**

Alexander L. Posey,
Muskogee, Indian Territory.

Dear Sir:

You are hereby advised that on **July 28, 1905** the Secretary of the Interior approved the enrollment of your minor child, **Wynema Torrans Posey**, as a citizen by blood of the **Creek** Nation, and that the name of said child appears upon the roll of new born citizens of the **Creek** Nation as Number **4**.

The child is now entitled to an allotment, and application therefor should be made without delay at the Land Office for the Nation in which the prospective allotment is located.

An entire allotment for said child must be selected at the time of the original application.

Respectfully,

Commissioner.

DEPARTMENT OF THE INTERIOR,
COMMISSION TO THE FIVE CIVILIZED TRIBES.
Muskogee, Ind. Terr. May 13, 1905.

In the matter of the application for the enrollment of Wynema Torrana Posey as a citizen by blood of the Creek Nation.

ALEXANDER POSEY, being duly sworn, testified as follows:

BY COMMISSION:
Q what is your name? A Alexander Posey.
Q How old are you? A Thirty-one.
Q What is your post office address? A Muskogee.
Q Are you a citizen of the Creek Nation? A Yes, sir.
Q To what town do you belong? A Tuckagee.
Q Have you a child named Wynema Torrana Posey? A Yes, sir.
Q Is that child living? A yes, sir.
Q Where is she living? A Muskogee.
Q When was the last time you saw the child? A This noon.

Q Why have you not produced the affidavit of the mid-wife in this case?   A Because I have been doing field work for the Commission and have had no opportunity to hunt the mid-wife up and have her execute an affidavit as to when my child was born.

Q What is her name?   A Mrs. Phillips, a negro woman.

Q What is her post office address?   A I do not know her present post office address but at that time she was living at Eufaula.

---oooOOOooo---

I, D.C. Skaggs, on my oath state that the above and foregoing is a full and true transcript of my stenographic notes as taken in said cause on said date.

DC Skaggs

Subscribed and sworn to before me this 13 day of May, 1905.

Edw C Griesel

Notary Public.

BIRTH AFFIDAVIT.

DEPARTMENT OF THE INTERIOR,
COMMISSION TO THE FIVE CIVILIZED TRIBES.

IN RE APPLICATION FOR ENROLLMENT, as a citizen of the Creek Nation, of Wynema Torrans Posey, born on the 6 day of February, 1902.

Name of Father: Alexander Posey   a citizen of the   Creek   Nation.
     Tuskegee Town
Name of Mother: Minnie Posey   a citizen of the United States Nation.

Postoffice Muskogee, I.T.

AFFIDAVIT OF MOTHER.

UNITED STATES OF AMERICA, Indian Territory, ⎤
                Western   DISTRICT. ⎦

I, Minnie Posey, on oath state that I am 32 years of age and a citizen by ----- , of the United States ~~Nation~~, that I am the lawful wife of Alexander Posey, who is a citizen, by blood of the Creek Nation; that a female child was born to me on 6 day of February, 1902; that said child has been named Wynema Torrans Posey, and ~~is now~~ was living March 4, 1905.

Minnie Posey

Witnesses To Mark:

{

Subscribed and sworn to before me this 13" day of May, 1905.

Drennan C Skaggs
Notary Public.

BIRTH AFFIDAVIT.

DEPARTMENT OF THE INTERIOR,
COMMISSION TO THE FIVE CIVILIZED TRIBES.

IN RE APPLICATION FOR ENROLLMENT, as a citizen of the Creek Nation, of Wynema Torrans Posey, born on the 6 day of February, 1902.

Name of Father:	Alex Posey	a citizen of the	Creek	Nation.
Name of Mother:	Minnie Posey	a citizen of the	U. S.	Nation.

Postoffice Muskogee, I.T.

AFFIDAVIT OF ATTENDING PHYSICIAN OR MID-WIFE.

UNITED STATES OF AMERICA, Indian Territory, ⎫
     Western   **DISTRICT.** ⎰

I, Adaline Philips, Midwife, on oath state that I attended on Mrs. Minnie Posey, wife of Alex Posey on the 6th day of February, 1902; that there was born to her on said date a Female child; that said child is now living and is said to have been named Wynema Torrans Posey.

Adeline Philips

Witnesses To Mark:
  { D.M. Whitaker
  { J.C. Hall

Subscribed and sworn to before me this 15th day of May, 190?.

(Name Illegible)
Notary Public.
My Commission expires Jul 10th 1906.

BIRTH AFFIDAVIT.

DEPARTMENT OF THE INTERIOR,
COMMISSION TO THE FIVE CIVILIZED TRIBES.

IN RE APPLICATION FOR ENROLLMENT, as a citizen of the Creek Nation, of Wynema Torrans Posey, born on the 6th day of February, 1902.

10

Applications for Enrollment of Creek Newborn
Act of 1905 Volume I

Name of Father: Alexander Posey   a citizen of the   Creek   Nation.
Name of Mother: Minnie Posey   a citizen of the United States Nation.

Postoffice Muskogee, Indian Territory

Father
AFFIDAVIT OF ~~MOTHER~~.

UNITED STATES OF AMERICA, Indian Territory,   ⎫
       Western   **DISTRICT.**   ⎬
                 ⎭

I, Alexander Posey, on oath state that I am 31 years of age and a citizen by blood, of the Creek Nation, that I am the lawful ~~wife~~ husband of Minnie Posey, who is a citizen, ~~by~~ of the United States Nation; that a female child was born to ~~me~~ her on 6th day of February, 1902; that said child has been named Wynema Torrans Posey, and was living March 4, 1905.

Alexander Posey

Witnesses To Mark:

{

Subscribed and sworn to before me this 13" day of March, 1905.
Drennan C. Skaggs
Notary Public.

BA 321 B

Muskogee, Indian Territory, May 15, 1905.

Roley C. McIntosh,
      Checotah, Indian Territory.
Dear Sir:

There is on file with the Commission an affidavit relative to the birth of your minor child, Cheesie McIntosh. You are advised that the Commission requires the affidavit of the midwife or physician in attendance at the birth of said child.

Where is herewith enclosed a blank form of birth affidavit, and in executing same care should be exercised to see that all blanks are properly filled, all names written in full and in the event that the person signing the affidavit is unable to write, signature by mark must be attested by two witnesses. Each affidavit must be executed before a Notary Public and the notarial seal and signature of the officer must be attached to each separate affidavit.

Respectfully,

BC.   Chairman.

Applications for Enrollment of Creek Newborn
Act of 1905   Volume I

United States of America ⎧
   Indian Territory   ⎬ ss.
   Western District   ⎩

    Rachel Thornberry, being first duly sworn on her oath deposes and says: My name is Rachel Thornberry, my age is 65, my residence is 8 miles south East of Checotah, I.T. I am by profession a midwife. I have been well acquainted with Roley C. McIntosh and Fannie McIntosh, his wife, for more than 30 years. I was present as midwife at the birth of their second youngest child, a son, born to them on the 4th day of October A.D. 1902 at their home about 4 miles south of Checotah I.T. This son was named "Sequoah" and is <u>now</u> living with his parents at their home, both Roley C. and Fannie McIntosh, the parents of this child, are citizens by blood of the Creek Nation.

Witnesses to mark.
    Cheesie McIntosh   her
Thomas McIntosh   Rachel x Thornberry
                          mark

Subscribed and sworn to before me this 13th day of March 1905.
                               Charles Buford
My commission expires July 3rd 1906.   Notary Public

BIRTH AFFIDAVIT.
DEPARTMENT OF THE INTERIOR,
COMMISSION TO THE FIVE CIVILIZED TRIBES.

    IN RE APPLICATION FOR ENROLLMENT, as a citizen of the Creek Nation, of Cheesie McIntosh, born on the 10 day of Jan, 1905

Name of Father: Roley C McIntosh   a citizen of the   Creek   Nation.
Name of Mother: Fannie   "   a citizen of the   "   Nation.

                        Postoffice Checotah

AFFIDAVIT OF ~~MOTHER~~. **Father**

UNITED STATES OF AMERICA, Indian Territory, ⎫
    Western   DISTRICT. ⎭

    I, Roley C. McIntosh, on oath state that I am 48 years of age and a citizen by blood, of the Creek Nation, that I am the lawful ~~wife~~ husband of of[sic] Fannie McIntosh, who is a citizen, by blood of the Creek Nation; that a male child was born to me on 10 day of Jan 1905; that said child has been named Cheesie McIntosh, and is now living.

Roley C McIntosh

Witnesses To Mark:

{

Subscribed and sworn to before me this 14 day of March, 1905.

Edw C Griesel
Notary Public.

BIRTH AFFIDAVIT.

DEPARTMENT OF THE INTERIOR,
COMMISSION TO THE FIVE CIVILIZED TRIBES.

IN RE APPLICATION FOR ENROLLMENT, as a citizen of the Creek Nation, of Cheesie McIntosh, born on the 10th day of January, 1905.

Name of Father: Roley C McIntosh	a citizen of the	Creek	Nation.
Name of Mother: Fannie McIntosh	a citizen of the	Creek	Nation.

Postoffice Checotah, Ind. Terr.

AFFIDAVIT OF ATTENDING PHYSICIAN OR MID-WIFE.

UNITED STATES OF AMERICA, Indian Territory, ⎫
    Western   **DISTRICT.** ⎭

I, Ella Blanche Baker, a citizen by blood of the Creek Nation, on oath state that I am the nearest neighbor of and well acquainted with Mrs. Fannie McIntosh, wife of Roley C. McIntosh: on or about the first week of the month of January 1905 there was born to her male that this child was born to her about the first week in the month of January[sic] and that said child was living March 4, 1905, and is said to have been named Cheesie McIntosh; that this same child is living at the date of this affidavit.

Ella Blanche Baker.

Witnesses To Mark:

{

Subscribed and sworn to before me this 27th day of May, 1905.

Charles Buford
Notary Public.

my commission expires July 3rd 1906.

13

Applications for Enrollment of Creek Newborn
Act of 1905   Volume I

BIRTH AFFIDAVIT.

DEPARTMENT OF THE INTERIOR,
COMMISSION TO THE FIVE CIVILIZED TRIBES.

IN RE APPLICATION FOR ENROLLMENT, as a citizen of the Creek Nation, of Cheesie McIntosh, born on the 10th day of January, 1905.

Name of Father: Roley C McIntosh	a citizen of the	Creek	Nation.
Name of Mother: Fannie McIntosh	a citizen of the	Creek	Nation.

Postoffice Checotah, Ind. Terr.

AFFIDAVIT OF ATTENDING PHYSICIAN OR MID-WIFE.

UNITED STATES OF AMERICA, Indian Territory,
Western   **DISTRICT.**

I, Alice McIntosh, wife of D.N. McIntosh, Jr. on oath state that I am well aquainted[sic] with Mrs. Fannie McIntosh, wife of Riley[sic] C. McIntosh, that I visited Mrs. Fannie McIntosh, wife of Roley C. McIntosh about three days before the birth of her last child, Cheesie McIntosh, on the 6th or 7th day of January, 1905; that there was born to her on the 10th day of January 1905 a male child; that said child was living March 4, 1905, and is said to have been named Cheesie McIntosh that about 2 days after the birth of this child I again visited Fannie McIntosh and saw the child; I know this child well and have seen it almost dailey[sic].

Alice McIntosh

Witnesses To Mark:

{

Subscribed and sworn to before me this 29th day of January, 1905.

Charles Buford
Notary Public.

my commission expires July 3rd 1906.

14

Applications for Enrollment of Creek Newborn
Act of 1905   Volume I

BIRTH AFFIDAVIT.

DEPARTMENT OF THE INTERIOR,
COMMISSION TO THE FIVE CIVILIZED TRIBES.

(child present)JMcD _____

IN RE APPLICATION FOR ENROLLMENT, as a citizen of the Creek Nation, of Cheesie McIntosh, born on the 10 day of Jan, 1905

Name of Father: Cub McIntosh	a citizen of the	Creek	Nation.
Name of Mother: Fannie "	a citizen of the	Creek	Nation.

Postoffice Checotah, I.T.

_____

AFFIDAVIT OF MOTHER.

UNITED STATES OF AMERICA, Indian Territory, ⎫
WESTERN   DISTRICT. ⎭

I, Fannie McIntosh, on oath state that I am 36 years of age and a citizen by blood, of the Creek Nation; that I am the lawful wife of Cub McIntosh, who is a citizen, by blood, of the Creek Nation; that a male child was born to me on 10" day of January, 1905, that said child has been named Cheesie McIntosh, and is now living.

Fannie McIntosh

Witnesses To Mark:

{

Subscribed and sworn to before me this 14 day of March, 1905.

Edw C. Griesel
Notary Public.

_____

BIRTH AFFIDAVIT.

DEPARTMENT OF THE INTERIOR,
COMMISSION TO THE FIVE CIVILIZED TRIBES.

_____

IN RE APPLICATION FOR ENROLLMENT, as a citizen of the Creek Nation, of Sequoah McIntosh, born on the 4 day of Oct, 1902

Name of Father: Cub McIntosh	a citizen of the	Creek	Nation.
Name of Mother: Fannie "	a citizen of the	Creek	Nation.

Postoffice Checotah, I.T.

_____

Applications for Enrollment of Creek Newborn
Act of 1905   Volume I

AFFIDAVIT OF MOTHER.

UNITED STATES OF AMERICA, Indian Territory, ⎫
    WESTERN   DISTRICT. ⎭

    I, Fannie McIntosh, on oath state that I am 36 years of age and a citizen by blood, of the Creek Nation; that I am the lawful wife of Cub McIntosh, who is a citizen, by blood, of the Creek Nation; that a male child was born to me on 4 day of Oct, 1902, that said child has been named Sequoah McIntosh, and is now living.

                                    Fannie McIntosh

Witnesses To Mark:

    Subscribed and sworn to before me this 14 day of March, 1905.

                                      Edw C. Griesel
                                            Notary Public.

BIRTH AFFIDAVIT.

DEPARTMENT OF THE INTERIOR,
COMMISSION TO THE FIVE CIVILIZED TRIBES.

IN RE APPLICATION FOR ENROLLMENT, as a citizen of the Creek Nation, of Sequoah McIntosh, born on the 4 day of Oct, 1902

Name of Father: Cub McIntosh	a citizen of the	Creek	Nation.
Name of Mother: Fannie McIntosh	a citizen of the	"	Nation.

                        Postoffice   Checotah

AFFIDAVIT OF ~~MOTHER~~. Father

UNITED STATES OF AMERICA, Indian Territory, ⎫
    Western   DISTRICT. ⎭

    I, Roley C. McIntosh, on oath state that I am 48 years of age and a citizen by blood, of the Creek Nation, that I am the lawful ~~wife~~ Husband of Fannie McIntosh, who is a citizen, by blood of the Creek Nation; that a male child was born to me on 4 day of October, 1902; that said child has been named Sequoah McIntosh, and is now living.

                                    Roley C McIntosh

Witnesses To Mark:

16

Subscribed and sworn to before me this 14 day of March, 1905.

Edw C Griesel
Notary Public.

NC 5.

Muskogee, Indian Territory, **July 5, 1905.**

Blanche E. Baker,
Checotah, Indian Territory.

In the matter of the application for the enrollment of your minor child, **Eula Blanche Baker**, as a citizen of the **Creek** Nation, you are advised that there is on file at this office an affidavit executed by you in which your name is given as **Ella B. and Blanche E. Baker.**

For the correction of this discrepancy there is herewith enclosed a blank form of birth affidavit, and in executing same care should be exercised to see that all blanks are properly filled, all names written in full and in the event that you are unable to write, signature by mark must be attested by two witnesses. The affidavit must be executed before a Notary Public and the notarial seal and signature of the officer must be attached to the affidavit.

Respectfully,

1 BA.

Commissioner.

Cheesie McIntosh,   Copy
    Attorney at Law,
Supt. Creek Schools.

Checotah, I.T. 8th July 1905.
The Commission to the Five Civilized Tribes,

Muskogee, Ind. Ter.
Gentlemen:

Enclosed I send renewed application for the enrollment of my daughter Ella Blanche Baker in compliance with yours of July 5th 1905.

I have signed my full name to the application as you request.

I sometimes sign my name Ella B. Baker but as I say that I have signed my full name.

17

Applications for Enrollment of Creek Newborn
Act of 1905   Volume I

Respectfully,

Ella Blanche Baker

BIRTH AFFIDAVIT.

DEPARTMENT OF THE INTERIOR,
COMMISSION TO THE FIVE CIVILIZED TRIBES.

IN RE APPLICATION FOR ENROLLMENT, as a citizen of the Creek Nation, of Eula Blanche Baker, born on the 7th day of March, 1902

Name of Father:	Sam Baker	a citizen of the United States Nation.
Name of Mother:	Ella Blanche Baker	a citizen of the Creek Nation.

Postoffice Checotah, Ind. Ter.

AFFIDAVIT OF MOTHER.

UNITED STATES OF AMERICA, Indian Territory, ⎱
Western   DISTRICT. ⎰

I, Ella Blanche Baker, on oath state that I am 25 years of age and a citizen by blood, of the Creek Nation, that I am the lawful wife of Sam Baker, who is a citizen, by birth of the United States Nation; that a female child was born to me on 7th day of March, 1902; that said child has been named Eula Blanche Baker, and is now living.

Ella Blanche Baker

Witnesses To Mark:

{

Subscribed and sworn to before me this 8th day of July, 1905.

Ben D. Gross
Notary Public.

AFFIDAVIT OF ATTENDING PHYSICIAN OR MID-WIFE.

UNITED STATES OF AMERICA, Indian Territory, ⎱
Western   DISTRICT. ⎰

I, D.M. Pate, a physician, on oath state that I attended on Mrs. Ella Blanche Baker, wife of Sam Baker on the 7th day of March, 1902; that there was born to her on said date a female child; that said child is now living and is said to have been named Eula Blanche Baker.

Applications for Enrollment of Creek Newborn
Act of 1905   Volume I

D.M. Pate, M.D.

Witnesses To Mark:

{

Subscribed and sworn to before me this 6th day of July, 1905.

Ben D. Gross
Notary Public.

BIRTH AFFIDAVIT.

DEPARTMENT OF THE INTERIOR,
COMMISSION TO THE FIVE CIVILIZED TRIBES.

IN RE APPLICATION FOR ENROLLMENT, as a citizen of the Creek Nation, of Eula Blanche Baker, born on the 6 day of March, 1902

Name of Father: Sam Baker   a citizen of the U.S. Nation
Name of Mother: Ella B. "   a citizen of the Creek Nation

Postoffice Checotah

AFFIDAVIT OF MOTHER.

UNITED STATES OF AMERICA, Indian Territory,
    Western   DISTRICT.

I, Ella B Baker, on oath state that I am 24 years of age and a citizen by blood, of the Creek Nation; that I am the lawful wife of Sam Baker, who is a citizen, by ----- of the U.S. Nation; that a female child was born to me on 6 day of march, 1904, that said child has been named Eula Blanche Baker, and is now living.

Child Present –   Blanche E. Baker

AFFIDAVIT OF ATTENDING PHYSICIAN OR MID-WIFE.

UNITED STATES OF AMERICA, Indian Territory,
    Western   DISTRICT.

I, Fannie McIntosh, a Assistant Midwife, on oath state that I attended on Mrs. Ella B. Baker, wife of Sam Baker on the 6 day of March, 1902; that there was born to her on said date a female child; that said child is now living and is said to have been named Eula Blanche Baker

Fannie McIntosh

19

Applications for Enrollment of Creek Newborn
Act of 1905 Volume I

Witnesses To Mark:

{

Subscribed and sworn to before me this 14 day of March, 1905.

Edw C. Griesel
Notary Public.

DEPARTMENT OF THE INTERIOR,
COMMISSIONER TO THE FIVE CIVILIZED TRIBES.

REFER IN REPLY TO THE FOLLOWING:
N.C. -6.

Muskogee, Indian Territory, **August 3, 1905**

Lisa Farmer,
Care of Nathan K. Farmer,
Muskogee, Indian Territory.

Dear Madam:

You are hereby advised that on **July 28, 1905.** , the Secretary of the Interior approved the enrollment of your minor child, **Natalie Farmer**, as a citizen by blood of the **Creek** Nation, and that the name of said child appears upon the roll of new born citizens of the **Creek** Nation as Number **6**.

The child is now entitled to an allotment, and application therefor should be made without delay at the Land Office for the Nation in which the prospective allotment is located.

An entire allotment for said child must be selected at the time of the original application.

Respectively,

Commissioner.

BIRTH AFFIDAVIT.

DEPARTMENT OF THE INTERIOR,
COMMISSION TO THE FIVE CIVILIZED TRIBES.

IN RE APPLICATION FOR ENROLLMENT, as a citizen of the Creek Nation, of Natalie Farmer, born on the 6th day of July, 1903

Name of Father:	Nathan K. Farmer	a citizen of the United States ~~Nation.~~
Name of Mother:	Liza Farmer	a citizen of the Creek Nation.

Applications for Enrollment of Creek Newborn
Act of 1905   Volume I

Postoffice   Muskogee Ind Ter

AFFIDAVIT OF MOTHER.

UNITED STATES OF AMERICA, Indian Territory, ⎤
    Western   DISTRICT. ⎰

    I, Liza Farmer, on oath state that I am 37 years of age and a citizen by Blood, of the Creek Nation; that I am the lawful wife of Nathan K Farmer, who is a citizen by ----- of the United States ~~Nation~~, that a Female child was born to me on 6th day of July 1903, that said child has been named Natalie Farmer, and is now living.

Liza Farmer

Witnesses To Mark:

    {

    Subscribed and sworn to before me this 23rd day of March, 1905.

My com. expires   R.R. Cravens
  October 8 – 1907   Notary Public.

AFFIDAVIT OF ATTENDING PHYSICIAN OR MID-WIFE.

UNITED STATES OF AMERICA, Indian Territory, ⎤
    Western   DISTRICT. ⎰

    I, J.L. Blakemore, a Physician, on oath state that I attended on Mrs. Liza Farmer, wife of Nathan K Farmer on the 6th day of July, 1903; that there was born to her on said date a Female child; that said child is now living and is said to have been named Natalie Farmer.

J.L. Blakemore

Witnesses To Mark:

    {

    Subscribed and sworn to before me this 23rd day of March, 1905.

R.R. Cravens
Notary Public.

My com. expires
  October 8 – 1907

21

BIRTH AFFIDAVIT.

DEPARTMENT OF THE INTERIOR,
COMMISSION TO THE FIVE CIVILIZED TRIBES.

IN RE APPLICATION FOR ENROLLMENT, as a citizen of the Creek Nation, of Natalie Farmer, born on the 6 day of July, 1903

Name of Father: Nathan K Farmer	a citizen of the	U.S.	Nation.
Name of Mother: Liza Farmer	a citizen of the	Creek	Nation.

Postoffice Muskogee, I.T.

AFFIDAVIT OF ~~MOTHER.~~ father

UNITED STATES OF AMERICA, Indian Territory,⎱
      Western   DISTRICT. ⎰

I, Nathan K. Farmer, on oath state that I am 49 years of age and a citizen by ----- of the U.S. Nation; that I am the lawful ~~wife~~ husb of Liza Farmer, who is a citizen by blood, of the Creek Nation; that a female child was born to me on 6 day of July, 1903; that said child has been named Natalie Farmer, and is now living.

Nathan K Farmer

Witnesses To Mark:

{

Subscribed and sworn to before me this 6 day of March, 1905.

Edw C. Griesel
Notary Public.

BA 66 B.

Muskogee, Indian Territory, May 15, 1905.

W. H. Harris,
      Muskogee, Indian Territory.

Dear Sir:

There is on file with the Commission an affidavit relative to the birth of your minor child, Charlie Harris. The affidavits of the mother and midwife or physician in attendance at the birth of said child should be furnished.

Applications for Enrollment of Creek Newborn
Act of 1905   Volume I

There is therewith enclosed a blank form of birth affidavit, and in executing same care should be exercised to see that all blanks are properly filled out, all names written in full and in the event that either of the persons signing the affidavits is unable to write, signatures by mark must be attested by two witnesses. Each affidavit must be executed before a Notary Public and the notarial seal and signature of the officer must be attached to each separate affidavit.

Respectfully,

BC.   Chairman.

DEPARTMENT OF THE INTERIOR,
COMMISSIONER TO THE FIVE CIVILIZED TRIBES.

> REFER IN REPLY TO THE FOLLOWING:
> **N.C. -7.**

Muskogee, Indian Territory, **August 3, 1905**

William R. Harris,
   Muskogee, Indian Territory.

Dear Sir:

You are hereby advised that on **July 28, 1905,** the Secretary of the Interior approved the enrollment of your minor child, **Charlie Harris**, as a citizen by blood of the **Creek** Nation, and that the name of said child appears upon the roll of new born citizens of the Nation as Number **7.**

The child is now entitled to an allotment, and application therefor should be made without delay at the Land Office for the Nation in which the prospective allotment is located.

An entire allotment for said child must be selected at the time of the original application.

Respectively,

Commissioner.

AFFIDAVIT OF MOTHER.

UNITED STATES OF AMERICA, Indian Territory,
   Western   DISTRICT. }

I, William R. Harris, on oath state that I am 40 years of age and a citizen by blood, of the Creek Nation; that I am the ~~lawful wife~~ husband of Lela Harris, who is a citizen ~~by~~ -----
of the United States Nation; that a male child was born to ~~me~~ her on 2 day of October, 1902; that said child has been named Charles W. Harris, and is now living.

W. R. Harris

23

Applications for Enrollment of Creek Newborn
Act of 1905   Volume I

Witnesses To Mark:

{

Subscribed and sworn to before me this 29 day of February, 1904.

Wm T. Martin, Jr
Notary Public.
My Commission Expires January 10th 1908.

BIRTH AFFIDAVIT.

DEPARTMENT OF THE INTERIOR,
COMMISSION TO THE FIVE CIVILIZED TRIBES.

IN RE APPLICATION FOR ENROLLMENT, as a citizen of the Creek Nation, of Charlie Harris, born on the 2 day of October , 1902

Name of Father: W. R. Harris   a citizen of the   Creek   Nation.
Name of Mother: Lela Harris   a citizen of the   U.S.   Nation.
(3-7-05 child appeared)

Postoffice   Muskogee I.T.

AFFIDAVIT OF ~~MOTHER~~. father

UNITED STATES OF AMERICA, Indian Territory,⎱
    Western   DISTRICT.⎰
        W. ̶J̶ R
        I, ~~Charlie~~ Harris, on oath state that I am 43 years of age and a citizen by blood, of the Creek Nation; that I am the lawful ~~wife~~ husband of Lela Harris, who is a citizen, by - ---- of the U.S. Nation; that a male child was born to me on 2 day of October, 1902, that said child has been named Charlie Harris, and is now living.

W R Harris

Witnesses To Mark:

{

Subscribed and sworn to before me this 6 day of March, 1905.

Edw C. Griesel
Notary Public.

Applications for Enrollment of Creek Newborn
Act of 1905   Volume I

BIRTH AFFIDAVIT.

DEPARTMENT OF THE INTERIOR,
COMMISSION TO THE FIVE CIVILIZED TRIBES.

IN RE APPLICATION FOR ENROLLMENT, as a citizen of the Creek Nation, of Charlie Harris, born on the 2nd day of October, 1902

Name of Father:	William R Harris	a citizen of the	Creek	Nation.
Name of Mother:	Lela C Harris	a citizen of the	Creek	Nation.

Postoffice Muskogee, Ind. Ty.

AFFIDAVIT OF MOTHER.

UNITED STATES OF AMERICA, Indian Territory,
    Western   DISTRICT.

I, Lela C. Harris, on oath state that I am 33 years of age and a citizen by adoption, of the Creek Nation; that I am the lawful wife of William R. Harris, who is a citizen, by Birth, of the Creek Nation; that a male child was born to me on 2nd day of October, 1902, that said child has been named Charlie Harris, and was living March 4, 1905.

Lela C Harris

Witnesses To Mark:

{

Subscribed and sworn to before me this 16th day of May, 1905.

My Commission Expires March 24th, 1907   W E Abney
                                       Notary Public.

AFFIDAVIT OF ATTENDING PHYSICIAN OR MID-WIFE.

UNITED STATES OF AMERICA, Indian Territory,
    Western   DISTRICT.

I, Nella A Harris, a Midwife, on oath state that I attended on Mrs. Lela C. Harris, wife of William R. Harris, on the 2nd day of October, 1902; that there was born to her on said date a *(blank)* child; that said child was living March 4, 1905, and is said to have been named Charlie Harris

Nellie A Harris

Witnesses To Mark:

{

Subscribed and sworn to before me this 16th day of May, 1905.

My Commission Expires March 24th, 1907   W E Abney
                                                        Notary Public.

                                                        BA 69 B.

                                        Muskogee, Indian Territory, May 15, 1905.

William A. Porter,
        Muskogee, Indian Territory.

Dear Sir:

        There is on file with the Commission an affidavit relative to the birth of Mildred Porter. The affidavits of the mother or said child and of the midwife or physician in attendance at the birth of said child should be furnished.

        There is enclosed herewith a blank form of birth affidavit, and in executing same care should be exercised to see that all blanks are properly filled out, all names written in full and in the event that either of the persons signing the affidavits is unable to write, signatures by mark must be attested by two witnesses. Each affidavit must be executed before a Notary Public and the notarial seal and signature of the officer must be attached to each separate affidavit.

                                        Respectfully,

BC.   Chairman.

DEPARTMENT OF THE INTERIOR, **COMMISSIONER TO THE FIVE CIVILIZED TRIBES.**	REFER IN REPLY TO THE FOLLOWING: **N.C. -8.**

                                Muskogee, Indian Territory, **August 4, 1905.**

William A. Porter,
        Muskogee, Indian Territory.

Dear Sir:

        You are hereby advised that on **July 28, 1905. ,** the Secretary of the Interior approved the enrollment of your minor child, **Mildred Porter** , as a citizen by blood of the **Creek** Nation, and that the name of said child appears upon the roll of new born citizens of the **Creek** Nation as Number **7.**

Applications for Enrollment of Creek Newborn
Act of 1905   Volume I

The child is now entitled to an allotment, and application therefor should be made without delay at the Land Office for the Nation in which the prospective allotment is located.

An entire allotment for said child must be selected at the time of the original application.

Respectively,

Commissioner.

BIRTH AFFIDAVIT.

DEPARTMENT OF THE INTERIOR,
COMMISSION TO THE FIVE CIVILIZED TRIBES.

IN RE APPLICATION FOR ENROLLMENT, as a citizen of the Creek Nation, of Mildred Porter , born on the 17 day of July, 1902

Name of Father: William A. Porter	a citizen of the Creek	Nation.
Name of Mother: Mildred M. "	a citizen of the U.S.	Nation.

Postoffice   Muskogee, I.T.

AFFIDAVIT OF ~~MOTHER~~. father

UNITED STATES OF AMERICA, Indian Territory, ⎫
          Western   DISTRICT. ⎰

I, William A. Porter, on oath state that I am 30 years of age and a citizen by blood, of the Creek Nation; that I am the lawful ~~wife~~ hus of Mildred M. Porter, who is a citizen, by ----- of the U.S. Nation; that a female child was born to me on 17 day of July, 1902, that said child has been named Mildred Porter, and is now living.

W.A. Porter.

Witnesses To Mark:

{

Subscribed and sworn to before me this 6 day of March, 1905.

Edw C. Griesel
Notary Public.

27

Applications for Enrollment of Creek Newborn
Act of 1905   Volume I

BIRTH AFFIDAVIT.

DEPARTMENT OF THE INTERIOR,
COMMISSION TO THE FIVE CIVILIZED TRIBES.

IN RE APPLICATION FOR ENROLLMENT, as a citizen of the Creek Nation, of Mildred Porter, born on the 17 day of July, 1902

Name of Father: William Adair Porter	a citizen of the Creek	Nation.
Name of Mother: Mildred M Porter	a citizen of the U.S.	Nation.

Postoffice Muskogee, Ind. Ter.

AFFIDAVIT OF MOTHER.

UNITED STATES OF AMERICA, Indian Territory,⎱
    Western   DISTRICT. ⎰

I, Mildred M Porter, on oath state that I am 29 years of age and a citizen by Blood of the U.S. ~~Nation~~; that I am the lawful wife of Wm Adair Porter, who is a citizen, by blood, of the Creek Nation; that a *(blank)* child was born to me on 17th day of July, 1902, that said child has been named Mildred Porter, and was living March 4, 1905.

Mildred M. Porter

Witnesses To Mark:

{

Subscribed and sworn to before me this 16th day of May, 1905.

G.P. Spaulding

My Com Exp July 14 – 06.   Notary Public.

AFFIDAVIT OF ATTENDING PHYSICIAN OR MID-WIFE.

UNITED STATES OF AMERICA, Indian Territory,⎱
    Western   DISTRICT. ⎰

            Mildred M.

I, M. F. Williams, a Physician, on oath state that I attended on Mrs. W.A. Porter,
     William Adair

wife of W.A. Porter on the day of, 1904; that there was born to her on said date a Female child; that said child was living March 4, 1905, and is said to have been named Mildred Porter.

M. F. Williams, M.D.

Witnesses To Mark:

{

28

Applications for Enrollment of Creek Newborn
Act of 1905 Volume I

Subscribed and sworn to before me this 16th day of May, 1905.

G.P. Spaulding

My Com Exp July 14 – 06.   Notary Public.

DEPARTMENT OF THE INTERIOR,
COMMISSIONER TO THE FIVE CIVILIZED TRIBES.

REFER IN REPLY TO THE FOLLOWING:

N.C. -1.

Muskogee, Indian Territory, **August 4, 1905**

James Bell,
Natura, Indian Territory

Dear Sir:

You are hereby advised that on **July 28, 1905.**, the Secretary of the Interior approved the enrollment of your minor child, **Agnes Bell**, as a citizen by blood of the **Creek** Nation, and that the name of said child appears upon the roll of new born citizens of the **Creek** Nation as Number **8**.

The child is now entitled to an allotment, and application therefor should be made without delay at the Land Office for the Nation in which the prospective allotment is located.

An entire allotment for said child must be selected at the time of the original application.

Respectfully,

Commissioner.

BIRTH AFFIDAVIT.

DEPARTMENT OF THE INTERIOR,
COMMISSION TO THE FIVE CIVILIZED TRIBES.

IN RE APPLICATION FOR ENROLLMENT, as a citizen of the Creek Nation, of Agnes Bell, born on the 13 day of Oct, 1902

Name of Father: James Bell   a citizen of the   Creek   Nation.
(Cussehta)[sic]
Name of Mother: Emma Bell (nee Checotah)   a citizen of the   Nation.
(Coweta)

Postoffice   Natura

29

AFFIDAVIT OF MOTHER.

UNITED STATES OF AMERICA, Indian Territory, ⎫
    Western   DISTRICT. ⎭

I, Emma Bell, on oath state that I am 30 years of age and a citizen by blood, of the Creek Nation; that I am the lawful wife of lawful wife of James Bell, who is a citizen by blood, of the Creek Nation; that a female child was born to me on 13 day of October, 1902, that said child has been named Agnes Bell, and was living March 4, 1905.

Emma Bell

Witnesses To Mark:

{

Subscribed and sworn to before me this 12 day of April, 1905.

(Seal)   Edw C Griesel
                                   Notary Public.

AFFIDAVIT OF ATTENDING PHYSICIAN OR MID-WIFE.

UNITED STATES OF AMERICA, Indian Territory, ⎫
    Western   DISTRICT. ⎭

I, Eliza Brown, a Mid Wife, on oath state that I attended on Mrs. Emma Bell, wife of James Bell on or about the 13 day of Oct, 1902; that there was born to her on said date a female child; that said child was living March 4, 1905, and is said to have been named Agnes Bell.

Eliza Brown

Witnesses To Mark:

{

Subscribed and sworn to before me this 12 day of April, 1905.

(Seal)   Edw C Griesel
                                   Notary Public.

BIRTH AFFIDAVIT.

DEPARTMENT OF THE INTERIOR,
COMMISSION TO THE FIVE CIVILIZED TRIBES.

———————

IN RE APPLICATION FOR ENROLLMENT, as a citizen of the Creek Nation, of Agnes Bell, born on the 13 day of Oct, 1902

Name of Father:	James Bell	a citizen of the	Creek	Nation.
Name of Mother:	Emma Bell	a citizen of the	"	Nation.

Postoffice

———————

AFFIDAVIT OF ~~MOTHER~~. father

UNITED STATES OF AMERICA, Indian Territory,⎫
    Western   DISTRICT.⎰

I, James Bell, on oath state that I am 33 years of age and a citizen by blood, of the Creek Nation; that I am the lawful ~~wife~~ husband of Emma Bell, who is a citizen by blood, of the Creek Nation; that a female child was born to me on 13 day of October, 1902, that said child has been named Agnes Bell, and is now living.

James Bell

Witnesses To Mark:

{

Subscribed and sworn to before me this 6 day of March, 1905.

Edw C Griesel
Notary Public.

———————————————

N C 10

Muskogee, Indian Territory, May 22, 1905.

William J. Roberts,
    Natura, Indian Territory.

Dear Sir:

In the matter of the application for the enrollment of your minor child, you are advised that the Commission requires further evidence as to the birth of said child.

Applications for Enrollment of Creek Newborn
Act of 1905   Volume I

You will be allowed fifteen days from date within which to appear before the Commission at the office in Muskogee, Indian Territory, for the purpose of being examined under oath.

Respectfully,

Register.   Chairman.

Cr NC-10

DEPARTMENT OF THE INTERIOR,
COMMISSION TO THE FIVE CIVILIZED TRIBES.

Muskogee, Indian Territory, June 1, 1905.

In the matter of the application for the enrollment of Walter H. Roberts, et al. as citizens of the Creek Nation.

William J. Roberts, being duly sworn, testified as follows:

EXAMINATION BY THE COMMISSION:
Q What is your name? A William J. Roberts.
Q How old are you? A 39.
Q What is your post office address? A Natura.
Q When was your child, Walter H. Roberts, born? A On the 13th day of February, 1905.
Q Do you know what day of the week the child was born on?
A No sir: I declare I could not tell you.
Q You don't recollect? A No sir.
Q Is the child Edith L. Roberts living? A No sir: dead.
Q On what day did it die? A On the 22nd day of February, 1904.
Q I thought you said long before? A I could be mistaken; I am not positive. I think it is February.

Indian TERRITORY, Western District.
I, J. Y. Miller, a stenographer to the Commission to the Five Civilized Tribes, do hereby certify that the above and foregoing is a true and complete translation of my notes as same appear in my stenographic report of this case.

JE Micleb *(difficult to read)*

Sworn to and subscribed before me
this the 17 day of June, 1905.

Edw C Griesel
Notary Public.

32

Applications for Enrollment of Creek Newborn
Act of 1905   Volume I

BIRTH AFFIDAVIT.

DEPARTMENT OF THE INTERIOR,
COMMISSION TO THE FIVE CIVILIZED TRIBES.

IN RE APPLICATION FOR ENROLLMENT, as a citizen of the Creek Nation, of Edith Roberts, born on the 21 day of Oct , 1903 died ~~Jany~~ Feb 22, 1904

Name of Father: W.J. Roberts   a citizen of the   Creek   Nation.
 Hickory Ground Town
Name of Mother: Annie A Roberts   a citizen of the United States ~~Nation.~~

Postoffice   Naturia, Ind. Ter.

AFFIDAVIT OF MOTHER.

UNITED STATES OF AMERICA, Indian Territory,⎫
        Western   DISTRICT.⎬

I, Annie A. Roberts, on oath state that I am 31 years of age and a citizen by (*blank*), of the United States ~~Nation~~; that I am the lawful wife of lawful wife of W.J. Roberts, who is a citizen, by blood, of the Creek Nation; that a female child was born to me on 21 day of October, 1903; that said child has been named Edith Roberts, and ~~was living March 4, 1905~~. died ~~Jan.~~ Feb. 22, 1904

Annie A Roberts
Witnesses To Mark:

⎰

Subscribed and sworn to before me this 11 day of April, 1905.

(Seal)   Edw C Griesel
                                    Notary Public.

AFFIDAVIT OF ATTENDING PHYSICIAN OR MID-WIFE.

UNITED STATES OF AMERICA, Indian Territory,⎫
        Western   DISTRICT.⎬

I, Wm Catt, a physician, on oath state that I attended on Mrs. Annie A Roberts, wife of W J Robert on the 21 day of Oct, 1903; that there was born to her on said date a
died on or about Feb 21-1904
female child; that said child ~~was living March 4, 1905~~, and is said to have been named Edith Roberts.

Wm Catt

33

Applications for Enrollment of Creek Newborn
Act of 1905   Volume I

Witnesses To Mark:

{

Subscribed and sworn to before me this 11 day of April, 1905.

(Seal)   Edw C Griesel
                                                  Notary Public.

BIRTH AFFIDAVIT.

DEPARTMENT OF THE INTERIOR,
COMMISSION TO THE FIVE CIVILIZED TRIBES.

IN RE APPLICATION FOR ENROLLMENT, as a citizen of the Creek Nation, of Edith L
Roberts , born on the 21 day of Oct , 1903
W. J.

Name of Father: ~~Edith L~~ Roberts	a citizen of the Creek	Nation.
Name of Mother: Annie Roberts	a citizen of the U.S.	Nation.

Postoffice   Natura Ind Ter

AFFIDAVIT OF ~~MOTHER~~. father

UNITED STATES OF AMERICA, Indian Territory,
Western   **DISTRICT.**

I, W.J. Roberts, on oath state that I am 39 years of age and a citizen by blood, of
the Creek Nation; that I am the lawful wife of lawful ~~wife~~ husb of Annie Roberts, who is
a citizen, by ----- of the U.S. Nation; that a Female child was born to me on 21 day of
Oct. 1903; that said child has been named Edith L. Roberts, and ~~is now living~~. she died
Feb. 22 – 1904.

Witnesses To Mark:

{

Subscribed and sworn to before me this 6 day of March, 1905.

Edw C Griesel
                                                  Notary Public.

34

NC 10   JLD

DEPARTMENT OF THE INTERIOR
COMMISSIONER TO THE FIVE CIVILIZED TRIBES

———————

In the matter of the application for the enrollment of your minor child, you are advised that the Commission requires further evidence as to the birth of said child. of Edith L. Roberts, deceased, as a citizen by blood of the Creek Nation.

———————

STATEMENT AND ORDER.

The record in this case shows that on March 6, 1905, application was made, in affidavit form, supplemented by sworn testimony taken June 1, 1905, for the enrollment of Edith L. Roberts, deceased, as a citizen by blood of the Creek Nation, under the provisions of the act of Congress approved March 3, 1905.

It appears from the evidence filed in this matter that said Edith L. Roberts, deceased, was born October 21, 1903, and died February 22, 1904.

The act of Congress approved March 3, 1905, (33 Stats., 1048), provides:

That the Commission to the Five Civilized Tribes is authorized for sixty days after the date of the approval of this act to receive and consider applications for enrollment, of children, <u>born subsequent to May twenty-fifth, nineteen hundred and one, and prior to March fourth, nineteen hundred and five, and living on said latter date, to</u> citizens of the Creek tribe of Indians whose enrollment has been approved by the Secretary of the Interior prior to the approval of this act; and to enroll and make allotments to such children.

It is, therefore, ordered that the application for the enrollment of Edith L. Roberts, deceased, as a citizen by blood of the Creek Nation, be, and the same is, hereby dismissed.

(Name Illegible) Commissioner.

Muskogee, Indian Territory.
JAN 15 1907

———————

DEPARTMENT OF THE INTERIOR,
COMMISSIONER TO THE FIVE CIVILIZED TRIBES.

REFER IN REPLY TO THE FOLLOWING:
N.C. 10.

Muskogee, Indian Territory, **August 4, 1905.**

William J. Roberts,
        Natura, Indian Territory.

Dear Sir:

You are hereby advised that on **July 28, 1905,** the Secretary of the Interior approved the enrollment of your minor child, **Walter H. Roberts** , as a citizen by blood of the **Creek** Nation, and that the name of said child appears upon the roll of new born citizens of the **Creek** Nation as Number **10.**

Applications for Enrollment of Creek Newborn
Act of 1905   Volume I

The child is now entitled to an allotment, and application therefor should be made without delay at the Land Office for the Nation in which the prospective allotment is located.

An entire allotment for said child must be selected at the time of the original application.

Respectively,

Commissioner.

DEPARTMENT OF THE INTERIOR,
COMMISSIONER TO THE FIVE CIVILIZED TRIBES.

REFER IN REPLY TO THE FOLLOWING:
_____

N.C. -10.

Muskogee, Indian Territory, **August 4, 1905.**

William J. Roberts,
Natura, Indian Territory.

Dear Sir:

You are hereby advised that on **July 28, 1905,** the Secretary of the Interior approved the enrollment of your minor child, **Tura E. Roberts** , as a citizen by blood of the **Creek** Nation, and that the name of said child appears upon the roll of new born citizens of the **Creek** Nation as Number **9.**

The child is now entitled to an allotment, and application therefor should be made without delay at the Land Office for the Nation in which the prospective allotment is located.

An entire allotment for said child must be selected at the time of the original application.

Respectively,

Commissioner.

BIRTH AFFIDAVIT.

DEPARTMENT OF THE INTERIOR,
COMMISSION TO THE FIVE CIVILIZED TRIBES.

IN RE APPLICATION FOR ENROLLMENT, as a citizen of the Creek Nation, of Walter H Roberts , born on the 13 day of Feb , 1905

Name of Father: Wm J Roberts   a citizen of the Creek   Nation.
Name of Mother: Annie Roberts   a citizen of the U.S.   Nation.

Postoffice   Natura, Ind. Terr.

Applications for Enrollment of Creek Newborn
Act of 1905   Volume I

AFFIDAVIT OF ~~MOTHER~~. father

UNITED STATES OF AMERICA, Indian Territory,
Western   DISTRICT.

I, W.J. Roberts, on oath state that I am 39 years of age and a citizen by blood, of the Creek Nation; that I am the lawful ~~wife~~ husb of Annie Roberts, who is a citizen, by --- of the U.S. Nation; that a male child was born to me on 13 day of Feb 1905; that said child has been named Walter H. Roberts, and is now living.

W.J. Roberts

Witnesses To Mark:

Subscribed and sworn to before me this 6 day of March, 1905.

Edw C Griesel C Griesel
Notary Public.

BIRTH AFFIDAVIT.

DEPARTMENT OF THE INTERIOR,
COMMISSION TO THE FIVE CIVILIZED TRIBES.

IN RE APPLICATION FOR ENROLLMENT, as a citizen of the Creek Nation, of Walter H. Roberts, born on the 13 day of Feb., 1905

Name of Father: W.J. Roberts   a citizen of the Creek   Nation.
Hickory Ground Town
Name of Mother: Anna A Roberts   a citizen of the United States ~~Nation~~.

Postoffice   Natura, Ind. Ter.

AFFIDAVIT OF MOTHER.

UNITED STATES OF AMERICA, Indian Territory,
Western   DISTRICT.

I, Annie A. Roberts, on oath state that I am 31 years of age and a citizen by *(blank)*, of the United States ~~Nation~~; that I am the lawful wife of W.J. Roberts, who is a citizen, by blood, of the Creek Nation; that a male child was born to me on 13 day of February, 1905; that said child has been named Walter H. Roberts, and was living March 4, 1905.

Annie A Roberts

37

Witnesses To Mark:

{

Subscribed and sworn to before me this 11 day of April, 1905.

Drennan C Skaggs
Notary Public.

AFFIDAVIT OF ATTENDING PHYSICIAN OR MID-WIFE.

UNITED STATES OF AMERICA, Indian Territory,
Western   DISTRICT.

I, Mollie Throckmorton, a midwife, on oath state that I attended on Mrs. Annie A Roberts, wife of W.J. Roberts on the 13 day of Feb , 1905 ; that there was born to her on said date a male child; that said child was living March 4, 1905, and is said to have been named Walter H. Roberts.

Mollie Throckmorton

Witnesses To Mark:

{

Subscribed and sworn to before me this 11 day of April, 1905.

Drennan C Skaggs
Notary Public.

BIRTH AFFIDAVIT.

DEPARTMENT OF THE INTERIOR,
COMMISSION TO THE FIVE CIVILIZED TRIBES.

IN RE APPLICATION FOR ENROLLMENT, as a citizen of the Creek Nation, of Tura E Roberts , born on the 21 day of May , 1902

Name of Father: W.J. Roberts   a citizen of the Creek   Nation.
Hickory Ground Town
Name of Mother: Annie A Roberts   a citizen of the United States Nation.

Postoffice   Naturia, Ind. Terr.

Applications for Enrollment of Creek Newborn
Act of 1905   Volume I

AFFIDAVIT OF MOTHER.

UNITED STATES OF AMERICA, Indian Territory, } Child is present
Western   DISTRICT.

I, Annie A. Roberts, on oath state that I am 31 years of age and a citizen by *(blank)*, of the United States ~~Nation~~; that I am the lawful wife of W.J. Roberts, who is a citizen, by blood, of the Creek Nation; that a female child was born to me on 21 day of May, 1902; that said child has been named Tura E. Roberts, and as living March 4, 1905.

Annie A Roberts

Witnesses To Mark:

{

Subscribed and sworn to before me this 11 day of April, 1905.

Drennan C Skaggs
Notary Public.

AFFIDAVIT OF ATTENDING PHYSICIAN OR MID-WIFE.

UNITED STATES OF AMERICA, Indian Territory,
Western   DISTRICT.

I, Mollie Throckmorton, a midwife, on oath state that I attended on Mrs. Annie A Roberts, wife of W.J. Roberts on the 21 day of May , 1902; that there was born to her on said date a female child; that said child was living March 4, 1905, and is said to have been named Tura E. Roberts.

Mollie Throckmorton

Witnesses To Mark:

{

Subscribed and sworn to before me this 11 day of April, 1905.

Drennan C Skaggs
Notary Public.

Applications for Enrollment of Creek Newborn
Act of 1905   Volume I

BIRTH AFFIDAVIT.
DEPARTMENT OF THE INTERIOR,
COMMISSION TO THE FIVE CIVILIZED TRIBES.

IN RE APPLICATION FOR ENROLLMENT, as a citizen of the Creek Nation, of Tura E. Roberts , born on the 21 day of May , 1902

Name of Father: W.J. Roberts	a citizen of the Creek	Nation.
Name of Mother: Annie Roberts	a citizen of the U.S.	Nation.

Postoffice   Natura, I.T.

AFFIDAVIT OF ~~MOTHER~~. father

UNITED STATES OF AMERICA, Indian Territory, ⎫
Western   DISTRICT. ⎰

I, W.J. Roberts, on oath state that I am 39 years of age and a citizen by blood, of the Creek Nation; that I am the lawful ~~wife~~ husband of Annie Roberts, who is a citizen, by ~~blood~~ of the ~~Creek~~ U.S. Nation; that a female child was born to me on 21 day of May 1902; that said child has been named Tura E. Roberts, and is now living.

W.J. Roberts

Witnesses To Mark:

⎧
⎨
⎩

Subscribed and sworn to before me this 6 day of March, 1905.

Edw C Griesel
Notary Public.

NC 10

Muskogee, Indian Territory, January 17, 1907.

Annie A. Roberts.
c/o William J. Roberts.
Natura, Indian Territory.

Dear Madam:

There is herewith enclosed one copy of the Statement and Order of the Commissioner of the Five Civilized Tribes, dated January 15, 1907, dismissing the application made by you for the enrollment of your minor child, Edith L. Roberts, deceased, as a citizen by blood of the Creek Nation.

40

Applications for Enrollment of Creek Newborn
Act of 1905   Volume I

Respectfully,

Commissioner.

BA 17 B.

Muskogee, Indian Territory, May 13, 1905.

John Brook
 Eufaula, Indian Territory.

Dear Sir:

There is on file with the Commission an affidavit executed by you relative to the birth of your minor child, Annetta May Brook. The affidavit of the mother and midwife or physician in attendance at the birth of said child must be furnished.

There is herewith enclosed a blank form of birth affidavit, and in executing same care should be exercised to see that all blanks are properly filled, all names written in full and in the event that either of the persons signing the affidavit is unable to write, signatures by mark must be attested by two witnesses. Each affidavit must be executed before a Notary Public and the notarial seal and signature of the officer must be attached to each separate affidavit.

Respectfully,

BC.   Chairman.

BIRTH AFFIDAVIT.

DEPARTMENT OF THE INTERIOR,
COMMISSION TO THE FIVE CIVILIZED TRIBES.

IN RE APPLICATION FOR ENROLLMENT, as a citizen of the Creek Nation, of Winthrope Brook , born on the 23 day of April, 1903

Name of Father: John Brook   a citizen of the   U.S.   Nation.
Name of Mother: Jeanetta A. Brook a citizen of the   Creek   Nation.

Postoffice   Eufaula

41

AFFIDAVIT OF MOTHER. father

UNITED STATES OF AMERICA, Indian Territory, ⎫
Western   **DISTRICT.** ⎰

I, John Brook, on oath state that I am 33 years of age and a citizen by ~~bl~~, of the U.S. Nation; that I am the lawful ~~wife~~ husb of Jeanetta A. Brook, who is a citizen, by blood, of the Creek Nation; that a female[sic] child was born to me on 23 day of April, 1903; that said child has been named Winthrope Brook, and ~~is now living~~. died July 5 – 1903

John Brook

Witnesses To Mark:

{

Subscribed and sworn to before me this 6 day of March, 1905.

Edw C Griesel
Notary Public.

NC 11   JLD

DEPARTMENT OF THE INTERIOR,
COMMISSIONER TO THE FIVE CIVILIZED TRIBES.

....

In the matter of the application for the enrollment of Winthrope Brook, deceased, as a citizen by blood of the Creek Nation.

....

STATEMENT AND ORDER.

The record in this case shows that on March 5, 1905, application was made, in affidavit form, for the enrollment of Winthrope Brook, deceased, as a citizen by blood of the Creek Nation, under the provisions of the act of Congress approved March 3, 1905.

It appears from the affidavit filed in this matter that said Winthrope Brook, deceased, was born April 23, 1903, and died July 5, 1903.

The act of Congress approved March 3, 1905 (33 Stats., 1048), provides:

"That the Commission to the Five Civilized Tribes is authorized for sixty days after the date of the approval of this act to receive and consider applications for enrollment, of children, <u>born subsequent to May twenty-fifth, nineteen hundred and one, and prior to March fourth, nineteen hundred and five, and living on said latter date</u>, to citizens of the Creek tribe of Indians whose enrollment has been approved by the Secretary of the Interior prior to the approval of this act; and to enroll and make and make allotments to such children."

Applications for Enrollment of Creek Newborn
Act of 1905   Volume I

It is, therefore, ordered that the application for the enrollment of Winthrope Brook, deceased, as a citizen by blood of the Creek Nation, be, and the same is, hereby dismissed.

(Name Illegible) Commissioner.

Muskogee, Indian Territory.
JAN 15 1907

BIRTH AFFIDAVIT.

DEPARTMENT OF THE INTERIOR,
COMMISSION TO THE FIVE CIVILIZED TRIBES.

IN RE APPLICATION FOR ENROLLMENT, as a citizen of the Creek Nation, of Annetta May Brook , born on the 31 day of August, 1904

Name of Father: John Brook	a citizen of the U.S.	Nation.
Name of Mother: Jeanetta A. Brook	a citizen of the Creek	Nation.

Postoffice   Eufaula

AFFIDAVIT OF ~~MOTHER~~. father

UNITED STATES OF AMERICA, Indian Territory,⎫
Western   DISTRICT. ⎰

I, John Brook, on oath state that I am 33 years of age and a citizen by ----- , of the U.S. Nation; that I am the lawful ~~wife~~ husb of Jeanetta A. Brook, who is a citizen, by blood, of the Creek Nation; that a female child was born to me on 31 day of August, 1904; that said child has been named Annetta May Brook, and is now living.

John Brook

Witnesses To Mark:

{

Subscribed and sworn to before me this 6 day of March, 1905.

Edw C Griesel
Notary Public.

BIRTH AFFIDAVIT.

DEPARTMENT OF THE INTERIOR,
COMMISSION TO THE FIVE CIVILIZED TRIBES.

IN RE APPLICATION FOR ENROLLMENT, as a citizen of the Creek Nation, of Annetta May Brook , born on the 31 day of August , 1904

Name of Father: John H. Brook   a citizen of the United States ~~Nation~~.

(nee Harvison)

Name of Mother: Jeanetta A. Brook   a citizen of the   Creek   Nation.

Postoffice   Eufaula, Ind. Terr.

---

child present

AFFIDAVIT OF MOTHER.

UNITED STATES OF AMERICA, Indian Territory, ⎤
     Western   DISTRICT. ⎦

I, Jeanetta A. Brook, on oath state that I am 32 years of age and a citizen by blood, of the Creek Nation; that I am the lawful wife of John H. Brook, who is a citizen ~~by (blank), of the~~ United States Nation; that a female child was born to me on 31 day of August, 1904; that said child has been named Annetta May Brook, and was living March 4, 1905.

Jennetta A. Brook

Witnesses To Mark:

{

Subscribed and sworn to before me this 6 day of April, 1905.

Drennan C. Skaggs
Notary Public.

AFFIDAVIT OF ATTENDING PHYSICIAN OR MID-WIFE.

UNITED STATES OF AMERICA, Indian Territory, ⎤
     Western   DISTRICT. ⎦

I, Adeline White, a mid-wife, on oath state that I attended on Mrs. Jennetta A. Brook, wife of John H. Brook on the 31 day of August , 1904 ; that there was born to her on said date a female child; that said child was living March 4, 1905, and is said to have been named Annetta May Brook.

her

Adeline x White

mark

Witnesses To Mark:

{   DC Skaggs
    (Illegible) Posey

Applications for Enrollment of Creek Newborn
Act of 1905   Volume I

Subscribed and sworn to before me this 6 day of April, 1905.

Drennan C Skaggs

Notary Public.

NC 11.

Muskogee, Indian Territory, January 17, 1907.

Jennetta A. Brook,
c/o John Brook,
Eufaula, Indian Territory.

Dear Madam:

There is herewith enclosed one copy of the Statement and Order of the Commissioner to the Five Civilized Tribes, dated January 15, 1907, dismissing the application made by you for the enrollment of your minor child, Winthrope Brook, deceased, as a citizen by blood of the Creek Nation.

Respectfully,

Commissioner.

LM-72.

DEPARTMENT OF THE INTERIOR,
COMMISSIONER TO THE FIVE CIVILIZED TRIBES.

REFER IN REPLY TO THE FOLLOWING:

N.C. -12.

Muskogee, Indian Territory, **August 4, 1905.**

Adaline Orcutt,
Care of A.D. Orcutt,
Coweta, Indian Territory.

Dear Madam:

You are hereby advised that on **July 28, 1905** , the Secretary of the Interior approved the enrollment of your minor child, **Guy B. Orcutt** , as a citizen by blood of the **Creek** Nation, and that the name of said child appears upon the roll of new born citizens of the **Creek** Nation as Number **11** .

The child is now entitled to an allotment, and application therefor should be made without delay at the Land Office for the Nation in which the prospective allotment is located.

45

An entire allotment for said child must be selected at the time of the original application.

Respectively,

Commissioner.

Affidavit.

United States of America,   :
    Western District,   :
Indian Territory.   :

Before me, B.J. Beavers, a Notary Public, duly qualified and appointed and acting within and for the Western District of the Indian Territory, personally appeared Dr. A.E. Carder, to me personally know, who on oath, deposes and says that he is a resident of Coweta, Indian Territory, and duly licensed to practice medicine within the Western District of said territory; that he was the attending physician during the confinement of Mrs. Adeline Orcutt, a Creek Citizen by blood, on 26th day of July, 1903, when she gave birth to a boy, now know[sic] as "Cuy[sic] Bowman Orcutt," that said boy is still living and under the care of his parents of Coweta, Indian Territory.

Therefore, I have hereunto set my hand this 4th day of March, 1905.

A.E. Carder, M.D.

Subscribed and sworn to before me this 4th day of March, 1905.

B.J. Beavers
Notary Public.

My commission expires December 19, 1908.

BIRTH AFFIDAVIT.

DEPARTMENT OF THE INTERIOR,
COMMISSION TO THE FIVE CIVILIZED TRIBES.

IN RE APPLICATION FOR ENROLLMENT, as a citizen of the Creek Nation, of Guy B. Orcutt, born on the 26 day of July , 1903

Name of Father: A.D. Orcutt   a citizen of the   U.S.   Nation.
Name of Mother: Adaline "   a citizen of the   Creek   Nation.

(child is present)   Postoffice   Coweta, I.T.

46

Applications for Enrollment of Creek Newborn
Act of 1905   Volume I

AFFIDAVIT OF MOTHER.

UNITED STATES OF AMERICA, Indian Territory, ⎱
    Western   DISTRICT. ⎰

    I, Adaline Orcutt, on oath state that I am 35 years of age and a citizen by blood, of the Creek Nation; that I am the lawful wife of A.D. Orcutt, who is a citizen, by ----- of the U.S. Nation; that a boy child was born to me on 26 day of July, 1903; that said child has been named Guy B. Orcutt, and is now living.

Adaline Orcutt

Witnesses To Mark:
  {

    Subscribed and sworn to before me this 6 day of March, 1905.

Edw C Griesel
Notary Public.

BA 19 B.

Muskogee, Indian Territory, May 13, 1905.

David Cummings,
    Hanna, Indian Territory.

Dear Sir:

    The Commission is in receipt of affidavits executed by yourself and Louise Cummings relative to the birth of your minor child, Susie Cummings. The affidavit of the midwife or the physician in attendance at the birth of said child is required.

    There is herewith enclosed a blank form of birth affidavit, and in executing same care should be exercised to see that all blanks are properly filled, all names written in full and in the event that either of the persons signing the affidavit is unable to write, signature by mark must be attested by two witnesses. Each affidavit must be executed before a Notary Public and the notarial seal and signature of the officer must be attached to each separate affidavit.

Respectfully,

Chairman.

BC.

Applications for Enrollment of Creek Newborn
Act of 1905 Volume I

DEPARTMENT OF THE INTERIOR,
COMMISSIONER TO THE FIVE CIVILIZED TRIBES.

REFER IN REPLY TO THE FOLLOWING:

N.C. 13.

Muskogee, Indian Territory, **August 4, 1905.**

David Cummings,
Hanna, Indian Territory.

Dear Sir:

You are hereby advised that on **July 28, 1905** , the Secretary of the Interior approved the enrollment of your minor child, **Susie Cummings** , as a citizen by blood of the **Creek** Nation, and that the name of said child appears upon the roll of new born citizens of the **Creek** Nation as Number **29** .

The child is now entitled to an allotment, and application therefor should be made without delay at the Land Office for the Nation in which the prospective allotment is located.

An entire allotment for said child must be selected at the time of the original application.

Respectively,

Commissioner.

BIRTH AFFIDAVIT.
DEPARTMENT OF THE INTERIOR,
COMMISSION TO THE FIVE CIVILIZED TRIBES.

IN RE APPLICATION FOR ENROLLMENT, as a citizen of the Creek Nation, of Susie Cummings , born on the 20 day of May , 1902

Name of Father: David Cummings   a citizen of the Creek   Nation.
Name of Mother: Louisa "   a citizen of the "   Nation.

(child present)   Postoffice   Hanna, I.T.

48

AFFIDAVIT OF MOTHER.

UNITED STATES OF AMERICA, Indian Territory, ⎱
Western   DISTRICT. ⎰

I, Louisa Cummings, on oath state that I am 38 years of age and a citizen by blood, of the Creek Nation; that I am the lawful wife of David Cummings, who is a citizen by blood of the Creek Nation; that a female child was born to me on 20 day of May, 1902; that said child has been named Susie Cummings, and is now living.

Her
Louisa x Cummings
mark

Witnesses To Mark:
{ H.G. Harris
{ EC Griesel

Subscribed and sworn to before me this 9 day of March, 1905.

Edw C Griesel
Notary Public.

BIRTH AFFIDAVIT.

DEPARTMENT OF THE INTERIOR,
COMMISSION TO THE FIVE CIVILIZED TRIBES.

IN RE APPLICATION FOR ENROLLMENT, as a citizen of the Creek Nation, of Susie Cummings , born on the 20 day of May , 1902

Name of Father: David Cummings	a citizen of the Creek	Nation.
Name of Mother: Louisa "	a citizen of the "	Nation.

(Mar 9-'05 child present ECG)   Postoffice   Hanna, I.T.

AFFIDAVIT OF ~~MOTHER~~. father

UNITED STATES OF AMERICA, Indian Territory, ⎱
Western   DISTRICT. ⎰

I, David Cummings, on oath state that I am 65 years of age and a citizen by blood, of the Creek Nation; that I am the lawful ~~wife~~ hus of Louisa Cummings, who is a citizen, by blood of the Creek Nation; that a female child was born to me 20 day of May, 1902; that said child has been named Susie Cummings, and is now living.

David Cummings.

Witnesses To Mark:
{

49

Applications for Enrollment of Creek Newborn
Act of 1905 Volume I

Subscribed and sworn to before me this 6 day of March, 1905.

Edw C Griesel
Notary Public.

BIRTH AFFIDAVIT.

DEPARTMENT OF THE INTERIOR,
COMMISSION TO THE FIVE CIVILIZED TRIBES.

IN RE APPLICATION FOR ENROLLMENT, as a citizen of the Creek Nation, of Susie Cummings , born on the 20 day of May , 1902

Name of Father: David Cummings	a citizen of the Creek	Nation.
Name of Mother: Louisa "	a citizen of the Creek	Nation.

Postoffice   **HANNA, I.T.**

AFFIDAVIT OF MOTHER.

UNITED STATES OF AMERICA, Indian Territory,
Western   **DISTRICT.**

I, Louisa Cummings, on oath state that I am 38 years of age and a citizen by Blood, of the Creek Nation; that I am the lawful wife of David Cummings, who is a citizen, by Blood, of the Creek Nation; that a Female child was born to me on 20 day of May, 1902; that said child has been named Susie Cummings, and was living March 4, 1905.

her
Louisa x Cummings
mark

Witnesses To Mark:
{ Earnest Gauge
{ A. J. Pope

Subscribed and sworn to before me this 23 day of May, 1905.

(Name Illegible)
Notary Public.

AFFIDAVIT OF ATTENDING PHYSICIAN OR MID-WIFE.

UNITED STATES OF AMERICA, Indian Territory,
Western   **DISTRICT.**

I, Bell G. Gray, a Midwife, on oath state that I attended on Mrs. David Cummings, wife of David Cummings on the 20 day of May , 1902; that there was born to

50

her on said date a Female child; that said child was living March 4, 1905, and is said to have been named Susie Cummings.

Bell G. Gray

Witnesses To Mark:

{

    Subscribed and sworn to before me this 23 day of May, 1905.

(Name Illegible)
Notary Public.

Sept 19, 1907

BA 20 B.

Muskogee, Indian Territory, May 13, 1905.

Louisa Aultman.
    Eufaula, Indian Territory.

Dear Madam:

    There is on file with the Commission an affidavit executed by Benjamin Aultman relative to the birth of your child, Agnes Aultman. The Commission requires your affidavit and the affidavit of the midwife or physician in attendance at the birth of said child.

    There is enclosed herewith a blank form of affidavit and in executing the same care should be exercised to see that all blanks are properly filled, all names written in full and in the event that either of the persons signing the affidavit is unable to write, signatures by mark must be attested by two witnesses. Each affidavit must be executed before a Notary Public and the notarial seal and signature of the officer must be attached to each separate affidavit.

Respectfully,

B.C.
Chairman

NC 14

Muskogee, Indian Territory, July 13, 1905.

Benjamin Aultman.
    Eufaula, Indian Territory.

Dear Sir:

51

Applications for Enrollment of Creek Newborn
Act of 1905   Volume I

There is on file at this office an affidavit executed by you relative to the birth of your minor child, Agnes Aultman, as a citizen of the Creek Nation. The affidavit of the mother of said child and of the midwife or physician in attendance at the birth of said child are required.

There is herewith enclosed a blank form of birth affidavit, and in executing same care should be exercised to see that all blanks are properly filled, all names written in full and in the event that either of the persons signing the affidavit is unable to write, signatures by mark must be attested by two witnesses. Each affidavit must be executed before a Notary Public and the notarial seal and signature of the officer must be attached to each separate affidavit.

Respectfully,

1 BA   Commissioner.

NC-14

Muskogee, Indian Territory, August 22, 1905.

Benjamin Aultman,
    Eufaula, Indian Territory.

Dear Sir:

In the matter of the application for the enrollment of your minor daughter, Agnes Aultman, as a citizen by blood of the Creek Nation, there is on file with the records of this Office your affidavit, the affidavit of your wife, Louisa Aultman, and that of M.M. Horn as to the birth of said child. You state in your affidavit that said child was born October 13, 1903, while the other affidavits state that she was born October 13, 1904.

You are requested to immediately forward this Office the joint affidavit of yourself, your wife and the said M.M. Horn, setting forth the correct date of the birth of said child.

Respectfully,

Commissioner.

Birth Affidavit.

Department of the Interior,
Commission to the Five Civilized Tribes.

IN RE APPLICATION FOR ENROLLMENT, as a citizen of the Creek Nation, of Agnes Aultman, born on the 13th day of October, 1903.

Name of Father: Benjamin Aultman   a citizen of the   Creek   Nation.
Name of Mother: Louis[sic] Aultman, a non-citizen

Applications for Enrollment of Creek Newborn
Act of 1905   Volume I

Post office, Eufaula Indian Territory.

Affidavit of Father.

United States of America,)
Indian Territory,   ) SS.
Western District.   )

I, Benjamin Aultman, on oath state that I am 33 years of age and a citizen by blood of the Creek Nation; that I am the lawful wife of lawful husband of Louise Aultman a non citizen; that a female child was born to my said wife on the 13th day of October, 1903; that said child has been named Agnes Aultman, and was living March 4th, 1905.

Benjamin Aultman

Subscribed and sworn to before me this 4th day of September, 1905.

Seal
Charles
Whitaker

Charles Whitaker
My Commission expires August 29, 1909.   Notary public.

BIRTH AFFIDAVIT.

DEPARTMENT OF THE INTERIOR,
COMMISSION TO THE FIVE CIVILIZED TRIBES.

IN RE APPLICATION FOR ENROLLMENT, as a citizen of the Creek Nation, of Agnes Aultman , born on the 13 day of October , 1903

Name of Father: Benjamin Aultman   a citizen of the Creek   Nation.
Name of Mother: Louisa Aultman   a citizen of the   U.S.   ~~Nation~~.

Postoffice   Eufaula

AFFIDAVIT OF ~~MOTHER~~. father

UNITED STATES OF AMERICA, Indian Territory,⎤
       Western   DISTRICT.⎦

I, Benjamin Aultman, on oath state that I am 29 years of age and a citizen by blood, of the Creek Nation; that I am the lawful ~~wife~~ husband of Louisa Aultman, who is a citizen ~~by~~ (blank), of the U.S. ~~Nation~~; that a female child was born to ~~me~~ her on the 13 day of October, 1903; that said child has been named Agnes Aultman, and is now living.

Benjamin Aultman

53

Applications for Enrollment of Creek Newborn
Act of 1905   Volume I

Witnesses To Mark:

{

Subscribed and sworn to before me this 6 day of March, 1905.

Edw C Griesel
Notary Public.

BIRTH AFFIDAVIT.

DEPARTMENT OF THE INTERIOR,
COMMISSION TO THE FIVE CIVILIZED TRIBES.

IN RE APPLICATION FOR ENROLLMENT, as a citizen of the Creek Nation, of Agnes Aultman, born on the 13th day of Oct , 1904[sic]

Name of Father: Benjamin Aultman	a citizen of the Creek	Nation.
Name of Mother: Louise Aultman	a citizen of the -----	Nation.

Postoffice   Eufaula IT

AFFIDAVIT OF MOTHER.

UNITED STATES OF AMERICA, Indian Territory, ⎫
      Western   DISTRICT. ⎭

I, Louise Aultman, on oath state that I am 24 years of age and a citizen by ----- of the *(blank)*, Nation; that I am the lawful wife of Benjamin Aultman, who is a citizen, by blood, of the Creek Nation; that a female child was born to me on 13th day of Oct. 1904; that said child has been named Agnes Aultman, and was living March 4, 1905.

Louise Aultman

Witnesses To Mark:

{

Subscribed and sworn to before me this 12th day of Aug, 1905.

E.F. Saltsman

My commission expires Jan. 27, 1907   Notary Public.

54

AFFIDAVIT OF ATTENDING PHYSICIAN OR MID-WIFE.

UNITED STATES OF AMERICA, Indian Territory,⎤
　　　Western　　　DISTRICT. ⎦

I, M. M. Horn, a *(blank)*, on oath state that I attended on Mrs. Louise Aultman, wife of Benjamin Aultman on the 13th day of Oct , 1904 ; that there was born to her on said date a female child; that said child was living March 4, 1905, and is said to have been named Agnes Aultman.　　　　　　　　　　　　her

　　　　　　　　　　　　　　　　M.M. Horn   x

　　　　　　　　　　　　　　　　　　　　mark

Witnesses To Mark:
{ E.F. Saltsman
{ H T Ballard
　　Subscribed and sworn to before me this 12th day of Aug, 1905.

　　　　　　　　　　　　　　　E F Saltsman

My Com expires Jan 27 1907　　　　　　　Notary Public.

BIRTH AFFIDAVIT.

DEPARTMENT OF THE INTERIOR,
COMMISSION TO THE FIVE CIVILIZED TRIBES.

IN RE APPLICATION FOR ENROLLMENT, as a citizen of the Creek Nation, of Agnes Aultman , born on the 13th day of October , 1903

Name of Father: Benjamin Aultman　　　a citizen of the　Creek　　Nation.
Name of Mother: Louise Aultman　　　　a citizen of the　-----　　Nation.

　　　　　　　　Postoffice　　Eufaula Ind Ter

AFFIDAVIT OF MOTHER.

UNITED STATES OF AMERICA, Indian Territory, ⎤
　　　Western　　　DISTRICT. ⎦

I, Louise Aultman, on oath state that I am 24 years of age and a citizen by *(blank)*, of the non citizen Nation; that I am the lawful wife of Benjamin Aultman, who is a citizen, by Blood, of the creek Nation; that a Female child was born to me on 13th day of October, 1903; that said child has been named Agnes Aultman, and was living March 4, 1905.

　　　　　　　　　　　　Louise Aultman

Witnesses To Mark:
{

Applications for Enrollment of Creek Newborn
Act of 1905   Volume I

Subscribed and sworn to before me this 5th day of September, 1905.

> Seal
> Charles
> Whitaker

Charles Whitaker
Notary Public.

AFFIDAVIT OF ATTENDING PHYSICIAN OR MID-WIFE.

UNITED STATES OF AMERICA, Indian Territory,⎱
     Western   DISTRICT.⎰

I, M.M. Horn, a mid-wife, on oath state that I attended on Mrs. Louise Aultman, wife of Benjamin Aultman on the 13th day of October, 1903, that there was born to her on said date a female child; that said child was living March 4, 1905, and is said to have been named Louise[sic] Aultman.

her
M.M. x Horne[sic]
mark

Witnesses To Mark:
  { John Luke
     Charles Whitaker

Subscribed and sworn to before me this 5th day of September, 1905.

Charles Whitaker

> Seal
> Charles
> Whitaker

Notary Public.

DA 21 B.

Muskogee, Indian Territory, May 13, 1906

Margaret Bruner,
    Sapulpa, Indian Territory.

Dear Madam:

In the matter of the application for the enrollment of your minor child, J. Esther Bruner, it is required that you execute the enclosed affidavit, taking care that all blanks are properly filled, all names written in full, and in the event that you are unable to write signature by mark must be attested by two witnesses. The affidavit should be executed before a Notary Public and the notarial seal and signature of the officer must be attached to the affidavit.

Respectfully,

BC

Chairman.

Applications for Enrollment of Creek Newborn
Act of 1905   Volume I

DEPARTMENT OF THE INTERIOR,
COMMISSIONER TO THE FIVE CIVILIZED TRIBES.

REFER IN REPLY TO THE FOLLOWING:

N.C. -15.

Muskogee, Indian Territory, **August 4, 1905.**

Joseph Bruner,
Sapulpa, Indian Territory.

Dear Sir:

You are hereby advised that on **July 28, 1905** , the Secretary of the Interior approved the enrollment of your minor child, **J. Esther Bruner** , as a citizen by blood of the **Creek** Nation, and that the name of said child appears upon the roll of new born citizens of the **Creek** Nation as Number **12.**

The child is now entitled to an allotment, and application therefor should be made without delay at the Land Office for the Nation in which the prospective allotment is located.

An entire allotment for said child must be selected at the time of the original application.

Respectively,

Commissioner.

BIRTH AFFIDAVIT.

DEPARTMENT OF THE INTERIOR,
COMMISSION TO THE FIVE CIVILIZED TRIBES.

IN RE APPLICATION FOR ENROLLMENT, as a citizen of the Creek Nation, of J. Esther Bruner , born on the 7 day of August , 1901

Name of Father: Joseph Bruner   a citizen of the Creek   Nation.
Name of Mother: Margurite Bruner   a citizen of the   U.S.   Nation.
Mar 8-05 – Child Present. ECG

Postoffice   Sapulpa, I.T.

AFFIDAVIT OF MOTHER.

UNITED STATES OF AMERICA, Indian Territory,⎫
          Western   DISTRICT. ⎭

I, Joseph Bruner, on oath state that I am 32 years of age and a citizen by blood, of the Creek Nation; that I am the lawful ~~wife~~ husband of Margurite Bruner, who is a citizen

57

Applications for Enrollment of Creek Newborn
Act of 1905   Volume I

~~by~~ *(blank)* of the U.S. ~~Nation~~; that a female child was born to ~~me~~ her on 7 day of August, 1901; that said child has been named J. Esther Bruner, and is now living.

Joseph Bruner

Witnesses To Mark:

{

Subscribed and sworn to before me this 6 day of March, 1905.

Edw C Griesel
Notary Public.

BIRTH AFFIDAVIT.   See Previous App.
DEPARTMENT OF THE INTERIOR,
COMMISSION TO THE FIVE CIVILIZED TRIBES.

IN RE APPLICATION FOR ENROLLMENT, as a citizen of the Creek Nation, of J. Esther Bruner , born on the 7 day of Aug , 1901

Name of Father: Joseph Bruner   a citizen of the Creek   Nation.
Name of Mother: Marguerite "   a citizen of the U.S.   Nation.
(Yochapoet)

Postoffice   Sapulpa

AFFIDAVIT OF ATTENDING PHYSICIAN OR MID-WIFE.

UNITED STATES OF AMERICA, Indian Territory,
        Western   **DISTRICT.**

I, James S McAllister, a Physician, on oath state that I attended on Mrs. Marguerita Bruner , wife of Joseph Bruner on the 7 day of Aug , 1901 ; that there was born to her on said date a female child; that said child was living March 4, 1905, and is said to have been named J. Esther Bruner.

James S. McAllister

Witnesses To Mark:

{

Subscribed and sworn to before me this 28 day of April, 1905.

(Seal)   Edw C Griesel
Notary Public.

58

Applications for Enrollment of Creek Newborn
Act of 1905   Volume I

BIRTH AFFIDAVIT.

DEPARTMENT OF THE INTERIOR,
COMMISSION TO THE FIVE CIVILIZED TRIBES.

IN RE APPLICATION FOR ENROLLMENT, as a citizen of the Creek Nation, of J. Esther Bruner , born on the 7 day of August , 1901

Name of Father: Joseph Bruner   a citizen of the   Creek   Nation.
Name of Mother: Marguerite Bruner   a citizen of the United States Nation.

Postoffice   Sapulpa, I.T.

AFFIDAVIT OF MOTHER.

UNITED STATES OF AMERICA, Indian Territory, ⎤
     Western   DISTRICT. ⎦

     I, Marguerite Bruner, on oath state that I am *(blank)* years of age and a ~~citizen by~~ ~~(blank), of the~~ ----- Nation; that I am the lawful wife of Joseph Bruner, who is a citizen by Creek Nation; that a female child was born to me on 7th day of August, 1901; that said child has been named J. Esther Bruner, and was living March 4, 1905.

                               Marguerite Bruner
Witnesses To Mark:

{

    Subscribed and sworn to before me this 17th day of June, 1905.

                        Wm P Roo?
                        Notary Public.

DEPARTMENT OF THE INTERIOR
COMMISSION TO THE FIVE CIVILIZED TRIBES.

Muskogee, Indian Territory, March 6, 1905.

     In the matter of the application for the enrollment of Lonie Irene Throckmorton (deceased) as a citizen by blood of the Creek Nation.

     James W. Throckmorton, being sworn, testified as follows:

EXAMINATION BY THE COMMISSION:
Q What is your name? A James W. Throckmorton.
Q What is your age? A 29.

Applications for Enrollment of Creek Newborn
Act of 1905   Volume I

Q What is your Postoffice address?   A Natura.
Q Have you a child name Lonie Irene Throckmorton?   A I have one dead by that name.
Q What is the name of the mother of that child?   A Ida Throckmorton.
Q Is she a citizen of the Creek Nation?   A Yes sir.

The father and mother of Lonie Irene Throckmorton are identified on Creek Indian card, field No. 630, and their names are contained in the partial list of citizens by blood of the Creek Nation approved by the Secretary of the Interior March 13, 1902, Roll Nos. 2059 and 2060, respectively.

Q When was Lonie Irene Throckmorton born?   A October 16, 1904.
Q How long did she live?   A About a month.
Q What was the date of her death?   A December 6.
Q Have you any record of the birth and death of that child—did you write it down anywhere?   A No, sir, I can't say that I did.
Q Was anyone present at the birth of that child?   A Mrs. Mary Throckmorton was present.
Q Who else?   A Dr. H. Mitehener of Muskogee, Dr. Hinely, Elisa Brown.
Q What is the post office address of Mary Throckmorton and Elisa Brown?   A Natura.
Q Was anyone attending on the child when it died?   A No sir.
Q Do you know some people who were present at the funeral?   A R S Brown, W J Roberts and Jim Bell.

R.S. Brown, being duly sworn, testified as follows:

EXAMINATION BY THE COMMISSION:
Q What is your name?   A R S Brown.
Q What is your Postoffice?   A Natura.
Q Did you know a child of James W and Ida Throckmorton named Lonie Irene?   A I did know; it is dead.
Q Do you know when that child was born?   A I can't tell you the date, but I remember when it was born.
Q Do you know the year it was born?   A It died this past year, I had to do my own cooking when my wife -----
Q Do you know how long the child lived?   A No, I don't know.
Q Were you at the funeral?   A Yes sir.
Q About how old a child did it look to be when it died?   A It is a pretty hard question to answer. It looked to be about two or three months old.
Q When did it die?   A Died soon after Saturday.
Q Died the same year it was born?   A Yes sir.
Q Did it die in the winter time or in the Fall?   A In the fall.
Q How late do you call Fall here?   A Fall sometimes until Christmas in this country.
Q Then it was the beginning of winter?   A It might have been. I don't know. She was sick until I heard she was dead.

Applications for Enrollment of Creek Newborn
Act of 1905   Volume I

W. J. Roberts, being duly sworn, testified as follows:

EXAMINATION BY THE COMMISSION:
Q What is your name?   A W. J. Roberts.
Q What is your age?   A Past 39.
Q What is your Postoffice Address?   A Natura.
Q Did you know a child of James W and Ida Throckmorton named Lonie Irene Throckmorton?   A Yes sir.
Q How soon after it was born did you see it?   A I just—I think a day or two.
Q Do you remember when it was born?   A I think it was in October, as well as I can remember.
Q What year?   A 1904.
Q Do you know how long that child lived?   A No sir; not exactly; a month or six weeks.
Q Died in the same year it was born   A Yes sir.
Q Were you present at the funeral?   A Yes sir.
Q Do you know anybody else that was present at the funeral?   A Yes, Jim Bell, Mr. Brown, father of the child, W E Throckmorton.
Q Do you know the name of the child?   A Yes sir.
Q Will you state the name?   A Lonie Irene as well as I remember.

The witness is advised that the testimony of the mother of the child is desired at the earliest day practicable.

INDIAN TERRITORY, Western District.
I, J. Y. Miller, a stenographer to the Commission to the Five Civilized Tribes, do hereby certify upon oath that the above and foregoing is a true and complete translation of my notes as same appear in my stenographic report of this case.

J Y Miller

Sworn to and subscribed
before me this the
30 day of March
1905.

Edw C Griesel
Notary Public.

BIRTH AFFIDAVIT.

DEPARTMENT OF THE INTERIOR,
COMMISSION TO THE FIVE CIVILIZED TRIBES.

IN RE APPLICATION FOR ENROLLMENT, as a citizen of the Creek Nation, of Irene Throckmorton , born on the 16 day of Oct , 1904

Name of Father: James W Throckmorton   a citizen of the   Creek   Nation.
Name of Mother: Ida L. Throckmorton   a citizen of the   "   Nation.

Applications for Enrollment of Creek Newborn
Act of 1905   Volume I

Postoffice   Natura

UNITED STATES OF AMERICA, Indian Territory, ⎫
    Western   DISTRICT. ⎭

    I, Ida L Throckmorton, on oath state that I am 29 years of age and a citizen by blood, of the Creek Nation; that I am the lawful wife of James W. Throckmorton, who is a citizen, by blood, of the Creek Nation; that a female child was born to me on 16 day of Oct, 1904; that said child has been named Irene Throckmorton, and ~~was living March 4, 1905.~~ died Dec 5 – 1904

                               Ida L. Throckmorton

Witnesses To Mark:

    Subscribed and sworn to before me this 11 day of April, 1905.

    (seal)   Edw C Griesel
                                    Notary Public.

AFFIDAVIT OF ATTENDING PHYSICIAN OR MID-WIFE.

UNITED STATES OF AMERICA, Indian Territory, ⎫
    Western   DISTRICT. ⎭

    I, Elias T. Hensley, a Physician, on oath state that I attended on Mrs. Ida L. Throckmorton , wife of James W. Throckmorton on the 16 day of Oct , 1904 ; that there was born to her on said date a female child; that said child ~~was living March 4, 1905, and~~ is said to have been named Irene Throckmorton.

                               Elias T. Hensley

Witnesses To Mark:

    Subscribed and sworn to before me this 11 day of April, 1905.

    (Seal)   Edw C Griesel
                                     Notary Public.

Applications for Enrollment of Creek Newborn
Act of 1905   Volume I

BIRTH AFFIDAVIT.

DEPARTMENT OF THE INTERIOR,
COMMISSION TO THE FIVE CIVILIZED TRIBES.

———————

IN RE APPLICATION FOR ENROLLMENT, as a citizen of the Creek Nation, of Lonie Irene Throckmorton , born on the 16 day of October , 1904

Name of Father: James W Throckmorton   a citizen of the   Creek   Nation.
Name of Mother: Ida Throckmorton   a citizen of the   Creek   Nation.

Postoffice   Natura, I.T.

———————

AFFIDAVIT OF ~~MOTHER.~~ father

UNITED STATES OF AMERICA, Indian Territory,⎫
        Western   DISTRICT.⎭

I, James W Throckmorton, on oath state that I am 29 years of age and a citizen by blood, of the Creek Nation; that I am the lawful ~~wife~~ hus of Ida Throckmorton, who is a citizen by blood, of the Creek Nation; that a female child was born to me on 16 day of Oct. 1904; that said child has been named Lonie Irene Throckmorton, ~~and is now living~~. & died December 5, 1904.

James W Throckmorton

Witnesses To Mark:
{

Subscribed and sworn to before me this 6 day of March, 1905.

Edw C Griesel
Notary Public.

———————

NC 16   JLD
DEPARTMENT OF THE INTERIOR
COMMISSIONER TO THE FIVE CIVILIZED TRIBES
. . . .

In the matter of the application for the enrollment of Lonie Irene Throckmorton, deceased, as a citizen by blood of the Creek Nation.
. . . .

STATEMENT AND ORDER.

Applications for Enrollment of Creek Newborn
Act of 1905   Volume I

The record in this case shows that on March 6, 1905, application was made, in affidavit form, supplemented by sworn testimony, for the enrollment of Lonie Irene Throckmorton, deceased, as a citizen by blood of the Creek Nation, under the provisions of the act of Congress approved March 3, 1905.

It appears from the evidence filed in this matter, that said Lonie Irene Throckmorton, deceased, was born October 16, 1904, and died December 5, 1904.

The act of Congress approved March 3, 1905, (33 Stats., 1048), provides:

"That the Commission to the Five Civilized Tribes is authorized for sixty days after the date of the approval of this act to receive and consider applications for enrollment, of children, born subsequent to May twenty-fifth, nineteen hundred and five, and living on said latter date, to citizens of the Creek tribe of Indians whose enrollment has been approved by the Secretary of the Interior prior to the approval of this act; and to enroll and make allotments to such children."

It is, therefore, ordered that the application for the enrollment of said Lonie Irene Throckmorton, deceased, as a citizen by blood of the Creek Nation be, and the same is, hereby dismissed.

(Name Illegible) Commissioner.

Muskogee, Indian Territory.
JAN 15 1907

BIRTH AFFIDAVIT.

DEPARTMENT OF THE INTERIOR,
COMMISSION TO THE FIVE CIVILIZED TRIBES.

IN RE APPLICATION FOR ENROLLMENT, as a citizen of the Creek Nation, of David William Throckmorton , born on the 12 day of June , 1902

Name of Father: James W Throckmorton	a citizen of the Creek	Nation.
Name of Mother: Ida Throckmorton	a citizen of the Creek	Nation.

Postoffice   Natura

AFFIDAVIT OF MOTHER.

UNITED STATES OF AMERICA, Indian Territory,
    Western   DISTRICT.

I, James W. Throckmorton, on oath state that I am 29 years of age and a citizen by blood, of the Creek Nation; that I am the lawful ~~wife~~ husband of Ida Throckmorton, who is a citizen, by blood, of the Creek Nation; that a male child was born to me on 12 day of June, 1902; that said child has been named David William Throckmorton, and is now living.

James W. Throckmorton

Witnesses To Mark:

64

Applications for Enrollment of Creek Newborn
Act of 1905   Volume I

Subscribed and sworn to before me this 6 day of March, 1905.

Edw C Griesel
Notary Public.

AFFIDAVIT OF ATTENDING PHYSICIAN OR MID-WIFE.   Half Brother

UNITED STATES OF AMERICA, Indian Territory,
     Western   DISTRICT.

I, W J Roberts, a Half Brother, a citizen by blood, on oath state that I ~~attended on Mrs. (blank) , wife of (blank) on the 12 day of June , 1902~~ ; that there was born to her on said date a male child; that said child is now living and is said to have been named David Wm Throckmorton.

W.J. Roberts

Witnesses To Mark:
{

Subscribed and sworn to before me this 6 day of March, 1905.
Edw C Griesel
Notary Public.

BIRTH AFFIDAVIT.

DEPARTMENT OF THE INTERIOR,
COMMISSION TO THE FIVE CIVILIZED TRIBES.

IN RE APPLICATION FOR ENROLLMENT, as a citizen of the Creek Nation, of William D. Throckmorton , born on the 12 day of June , 1902

Name of Father: James W Throckmorton   a citizen of the   Creek   Nation.
Hickory Ground
Name of Mother: Ida L. Throckmorton   a citizen of the   Creek   Nation.
Coweta Town

Postoffice   Natura, Ind. Terr.

Child present.

AFFIDAVIT OF MOTHER.

UNITED STATES OF AMERICA, Indian Territory,
     Western   DISTRICT.

I, Ida L. Throckmorton, on oath state that I am 29 years of age and a citizen by blood, of the Creek Nation; that I am the lawful wife of James W. Throckmorton, who is a citizen, by blood, of the Creek Nation; that a male child was born to me on 12 day of

65

June, 1902; that said child has been named William D. Throckmorton and was living March 4, 1905.

Ida L. Throckmorton

Witnesses To Mark:

{

Subscribed and sworn to before me this 11 day of April, 1905.

Drennan C Skaggs
Notary Public.

AFFIDAVIT OF ATTENDING PHYSICIAN OR MID-WIFE.

UNITED STATES OF AMERICA, Indian Territory, ⎫
     Western   DISTRICT. ⎬

I, Mollie Throckmorton, a nurse, on oath state that I assisted the physician who attended on Mrs. Ida L. Throckmorton, wife of James W. Throckmorton on the 12 day of June, 1902; that there was born to her on said date a male child; that said child was living March 4, 1905, and is said to have been named William D. Throckmorton.

Mollie Throckmorton

Witnesses To Mark:

{

Subscribed and sworn to before me this 11 day of April, 1905.

Drennan C. Skaggs
Notary Public.

NC 16.

Muskogee, Indian Territory, July 1, 1905.

James W. Throckmorton,
    Natura, Indian Territory.

Dear Sir:

There are on file with the Commission affidavits relative to the enrollment of your minor child in which its name is given as David William and William D. Throckmorton. The former name appear[sic] in your affidavit and the latter in the affidavits of the mother and midwife.

It is necessary for you to correct this discrepancy, and a letter to that effect is requested by you and your wife at an early date.

Respectfully,

Commissioner.

NC 16.

Muskogee, Indian Territory, July 5, 1905.

James W. Throckmorton,
Natura, Indian Territory.

Dear Sir:

There are on file at this office affidavits relative to the enrollment of your minor child, in which its name is given as David William and William D. Throckmorton. The former name appears in your affidavit and the latter in the affidavits of the mother and midwife.

It is necessary for you to correct this discrepancy, and a letter to that effect is requested by you and your wife at an early date.

Respectfully,

Commissioner.

Natura, July 7, 1905.

Mr. Tams Bixby,
Muskogee, Ind. Ty.

Dear Sir:

Yours of the 5th inst. rec'd and will say in reply that the correct name of the child of is William D. Throckmorton. The child being named for his two grand fathers, caused the mistake in the name to be made, as it must have been given in backwards.

Respectfully,

(Signed)   James W. Throckmorton
Ida L. Throckmorton.

The father and the mother

NC 16.

Muskogee, Indian Territory, January 17, 1907.

Ida L. Throckmorton,
    c/o James W. Throckmorton,
        Natura, Indian Territory.

Dear Madam:

There is herewith enclosed one copy of the Statement and Order of the Commissioner to the Five Civilized Tribes, dated January 15, 1907, dismissing the application made by you for the enrollment of your minor child, Lonie Irene Throckmorton, deceased, as a citizen by blood of the Creek Nation.

Respectfully,

LM-74.

Commissioner.

Muskogee, Indian Territory, May 2, 1905.

Freeman & Lucas,
    Checotah, Indian Territory.

Gentlemen:

Receipt is hereby acknowledged of your letter of April 25, 1905, transmitting duly executed power of attorney given by Mary Lou Baughman to Bert Baughman for the purpose of filing their minor children, Guy L., Jefferson E., and Hila May Baughman, applicants for enrollment under the Act of March 3, 1905, also petition by said Bert Baughman that certain lands in the Creek Nation designated in said petition be allotted to them and protesting against the filing of any other citizens upon land so sought.

In reply you are advised that until the enrollment of said minor children has been approved by the Secretary of the Interior no reservation of land in the Creek Nation can be made. The petition and power of attorney transmitted by your letter are herewith returned.

Respectfully,

Enc. NEW 13.

Chairman.

DEPARTMENT OF THE INTERIOR,
COMMISSIONER TO THE FIVE CIVILIZED TRIBES.

REFER IN REPLY TO THE FOLLOWING:

N.C. -17.

Muskogee, Indian Territory, **August 4, 1905.**

Mary Lula Baughman,
    Care of Bert Baughman,
        Checotah, Indian Territory.

Dear Madam:

You are hereby advised that on **July 28, 1905** , the Secretary of the Interior approved the enrollment of your minor child, **Jefferson Euel Baughman**, as a citizen by blood of the **Creek** Nation, and that the name of said child appears upon the roll of new born citizens of the **Creek** Nation as Number **13**.

The child is now entitled to an allotment, and application therefor should be made without delay at the Land Office for the Nation in which the prospective allotment is located.

An entire allotment for said child must be selected at the time of the original application.

Respectively,

Commissioner.

DEPARTMENT OF THE INTERIOR,
COMMISSIONER TO THE FIVE CIVILIZED TRIBES.

REFER IN REPLY TO THE FOLLOWING:

N.C. -17.

Muskogee, Indian Territory, **August 4, 1905.**

Mary Lula Baughman,
    Care of Bert Baughman,
        Checotah, Indian Territory.

Dear Madam:

You are hereby advised that on **July 28, 1905** , the Secretary of the Interior approved the enrollment of your minor child, **Gay[sic] L. Baughman**, as a citizen by blood of the **Creek** Nation, and that the name of said child appears upon the roll of new born citizens of the **Creek** Nation as Number **14**.

The child is now entitled to an allotment, and application therefor should be made without delay at the Land Office for the Nation in which the prospective allotment is located.

An entire allotment for said child must be selected at the time of the original application.

Respectively,

Commissioner.

REFER IN REPLY TO THE FOLLOWING:

DEPARTMENT OF THE INTERIOR,
COMMISSIONER TO THE FIVE CIVILIZED TRIBES.   N.C. -17.

Muskogee, Indian Territory, **August 4, 1905.**

Mary Lula Baughman,
  Care of Bert Baughman,
    Checotah, Indian Territory.

Dear Madam:

You are hereby advised that on July 28, 1905 , the Secretary of the Interior approved the enrollment of your minor child, **Ella May Baughman**, as a citizen by blood of the **Creek** Nation, and that the name of said child appears upon the roll of new born citizens of the **Creek** Nation as Number **15.**

The child is now entitled to an allotment, and application therefor should be made without delay at the Land Office for the Nation in which the prospective allotment is located.

An entire allotment for said child must be selected at the time of the original application.

Respectively,

Commissioner.

Indian Territory   Checotah IT Mch. 7th – 1905
Western District

Personally appeared before me this 7th day of March 1905, Dr. B.J. Vance to me personally well known who being first duly sworn, states on his oath as follows: to-wit: On the 2nd day of May 1902 I attended on Mrs. Mary Lula Baughman on which day a male child was born to her which said child is still living and is said to be named Jefferson Euel Baughman.
Also, on the 8th day of December 1903, I attended on the said Mary Lula Baughman on which date a male child was born to her which said child is still living and is said to be named Gay[sic] L. Baughman.
Also, on the 11th day of February 1905, I attended on the said Mary Lula Baughman on which date a Female child was born to her, which said child is still living and is said to have been named Ella May Baughman.

B. J. Vance M.D.

70

Subscribed and sworn to before me this 7th day of March 1905.

JB Morrow

My Commission Expires July 1, 1906.

BIRTH AFFIDAVIT.

DEPARTMENT OF THE INTERIOR,
COMMISSION TO THE FIVE CIVILIZED TRIBES.

IN RE APPLICATION FOR ENROLLMENT, as a citizen of the Creek Nation, of Jefferson Euel Baughman , born on the 2nd day of May , 1902

Name of Father: Bert Baughman   a citizen of the United States Nation.

(nee Chapman)

Name of Mother: Mary Lula Baughman   a citizen of the   Creek   Nation.

Postoffice   Checotah, I.T.

AFFIDAVIT OF MOTHER.

UNITED STATES OF AMERICA, Indian Territory,
Western   DISTRICT.

I, Mary Lula Baughman, on oath state that I am 23 years of age and a citizen by Blood, of the Creek Nation; that I am the lawful wife of Bert Baughman, who is a citizen, by *(blank)*, of the United States Nation, that a male child was born to me on the 2nd day of May 1902, that said child has been named Jefferson Euel Baughman, and is now living.

Mary Lula Baughman

Witnesses To Mark:

Subscribed and sworn to before me this 7th day of March, 1905.

JB Morrow

My Commission Expires July 1, 1906.   Notary Public.

AFFIDAVIT OF ATTENDING PHYSICIAN OR MID-WIFE.

UNITED STATES OF AMERICA, Indian Territory,
Western   DISTRICT.

I, B.J. Vance M.D., a Physician on oath state that I attended on Mrs. Mary Lula Baughman, wife of Bert Baughman on the 2nd day of May , 1902 ; that there was born to her on said date a male child; that said child is now living, and is said to have been named Jefferson Euel Baughman.

71

BJ Vance, M.D.

Witnesses To Mark:

{

Subscribed and sworn to before me this 7th day of March, 1905.

JB Morrow

My Commission Expires July 1, 1906.   Notary Public.

BIRTH AFFIDAVIT.
DEPARTMENT OF THE INTERIOR,
COMMISSION TO THE FIVE CIVILIZED TRIBES.

IN RE APPLICATION FOR ENROLLMENT, as a citizen of the Creek Nation, of Jefferson E. Baughman , born on the 2 day of May , 1902

Name of Father: Bert Baughman	a citizen of the U.S.	Nation.
Name of Mother: Mary L "	a citizen of the Creek	Nation.

Postoffice   Checotah

AFFIDAVIT OF ~~MOTHER~~. father

UNITED STATES OF AMERICA, Indian Territory,
Western   **DISTRICT.**

I, Bert Baughman, on oath state that I am 24 years of age and a citizen by ----- of the U.S. Nation; that I am the lawful ~~wife~~ hus of Mary L. Baughman, who is a citizen, by blood, of the Creek Nation; that a male child was born to me on 2 day of May, 1902, that said child has been named Jefferson E. Baughman, and is now living.

Bert Baughman

Witnesses To Mark:

{

Subscribed and sworn to before me this 6 day of March, 1905.

Edw C Griesel
Notary Public.

BIRTH AFFIDAVIT.

DEPARTMENT OF THE INTERIOR,
COMMISSION TO THE FIVE CIVILIZED TRIBES.

IN RE APPLICATION FOR ENROLLMENT, as a citizen of the Creek Nation, of Gay L. Baughman , born on the 8th day of December , 1903

Name of Father: Bert Baughman	a citizen of the U.S.	Nation.
Name of Mother: Mary Lula Baughman	a citizen of the Creek	Nation.

Postoffice   Checotah I.T.

AFFIDAVIT OF MOTHER.

UNITED STATES OF AMERICA, Indian Territory,⎤
    Western   DISTRICT. ⎦

    I, Mary Lula Baughman, on oath state that I am 23 years of age and a citizen by Blood, of the Creek Nation; that I am the lawful wife of Bert Baughman, who is a citizen, by *(blank)*, of the United States Nation, that a male child was born to me on the 8th day of December 1903, that said child has been named Gay L. Baughman, and is now living.

Mary Lula Baughman

Witnesses To Mark:

{

    Subscribed and sworn to before me this 7th day of March, 1905.

My Commission Expires July 1, 1906.   JB Morrow
                                       Notary Public.

AFFIDAVIT OF ATTENDING PHYSICIAN OR MID-WIFE.

UNITED STATES OF AMERICA, Indian Territory,⎤
    Western   DISTRICT. ⎦

    I, B.J. Vance M.D., a Physician, on oath state that I attended on Mrs. Mary Lula Baughman, wife of Bert Baughman on the 8th day of December , 1903; that there was born to her on said date a male child; that said child is now living, and is said to have been named Gay L. Baughman.

BJ Vance, M.D.

Witnesses To Mark:

{

    Subscribed and sworn to before me this 7th day of March, 1905.

73

Applications for Enrollment of Creek Newborn
Act of 1905   Volume I

My Commission Expires July 1, 1906.

JB Morrow
Notary Public.

DEPARTMENT OF THE INTERIOR,
COMMISSION TO THE FIVE CIVILIZED TRIBES.

IN RE APPLICATION FOR ENROLLMENT, as a citizen of the Creek Nation, of Gay L. Baughman , born on the 8 day of Dec, 1903

Name of Father: Bert Baughman	a citizen of the	U.S.	Nation.
Name of Mother: Mary L "	a citizen of the	Creek	Nation.

Postoffice   Checotah

AFFIDAVIT OF ~~MOTHER~~. father

UNITED STATES OF AMERICA, Indian Territory,
        Western   **DISTRICT.**

I, Bert Baughman, on oath state that I am 24 years of age and a citizen by ----- of the U.S. Nation; that I am the lawful ~~wife~~ hus of Mary Lu Baughman, who is a citizen, by blood, of the Creek Nation; that a male child was born to me on 8 day of Dec, 1903, that said child has been named Gay L. Baughman, and is now living.

Bert Baughman

Witnesses To Mark:

Subscribed and sworn to before me this 6 day of March, 1905.

Edw C Griesel
Notary Public.

DEPARTMENT OF THE INTERIOR,
COMMISSION TO THE FIVE CIVILIZED TRIBES.

IN RE APPLICATION FOR ENROLLMENT, as a citizen of the Creek Nation, of Ella May Baughman , born on the 11 day of Feb, 1905

Name of Father: Bert Baughman	a citizen of the	U.S.	Nation.
Name of Mother: Mary Lu "	a citizen of the	Creek	Nation.

Applications for Enrollment of Creek Newborn
Act of 1905   Volume I

Postoffice   Checotah

AFFIDAVIT OF ~~MOTHER~~. father

UNITED STATES OF AMERICA, Indian Territory, ⎫
  Western   DISTRICT. ⎭

    I, Bert Baughman, on oath state that I am 24 years of age and a citizen by ----- of the U.S. Nation; that I am the lawful ~~wife~~ hus of Mary Lu Baughman, who is a citizen, by blood, of the Creek Nation; that a female child was born to me on 11 day of Feb, 1905, that said child has been named Ella May Baughman, and is now living.

Bert Baughman

Witnesses To Mark:
  {

    Subscribed and sworn to before me this 6 day of March, 1905.

Edw C Griesel
Notary Public.

BIRTH AFFIDAVIT.

DEPARTMENT OF THE INTERIOR,
COMMISSION TO THE FIVE CIVILIZED TRIBES.

IN RE APPLICATION FOR ENROLLMENT, as a citizen of the Creek Nation, of Ella May Baughman , born on the 11th day of February , 1905

Name of Father: Bert Baughman	a citizen of the U.S.	Nation.
Name of Mother: Mary Lula Baughman	a citizen of the Creek	Nation.

Postoffice   Checotah I.T.

AFFIDAVIT OF MOTHER.

UNITED STATES OF AMERICA, Indian Territory,⎫
  Western   DISTRICT. ⎭

    I, Mary Lula Baughman, on oath state that I am 23 years of age and a citizen by Blood, of the Creek Nation; that I am the lawful wife of Bert Baughman, who is a citizen, by *(blank)*, of the United States Nation, that a female child was born to me on the 11th day of February, 1905, that said child has been named Ella May Baughman, and is now living.

Mary Lula Baughman

75

Applications for Enrollment of Creek Newborn
Act of 1905   Volume I

Witnesses To Mark:

{

Subscribed and sworn to before me this 7th day of March, 1905.

My Commission Expires July 1, 1906.   JB Morrow
                                                                        Notary Public.

AFFIDAVIT OF ATTENDING PHYSICIAN OR MID-WIFE.

UNITED STATES OF AMERICA, Indian Territory,
          Western   **DISTRICT.**

I, B.J. Vance M.D., a Physician, on oath state that I attended on Mrs. Mary Lula Baughman, wife of Bert Baughman on the 11th day of February , 1905; that there was born to her on said date a Female child; that said child is now living, and is said to have been named Ella May Baughman.

                                                        BJ Vance, M.D.

Witnesses To Mark:

{

Subscribed and sworn to before me this 7th day of March, 1905.

My Commission Expires July 1, 1906.   JB Morrow
                                                                        Notary Public.

                                                                        N.C. 18

DEPARTMENT OF THE INTERIOR,
COMMISSIONER TO THE FIVE CIVILIZED TRIBES.
Muskogee, Indian Territory, August 23, 1905.

In the matter of the application for the enrollment of Josephine Sookey as a citizen by blood of the Creek Nation.

APPEARANCES: Thomas & Foreman attys. for applicant by J.P. Farnsworth.

Mamie Sookey, being duly sworn, testified as follows:

By Commissioner.

Q What is your name? A Mamie Sookey.
Q What is your age? A I will be 21 the 26th of this month.
Q What is your post office address? A Wybark.

Applications for Enrollment of Creek Newborn
Act of 1905 Volume I

Q Are you a citizen of the Creek Nation? A No, sir

Q Are you a citizen of any of the five tribes? A No sir

Q How long have you lived in Indian Territory? A About eight years

Q Have you a child named Josephine Sookey? A Yes, sir

Q Where is this child: A Here

Q What is the name of the father of this child? Boney Sookey

Q Is he living? A Dead

Q When did he die? A May 29, 1905

Q How old was he? A About 26

Q Do you know the name of his father? A Wiley Sookey

Q When was this child born? A January 19, 1903

Q How do you fix that date, anything help you to remember it? A I know she was born at that time

Q Are you pretty certain of that now? A Yes, sir

Q You haven't always been? A I made a mistake before

Q There are on file at this office affidavits executed by you on the 6th of March 1905 signed by you before a Commission Notary Public in which you state this child was born January 19 1901, also affidavit signed and sworn to before Thomas A Jenkins May 1905 along with affidavit of midwife in which it is given as January 19, 1902, how do you account for that? A I just made a mistake that's all the way I can account for it

Q When you came in here did you know it was 1903 the child was born? A I knew it but I made a mistake.

Q Were you conscious that you gave the year 1901? A I was conscious but I had a right smart of trouble.

Q Then you knew at that time that the child wasn't born in 1901 but just failed to give it? A Yes

Q How old will this child be next January, 1905? A Will be three years old

Q How old was it last January? A Two

Q Inspite[sic] of that you came in here and made an affidavit that it was 1901 and also went before another man and gave 1902 Q I did that but it was through a mistake

Q Were you married to Boney Sookey? A Yes, sir

      Attorney for applicant presents marriage license and certificate
      which is made a part of the record herein

Q When were you married? A October 27, 1902

Q What was your name before you were married? A Mamie Hohimar

Q Was this child born before or after you were married? A After

Q How long after? A Three months I guess

Q Was any person present when she was born? A Bell Smizer, Ivir Hohimar

Q Was Bell Smizer the midwife? A Yes, sir

Q Can you read and write? A Not to say well, I can sign my name

Q Did you have any trouble with Boney Sookey? A He and I were intending to marry but he kept putting me off, he didn't have the money and my father put up the money.

Q When you knew you were to have a child and he didn't marry you, you had him arrested and taken into court and instead of prosecuting him further he married you, is that correct? A Yes

Q How many months after that before you had this child? A Three

Q This is the child here? A Yes, sir

Q Did you ever have any other child? A No, sir

Q Did you live with him after you were married until he died? A Part of the time

Q How long did you live with him after that? A I guess about three months

Q Was he living with you at the time the child was born? A No we had parted about a week

Q Did you ever live with him again? A No, sir

> The record of the Commissioner of the U.S. Harlow A. Leekey
> is produced and it says the complaint states that in July
> 1902 this promise was made and in October the case was
> dismissed as he promised to marry th[sic] witness and did
> marry her before he left the courthouse.

By Mr. Farnsworth.

Q Why did you leave Boney Sookey? A Because he wouldn't support me

Q How long did you leave him before the child was born? A About a week

Belle Smyers being duly sworn testifies as follows:

Q What is your name? A Belle Smyers

Q What is your age? 42

Q What is your post office address? A Haynes

Q Are you a citizen of the Creek Nation? A No, sir

Q States woman? A Yes, sir

Q Do you know Mamie Sookey? A Yes, sir

Q Did you know Boney Sookey? A Yes, sir I have seen him

Q Do you know a child of theirs named Josephine Sookey? A Yes, sir

Q Is that child living? A Yes, sir she is right here

Q When did you first see her? A When I was with her mother

Q Did you wait on her a midwife? A Yes, sir

Q Do you know the years very well? A No, sir

Q When was this child born? A January 19

Q What year? A 1900 I forget it is 1903 ought

Q Are you sure it was born in 1903? A I cant[sic] count

Q You came in here once before and made an affidavit and at that time you said it was born in 1901? A I reckon she must have had it wrong

Q Do you know it better now that you did then? A No, sir

Q At that time you signed by mark before a notary public and you said it was born January 19, 1901? A It is about 2 years and 6 months old but I cant[sic] count

Q Are you sure it's just 2 years and 6 months? A It may be 7 months

Q You are sure of the two years? A Yes, sir

Applications for Enrollment of Creek Newborn
Act of 1905   Volume I

Q How do you account for having sworn it was born in 1901? A We ll[sic] I tell you to be honest I dont[sic] count

By Mr. Farnsworth.

Q Do you live near Mrs. Sookey? A Yes, sir
Q How far? A About 22o[sic] yards
Q Then you moved away from them? A Yes, sir
Q Soon after the child was born? A Yes, sir
Q How long since you moved away from them about? A This makes three crops
Q How did you happen to make that other affidavit did they read it over to you? A No not to my remembrance
Q What did they say? A They asked me if I was the midwife and I said yes and held up my hand

Commissioner

Q Did you ever see the child again? A Yes, sir
Q How long did you say when you acted as midwife? A Two or three times
Q Then you moved away? A I saw the child often
Q You know this child here is the same child? A Yes, sir
Q Do you know if she ever had any other child? A No, sir, that's all I ever knew of her having
Irving Hohimar being duly sworn testified as follows.?

Q What is your name? A Irving Hohimar.
Q How old are you? A 24
Q What is your post office address? A Muskogee
Q You are a States man? A Yes, sir
Q Do you know for a fact that she is your niece? A Yes, sir
Q Your sisters child? A Yes sir
Q Do you live near her? A No, sir
Q Did you at the time it was born? A Yes, sir
Q Were you present when it was born? A No, sir, I had gone for the doctor
Q Who was that? A Dr. Martin
Q Did you get him? A Yes, sir
Q Was he present when it was born? A No, sir, it was born when we got back
Q How old was it? A couple of hours Before I went for the doctor I got the midwife and she was present when it was born
Q When was this? A 1903
Q Are you sure of that? A Yes, sir
Q What was have you of remembering the year, the mother and midwife have confused it slightly? A I know that was the year I came to my place, I moved over from Vans Lake
Q You moved from Vans Lake to near Wybark in January 1903? A Yes
Q In this way you are certain it was 1903? A Yes, sir

Q You know there was trouble between Boney Sookey and your sister do you think that would help mix the dates in her mind or can you account for it in any way? A No, sir I cant[sic]
Q But you are certain this is her child and you have seen the child often? A Yes, sir
Q And you know that is the child that was born in January 1903 A Yes Sir
Q And you know positively that it is now about how old? A Two year
Q And not four? A No, sir
Q Did she ever have any other children that you know of? A No, sir
Q She didn't have any before nor since? A No, sir, I haven't been away from her over three months at a time
Q Are you positive that Boney Sookey was the father? A Yes, sir
Q Never saw any one else around there? A No, sir

By Mr. Farnsworth

Q Your father had a lease for five years on this place? A Yes, sir
Q When did that lease begin? A 1903
Q January 1903? A Yes, sir
Q And run for five years? A Yes, sir
Q When did your father move on this place? A Began moving the 17th and finished moving the 18th January 1903
I live in the house that he occupied and I moved about 300 yards west of the same place.

I, Anna Garrigues, state that the above and foregoing is a true and correct transcript of my stenographic notes as taken in said cause on said date.

Anna Garrigues

Subscribed and sworn to   Edw C Griesel
before me this 24th day of August 1905   Notary Public

MARRIAGE LICENSE.

United States of America
Indian Territory
Western District   ss   No. 371

To any person authorized by law to solemnize marriage-Greeting

You are hereby command to solemnize the rite and publish the Banns of matrimony between Mr. Barney[sic] Sookey of Wybark in the Indian Territory, aged 23 years and Miss Mamie Hohimar of Wybark in the Indian Territory aged 18 years according to law, and do you officially sign and return this license to the parties herein named.

Witness my hand and official seal at Muskogee Indian territory this 27 day of October AD 1902

Applications for Enrollment of Creek Newborn
Act of 1905   Volume I

R.P. Harrison
Clerk of the U S Court

By A Z England deputy

CERTIFICATE OF MARRIAGE

United states[sic] of America
Indian Territory
Western District

I R.P. Harrison Clerk U S Court ~~A minister of the gospel~~ do hereby certify that on the 27 day of Oct A D 1902 did duly and according to law as commanded in the foregoing license solemnize the rite and publish the banns of matrimony between the parties therein named

Witness my hand this 27 day of Oct A D 1902

My credentials are recorded in the office of the Clerk of the United States Court, Indian Territory Western District Book *(blank)* page

R P Harrison
Clerk U S Court
~~A Minister of the~~
~~Gospel~~
A Z England

Note This license and certificate of marriage must be returned to the office of the Clerk of the United States court in the Western District Indian Territory from whence it was issued within sixty days from the date thereof of the party to whom the license was issued will be liable in the amount of the one hundred dollars ($100.00)

BIRTH AFFIDAVIT.

DEPARTMENT OF THE INTERIOR,
COMMISSION TO THE FIVE CIVILIZED TRIBES.

IN RE APPLICATION FOR ENROLLMENT, as a citizen of the Creek Nation, of Josephine Sookey , born on the 19th day of January , 1901

Name of Father: Boney Sookey	a citizen of the Creek	Nation.
Name of Mother: Mammie Sookey	a citizen of the Creek	Nation.

Postoffice   Gibson Station

81

Applications for Enrollment of Creek Newborn
Act of 1905 Volume I

AFFIDAVIT OF MOTHER.

UNITED STATES OF AMERICA, Indian Territory, ⎱
    Western   **DISTRICT.** ⎰

    I, Mammie Sookey, on oath state that I am 21 years of age and a non citizen ~~by~~ of[sic], of the Creek Nation; that I am the lawful wife of Boney Sookey, who is a citizen, by blood, of the Creek Nation; that a female child was born to me on 19th day of January, 1901, that said child has been named Josephine Sookey, and was living March 4, 1905.

                                  Mamie Sookey

Witnesses To Mark:

{

    Subscribed and sworn to before me this 2nd day of May, 1905.

My Commission
expires on December 26th 1907   Thos A Jenkins
                                 Notary Public.

AFFIDAVIT OF ATTENDING PHYSICIAN OR MID-WIFE.

UNITED STATES OF AMERICA, Indian Territory, ⎱
    Western   **DISTRICT.** ⎰

    I, Bell Smyers, a midwife, on oath state that I attended on Mrs. Mammie Sookey, wife of Boney Sookey on the 19th day of January, 1901; that there was born to her on said date a female child; that said child was living March 4, 1905, and is said to have been named Josephine Sookey.

                                    her
                             Belle x Smyers
Witnesses To Mark: mark
{ C.W. Reid
{ J.N. Allen

    Subscribed and sworn to before me this 2nd day of May, 1905.

My Commission
expires on December 26th 1907   Thos A Jenkins
                                 Notary Public.

Applications for Enrollment of Creek Newborn
Act of 1905   Volume I

BIRTH AFFIDAVIT.

DEPARTMENT OF THE INTERIOR,
COMMISSION TO THE FIVE CIVILIZED TRIBES.

———————

IN RE APPLICATION FOR ENROLLMENT, as a citizen of the Creek Nation, of Josephine Sookey, born on the 19 day of January , 1901

Name of Father:	Boney Sookey	a citizen of the Creek	Nation.
Name of Mother:	Mammie "	a citizen of the U.S.	Nation.

Postoffice   Gibson Station, I.T.

———————

AFFIDAVIT OF MOTHER.

UNITED STATES OF AMERICA, Indian Territory,⎤
     Western   DISTRICT.⎦

I, Mamie Sookey, on oath state that I am 21 years of age and a citizen by ----- of the U.S. Nation; that I am the lawful wife of Boney Sookey, who is a citizen, by blood, of the Creek Nation; that a female child was born to me on 19 day of January, 1901, that said child has been named Josephine Sookey, and is now living.

                    Mamie Sookey
Witnesses To Mark:

{

Subscribed and sworn to before me this 6 day of March, 1905.

                    Edw C Griesel
                         Notary Public.

———————

BIRTH AFFIDAVIT.

DEPARTMENT OF THE INTERIOR,
COMMISSION TO THE FIVE CIVILIZED TRIBES.

———————

IN RE APPLICATION FOR ENROLLMENT, as a citizen of the Creek Nation, of Josephine Sookey, born on the 19 day of January , 1903

Name of Father:	Boney Sookey	a citizen of the Creek	Nation.
Name of Mother:	Mamie Sookey	a citizen of the U.S.	Nation.

Postoffice

———————

Applications for Enrollment of Creek Newborn
Act of 1905   Volume I

AFFIDAVIT OF MOTHER.

UNITED STATES OF AMERICA, Indian Territory,⎫
    Western   DISTRICT. ⎬

      I, Mamie Sookey, on oath state that I am 20 years of age and a citizen by ----- of the U.S. Nation; that I am the lawful wife of Boney Sookey, who is a citizen, by blood, of the Creek Nation; that a female child was born to me on 19 day of January, 1903, that said child has been named Josephine Sookey, and was living March 4, 1905.

                                    Mamie Sookey

Witnesses To Mark:

{

  Subscribed and sworn to before me this 23 day of August, 1905.

                  (Name Illegible Ink Smeared)
                            Notary Public.

                                    BA 27 B.

               Muskogee, Indian Territory, May 15, 1905.

Mr. Charles Gibson,
      Eufaula, Indian Territory.

Dear Sir:

      The Commission is in receipt of affidavits executed by you relative to the birth of your minor children, Verna Marie and Charles C. Gibson. The affidavits of the mother and midwife or physician in attendance at the birth of said child must be furnished.

      There is therewith enclosed two blank forms of birth affidavits, and in executing same care should be exercised to see that all blanks are properly filled, all names written in full and in the event that either of the persons signing the affidavits is unable to write, signatures by mark must be attested by two witnesses. Each affidavit must be executed before a Notary Public and the notarial seal and signature of the officer must be attached to each separate affidavit.

                          Respectfully,
BC.   Chairman.

Applications for Enrollment of Creek Newborn
Act of 1905   Volume I

NC 19.

Muskogee, Indian Territory, July 13, 1906.

Mrs. Modenia Gibson,
  Eufaula, Indian Territory.

Dear Madam:

There are on file at this office affidavits executed by you in which your name is given as Modenia M., Modina and Maud Gibson.

You are requested to advise this office as to your correct name.

Respectfully,

Commissioner.

DEPARTMENT OF THE INTERIOR,
COMMISSION TO THE FIVE CIVILIZED TRIBES.

NC.19.

Muskogee, Indian Territory, July 13, 1905.

Mrs. Modenia Gibson,
  Eufaula, Indian Territory.

Dear Madam:

There are on file at this office affidavits executed by you in which your name is given as Modenia M., Modina and Maud Gibson.
You are requested to advise this office as to your correct name.

Respectfully,
(Signed) Tams Bixby,
Commissioner.

To the Hon. T. Bixby,
  Dear Sir: July 16, 1905.
                        I will say in reply to above that my name is Modenia Muskogee Gibson i[sic] was in my childhood called Maud for short in my widow[sic] hood was known as Maud Perry i was filed as Maud Perry on my Land i had one babe boy when I marryed[sic] Mr. Charles Gibson who is well known To you of course i became Gibson. Therefore my name in full is Mrs. Modenia M. Gibson.   The middle name being

85

Applications for Enrollment of Creek Newborn
Act of 1905   Volume I

Muskogee I hope xx with this explanation the Coms. will be satisfyed[sic] my maden[sic] name was Modenia M. Aultman.

Yours
signed   Mrs. M.M. Gibson.

P.S. Mr .[sic] Gibson is now located for a few months at a new place on the Fort Smith & Western R.R. please address all communications to us if need be to Hanna, I.T. & oblige.

signed Mrs. M.M. Gibson.

BIRTH AFFIDAVIT.

DEPARTMENT OF THE INTERIOR,

COMMISSION TO THE FIVE CIVILIZED TRIBES.

IN RE APPLICATION FOR ENROLLMENT, as a citizen of the Creek Nation, of Verna Marie Gibson , born on the 5th day of October , 1901

Name of Father: Charles Gibson	a citizen of the	Creek	Nation.
Name of Mother: Modenia M. Gibson	a citizen of the	Creek	Nation.

Postoffice   Eufaula, I.T.

AFFIDAVIT OF MOTHER.

UNITED STATES OF AMERICA, Indian Territory,⎫

    Western   **DISTRICT.** ⎭

   I, Mrs. Modenia M. Gibson, on oath state that I am 25 years of age and a citizen by Blood, of the Creek Nation; that I am the lawful wife of Charles Gibson, who is a citizen, by Blood, of the Creek Nation; that a female child was born to me on 5th day of October, 1901, that said child has been named Verna Marie Gibson, and was living March 4, 1905.

Modenia M. Gibson

Witnesses To Mark:

{

Subscribed and sworn to before me this 17th day of May, 1905.

N R Allen
Notary Public.

Applications for Enrollment of Creek Newborn
Act of 1905   Volume I

AFFIDAVIT OF ATTENDING PHYSICIAN OR MID-WIFE.

UNITED STATES OF AMERICA, Indian Territory,⎤
 Western   DISTRICT. ⎰

I, R.M. Counterman, a Physician, on oath state that I attended on Mrs. M.M. Gibson, wife of Charles Gibson on the 5th day of October, 1901; that there was born to her on said date a girl "Female" child; that said child was living March 4, 1905, and is said to have been named Verna M. Gibson.

R.M. Counterman MD

Witnesses To Mark:

{

Subscribed and sworn to before me this 17 day of May, 1905.

N R Allen
Notary Public.

BIRTH AFFIDAVIT.

DEPARTMENT OF THE INTERIOR,
COMMISSION TO THE FIVE CIVILIZED TRIBES.

IN RE APPLICATION FOR ENROLLMENT, as a citizen of the Creek Nation, of Verna Marie Gibson , born on the 5 day of Oct, 1901

Name of Father: Charles Gibson	a citizen of the	Creek	Nation.
Name of Mother: Modina M. Gibson	a citizen of the	"	Nation.

Postoffice   Eufaula, I.T.

AFFIDAVIT OF ~~MOTHER~~. father

UNITED STATES OF AMERICA, Indian Territory,⎤
 Western   DISTRICT. ⎰

I, Charles Gibson, on oath state that I am 58 years of age and a citizen by blood, of the Creek Nation; that I am the lawful ~~wife~~ hus of Modina M. Gibson, who is a citizen, by blood, of the Creek Nation; that a female child was born to me on 5 day of Oct, 1901, that said child has been named Verna Marie Gibson, and is now living.

Charles Gibson

Witnesses To Mark:

{

Subscribed and sworn to before me this 6 day of March, 1905.

87

Applications for Enrollment of Creek Newborn
Act of 1905 Volume I

Edw C Griesel
Notary Public.

BIRTH AFFIDAVIT.

DEPARTMENT OF THE INTERIOR,
COMMISSION TO THE FIVE CIVILIZED TRIBES.

IN RE APPLICATION FOR ENROLLMENT, as a citizen of the Creek Nation, of Charles C. Gibson , born on the 28 day of March, 1903

Name of Father:	Charles Gibson	a citizen of the	Creek	Nation.
Name of Mother:	Modina M. "	a citizen of the	Creek	Nation.

Postoffice   Eufaula, I.T.

AFFIDAVIT OF ~~MOTHER~~. father

UNITED STATES OF AMERICA, Indian Territory,
Western   DISTRICT.

I, Charles Gibson, on oath state that I am 58 years of age and a citizen by blood, of the Creek Nation; that I am the lawful ~~wife~~ husband of Modina M. Gibson, who is a citizen, by blood, of the Creek Nation; that a male child was born to me on 28 day of March, 1903, that said child has been named Charles C. Gibson, and is now living.

Charles Gibson

Witnesses To Mark:

{

Subscribed and sworn to before me this 6 day of March, 1905.

Edw C Griesel
Notary Public.

BIRTH AFFIDAVIT.

DEPARTMENT OF THE INTERIOR.
COMMISSION TO THE FIVE CIVILIZED TRIBES.

IN RE APPLICATION FOR ENROLLMENT, as a citizen of the Creek Nation, of ~~Verna~~ Charles Counterman ~~Marie~~ Gibson , born on the 28 day of ~~October~~ March , 1903

Name of Father:	Charles Gibson	a citizen of the	Creek	Nation.
Name of Mother:	Modenia M. Gibson	a citizen of the	Creek	Nation.

Applications for Enrollment of Creek Newborn
Act of 1905 Volume I

Postoffice   Eufaula, I.T.

AFFIDAVIT OF MOTHER.

UNITED STATES OF AMERICA, Indian Territory,⎤
   Western   DISTRICT. ⎰

I, Mrs. Modenia M. Gibson, on oath state that I am 25 years of age and a citizen by Blood, of the Creek Nation; that I am the lawful wife of Charles Gibson, who is a citizen, by Blood, of the Creek Nation; that a male child was born to me on 28 day of March, 1903, that said child has been named Charles Counterman Gibson, and was living March 4, 1905.

Modenia M. Gibson

Witnesses To Mark:

{

Subscribed and sworn to before me this 17 day of May, 1905.

N R Allen
Notary Public.

AFFIDAVIT OF ATTENDING PHYSICIAN OR MID-WIFE.

UNITED STATES OF AMERICA, Indian Territory,⎤
   Western   DISTRICT. ⎰

I, R.M. Counterman, a Physician, on oath state that I attended on Mrs. M.M. Gibson, wife of Charles Gibson on the 28 day of March, 1903; that there was born to her on said date a male child; that said child was living March 4, 1905, and is said to have been named Charles Counterman Gibson.

R.M. Counterman MD

Witnesses To Mark:

{

Subscribed and sworn to before me this 17 day of May, 1905.

N R Allen
Notary Public.

Applications for Enrollment of Creek Newborn
Act of 1905   Volume I

BA 29 B.

Muskogee, Indian Territory, May 15, 1905.

John Baker,
  Weeletka[sic], Indian Territory.

Dear Sir:

The Commission is in receipt of an affidavit executed by you relative to the birth of your grandchild, Martha Baker. The affidavit of the mother and midwife or physician in attendance of the birth of said child must be furnished.

There is herewith enclosed a blank form of birth affidavit, and in executing same care should be exercised to see that all blanks are properly filled, all names written in full and in the event that either of the persons signing the affidavit is unable to write, signatures by mark must be attested by two witnesses. Each affidavit must be executed before a Notary Public and the notarial seal and signature of the officer must be attached to each separate affidavit.

Respectfully,

BC.   Chairman

NC 20.

Muskogee, Indian Territory, May 24, 1905.

Leslie Baker,
  Weeletka[sic], Indian Territory.

Dear Sir:

In the matter of the application for the enrollment of your minor child, Martha Baker, as a citizen of the Creek Nation, you are advised that it is impossible to obtain the affidavit of the midwife in attendance at the birth of said child, the affidavits of two disinterested parties should be furnished the Commission.

There are herewith enclosed two blank forms of birth affidavits, and in executing same care should be exercised to see that all blanks are properly filled, all names written in full and in the event that the persons signing the affidavits are unable to write, signatures by mark must be attested by two witnesses. Each affidavit must be executed before a Notary Public and the notarial seal and signature of the officer must be attached to each separate affidavit.

Respectfully,

2 BA.   Chairman.

Applications for Enrollment of Creek Newborn
Act of 1905   Volume I

NC 20.

Muskogee, Indian Territory, July 13, 1905.

Anna Baker,
    c/o John Baker,
        Weleetka, Indian Territory.

Dear Madam:

    In the matter of the application for the enrollment of your minor child, Martha Baker, as a citizen of the Creek Nation, you are advised that it is impossible to obtain the affidavit of the midwife in attendance at the birth of said child, the affidavits of two disinterested parties should be furnished the Commission.

    There are herewith enclosed two blank forms of birth affidavits, and in executing same care should be exercised to see that all blanks are properly filled, all names written in full and in the event that the persons signing the affidavits are unable to write, signatures by mark must be attested by two witnesses. Each affidavit must be executed before a Notary Public and the notarial seal and signature of the officer must be attached to each separate affidavit.

    In the affidavit of John Baker relative to the birth of this child, the date is given as December 10, 1901, and your affidavit as November 14, 1901.

    You are requested to correct said discrepancies.

Respectfully,

2 BA   Commissioner.

N.C. 20

Muskogee, Indian Territory, July 25, 1905.

Anna Baker,
    Care John Baker,
        Weleetka, Indian Territory.

Dear Madam:

    This office is in receipt of an affidavit executed by you in which the date of the birth of your minor child, Martha Baker, is given as November 14, 1901, and affidavit executed by Joseph Brooks and Simson Tiger in which said date is given as July 14, 1901.

    Said affidavits are herewith returned on account of said discrepancy.

91

Applications for Enrollment of Creek Newborn
Act of 1905   Volume I

There is herewith enclosed a blank form of birth affidavit.   In having same executed, care should be exercised to see that all blanks are properly filled, all names written in full and in the event that the person signing the affidavit is unable to write, signature by mark must be attested by two witnesses.   Each affidavit must be executed before a Notary Public and the notarial seal and signature of the officer must be attached to each separate affidavit must be attested by two witnesses.

Respectfully,

AGE-7-25-05   Commissioner.

_____

NC-20

DEPARTMENT OF THE INTERIOR,
COMMISSION TO THE FIVE CIVILIZED TRIBES.

Muskogee, Indian Territory, August 1, 1905.

In the matter of the application for the enrollment of Martha Baker as a citizen by blood of the Creek Nation.

John Baker, being duly sworn, testified as follows (through Jesse McDermott, Official Interpreter):

EXAMINATION BY THE COMMISSIONER:
Q What is your name? A John Baker.
Q How old are you? A 49.
Q What is your postoffice address? A Weleetka.
Q Do you know Martha Baker? A Yes sir.
Q Is she your grand-daughter? A Yes sir.
Q Daughter of your son? A Yes sir.
Q Was there a midwife present when that child was born? A There was no one present when the child was born, only the father.
Q Where is he now? A He is in the Fort Leavenworth prison.
Q You made affidavit herein which you gave the date of the birth December 10, and the mother, Anna Baker, made another affidavit and gave the birth November 14, 1901; which one is correct? A The mother's affidavit is correct.
Q How do you explain the mistake? A I was not certain of the time when I made the affidavit, but the mother had a record of the birth of the child and I knew.
Q You know that hers is correct? A Yes sir.

Witness is advised that in lieu of the affidavit of the mid-wife or physician, there should be filed in this case the affidavit of two disinterested parties as to the birth of this child.

Q Ask him if he knows under what name Anna Baker was finally enrolled. A I am not certain, but I think she is enrolled as Anna Coachman.

Applications for Enrollment of Creek Newborn
Act of 1905   Volume I

INDIAN TERRITORY, Western District.

I, J. Y. Miller, a stenographer to the Commissioner to the Five Civilized Tribes, do hereby certify that the above and foregoing is a true and complete translation of my notes as same appear in my stenographic report of this case.

JY Miller

Sworn to and subscribed before me
this the 4th day of August, 1905

Edw C Griesel
Notary Public.

BIRTH AFFIDAVIT.

DEPARTMENT OF THE INTERIOR.
COMMISSION TO THE FIVE CIVILIZED TRIBES.

IN RE APPLICATION FOR ENROLLMENT, as a citizen of the Creek Nation, of Martha Baker, born on the 14th day of Nov , 1901

Name of Father: Leslie Baker	a citizen of the Creek	Nation.
Name of Mother: Anna Baker	a citizen of the Creek	Nation.

Postoffice   Weleetka, Ind. Ter.

AFFIDAVIT OF MOTHER.

UNITED STATES OF AMERICA, Indian Territory, ⎤
　　　Western Judicial　　DISTRICT. ⎦

I, Anna Baker, on oath state that I am 32 years of age and a citizen by birth, of the Creek Nation; that I am the lawful wife of Leslie Baker, who is a citizen, by birth, of the Creek Nation; that a female child was born to me on 14th day of Nov , 1901, that said child has been named Martha Baker , and was living March 4, 1905.

her
Anna Baker x
Witnesses To Mark: mark
　⎧ Nat Williams
　⎩ Chas Coachman

Subscribed and sworn to before me this 22nd day of July, 1905.

BH Mills
My Commission Expires Aug 15th 1906.   Notary Public.

93

Applications for Enrollment of Creek Newborn
Act of 1905   Volume I

UNITED STATES OF AMERICA, Indian Territory, ⎱
    Western Judicial   DISTRICT.⎰

I, Joseph Brooks, & Simson Tiger, a witnesses, on oath state that I attended on Mrs. Anna Baker , wife of Leslie Baker on the 14th day of Nov , 1901 ; that there was born to her on said date a Female child; that said child was living March 4, 1905, and is said to have been named Martha Baker.

Joe Brooks

Witnesses To Mark:
   ⎰ Nat Williams
   ⎱ Chas. Coachman

his
Simson Tiger   x
mark

Subscribed and sworn to before me this 22nd day of July, 1905.

B H Mills

Commission Expires Aug 15, 1906   Notary Public.

BIRTH AFFIDAVIT.
DEPARTMENT OF THE INTERIOR.
COMMISSION TO THE FIVE CIVILIZED TRIBES.

IN RE APPLICATION FOR ENROLLMENT, as a citizen of the Creek Nation, of Martha Baker, born on the 14th day of November , 1901

Name of Father: Lesley Baker   a citizen of the   Creek   Nation.
Name of Mother: Anna Baker (Coachman)   a citizen of the   Creek   Nation.

Postoffice   Weleetka, Ind. Ter.

AFFIDAVIT OF MOTHER.

UNITED STATES OF AMERICA, Indian Territory, ⎱
    Western Judicial   DISTRICT.⎰

I, Anna Baker, on oath state that I am 32 years of age and a citizen by birth, of the Creek Nation; that I am the lawful wife of Leslie Baker, who is a citizen, by birth, of the Creek Nation; that a female child was born to me on 14th day of Nov , 1901, that said child has been named Martha Baker , and was living March 4, 1905. And I also state that my husband, Lesley Baker, who is now in the penitentiary at Ft Leavenworth, Kansas, acted as my physician when the said child was born.

Anna Baker   her + mark

94

Applications for Enrollment of Creek Newborn
Act of 1905   Volume I

Witnesses To Mark:

{ Bernard B. Mooney
{ Chas Coachman

Subscribed and sworn to before me this 21st day of March, 1905.

(Name Illegible)
Notary Public.

BIRTH AFFIDAVIT.

DEPARTMENT OF THE INTERIOR.
COMMISSION TO THE FIVE CIVILIZED TRIBES.

IN RE APPLICATION FOR ENROLLMENT, as a citizen of the Creek Nation, of Martha Baker, born on the 10 day of December , 1901

Name of Father: Lesley Baker	a citizen of the Creek	Nation.
Name of Mother: Anna "	a citizen of the "	Nation.

Postoffice   Weleetka, I.T.

AFFIDAVIT OF ~~MOTHER.~~ grandfather

UNITED STATES OF AMERICA, Indian Territory, ⎤
        Western   **DISTRICT.** ⎦

I, John Baker, on oath state that I am 50 years of age and a citizen by blood, of the Creek Nation; that I am the ~~lawful wife~~ grandfather of Martha Baker, who is a citizen by blood of the Creek Nation; ~~that a (blank) child~~ who was born to ~~me,~~ on 10 day of December, 1901; that said child has been named Martha Baker, and is now living.

His
John x Baker
mark

Witnesses To Mark:

{ EC Griesel
{ J McDermott

Subscribed and sworn to before me this 6 day of March, 1905.

Edw C Griesel
Notary Public.

Creek Equalization
Supplemental Proof

State of Oklahoma)
) ss
Muskogee County)

John Baker, a Creek citizen of the age of about 64, post-office Weleetka, Okla., being duly sworn, deposes and says:

That he is the father of Sunday Baker, enrolled as a Creek citizen opposite number 5064;

That he is informed that John Baker, enrolled as minor Creek number 423, was said to be the son of said Sunday Baker, and that the mother of said child stated, or the testimony so shows, that she and the said Sunday Baker were husband and wife;

That affiant says that said Sunday Baker was never married, never lived with the mother of said John Baker; and if said John Baker was his child it was illegitimate and was never recognized by said Sunday Baker as such, to the best of my knowledge and belief.

		His
Witness to Mark:	John Baker *(Thumb print)*	thumb
Alvin C Hinkle		mark

Muskogee, Okla.
Subscribed and sworn to before me this 23 Feb. 1916.

Edward Merriet

My Com Exp 3/17/19.   Notary Public.

Felix *(Illegible)*, Interpreter
OCH

See other affidavit and letter from Johnson Tiger attached to proof for Sundy[sic] Lasly[sic]

OCH 2/24/16

DEPARTMENT OF THE INTERIOR,
COMMISSION TO THE FIVE CIVILIZED TRIBES.

Muskogee, Indian Territory, March 6, 1905.

In the matter of the application for the enrollment of Upakalitkee Brown as a citizen by blood of the Creek Nation.

R. S. Brown, being duly sworn, testified as follows:

Applications for Enrollment of Creek Newborn
Act of 1905   Volume I

EXAMINATION BY THE COMMISSION:
Q What is your name? A R S Brown.
Q What is your Age? A 41 years old.
Q You are not a citizen of the Creek Nation? A No sir.
Q Have you a child named Upakalitkee Brown? A No; I had, it's dead.
Q What is the name of the mother of the child? A Eliza.

Eliza Brown, mother of the child, is identified on Creek Indian care No. 629, and her[sic] is contained in the partial list of Creek citizens by blood approved by the Secretary of the Interior March 13, 1902, Roll No. 2053.

Q When was that child born? A September 12, 1901.
Q Who was present at its birth? A Myself, Mr. Bell here and a Dutch woman by the name of Whiteman.
Q Was there any doctor in attendance? A Not at the birth. We called for a doctor. The child was born when he came.
Q How long did the child live? A Five months.
Q It died when? A February 25, 1902.
Q Did you have a doctor in attendance at the death of the child? A Not at the death. We had a doctor coming to see it while it was sick.
Q Who was the doctor? A Dr. Scott (?)
Q What is his postoffice? A Muskogee.
Q Did you have the same doctor both times? A Yes sir.

James Bell, being duly sworn, testified as follows:

EXAMINATION BY THE COMMISSION:
Q What is your name? A James Bell.
Q Are you a citizen of the Creek Nation? A Yes sir.
Q Did you know a child of R S Brown named Upakalitkee Brown? A Yes sir.
Q Know the mother of the child? A Yes (?) sir.
Q What's her name? A Liza.
Q Were you present at the birth of the child? A Yes sir.
Q When was the child born? A September 12.
Q What year? A 1901.
Q Do you know how long that child lived? A Yes sir.
Q How long? A Five months.
Q Do you know the date of its death? A Yes sir.
Q What was it? A February 25, 1902.
Q Were you present when it died? A Yes sir.
Q Were you at the funeral? A Yes sir.
Q Do you know anyone else who was present at the birth of the child? A Mr. Brown was.
Q Any doctor or midwife? A No sir.
Q Were there any other women at all at the birth? A Mrs. Whitman.

Applications for Enrollment of Creek Newborn
Act of 1905 Volume I

James Throckmorton, being duly sworn, testified as follows:

EXAMINATION BY THE COMMISSION:
Q What is your name? A James Throckmorton.
Q What is your age? A 29.
Q What is your postoffice? A Natura.
Q Did you know a child of R S Brown and Eliza Brown named Upakalitkee? A I know he had a child; don't know what its name was.
Q Were you present when it was born? A No sir.
Q How long after it was born did you know it? A Well, I knew it had been born.
Q Did you ever see it? A Yes sir.
Q About how old was it when you saw it? A I saw it from the time it was two or three weeks old until it died.
Q About when was that? A It was born in the fall. It was a small baby.
Q What year was that? A 1903, I think.
Q You are sure about the year? A No, I am not. I saw the baby there; I helped bury it.

R. S. Brown, recalled.

Q Have you a record of the birth and death of the child—did you write it down? A Have it on a piece of paper with the rest of the children; have put it in the Bible. I did not keep it on the blank leaf in the Bible. It is not fastened in the Bible.

The witness is notified that when the mother of the child comes in to testify, to bring in the record of the birth and death of said child.

INDIAN TERRITORY, Western District.
I, J. Y. Miller, a stenographer to the Commission to the Five Civilized Tribes. Five Civilized Tribes, do hereby certify that the above and foregoing is a true and complete transcription of my notes as same appear in my stenographic report of this case.

J Y Miller
Sworn to and subscribed before me this the 30 day of March 1905.

Edw C Griesel
Notary Public.

———————

I.D.

Muskogee, Indian Territory, April. 20, 1905.

R. S. Brown,
        Natura, Indian Territory

Dear Sir:

Applications for Enrollment of Creek Newborn
Act of 1905   Volume I

The Commission is in receipt of your letter of April 16, 1905, relative to the application for the enrollment of your minor child, Upakalitkee Brown, asking if any further evidence is required in said matter.

In reply you are advised that, from an affidavit filed by you March 6, 1905, it appears that said Upakalitkee Brown was born on September 13, 1901, and that she died February 25, 1902.

There is herewith enclosed a circular containing information relative to the enrollment of children born since May 25, 1901, to citizens of the Creek Nation, and you are advised that it does not at this time appear that further evidence is necessary in the matter of the application for the enrollment of said Upakalitkee Brown.

Respectfully,

Circular.   Chairman.

BA 330 B.

Muskogee, Indian Territory, May 15, 1905.

Conzie Tiger,
Sapulpa, Indian Territory.

Dear Sir:

There are on file with the Commission affidavits relative to the birth of your minor children, Aby and Waxin Tiger. You are advised that the Commission required the affidavit of the midwife or physician in attendance at the birth of said children.

There is herewith enclosed a blank form of birth affidavit, and in executing same care should be exercised to see that all blanks are properly filled, all names written in full and in the event that either of the person signing the affidavit is unable to write, signature by mark must be attested by two witnesses. Each affidavit must be executed before a Notary Public and the notarial seal and signature of the officer must be attached to each separate affidavit.

Respectfully,

BC   Chairman.

99

Applications for Enrollment of Creek Newborn
Act of 1905   Volume I

COMMISSIONERS:
TAMS BIXBY,
THOMAS B. NEEDLES,
C.R. BRECKINBRIDGE.

WM. O. BEALL
Secretary

DEPARTMENT OF THE INTERIOR,
COMMISSIONER TO THE FIVE CIVILIZED TRIBES.

REFER IN REPLY TO THE FOLLOWING:

NC 22.

ADDRESS ONLY THE
COMMISSION TO THE FIVE CIVILIZED TRIBES.

Muskogee, Indian Territory, June 6, 1905.

Fancy Tiger,
Sapulpa, Indian Territory.

Dear Madam:

In the matter of the application for the enrollment of your minor children, Aby and Woxin[sic] Tiger, as citizens of the Creek Nation, you are advised that there are on file with the Commission affidavits signed by you under the name of Fancy Tiger and Frances Tiger.

You are identified on the Commission's rolls as Fancy Tiger. In the affidavits one of your children is given as Waxin and the other as Woxin.

For the purpose of correcting these discrepancies you will be allowed fifteen days from date within which to appear before the Commission at its office in Muskogee, Indian Territory.

Respectfully,

(Name Illegible)

Commissioner in Charge.

———

N.C. 22.

DEPARTMENT OF THE INTERIOR,
COMMISSION TO THE FIVE CIVILIZED TRIBES.
Muskogee, Ind. Ter., June 15, 1905.

In the matter of the application for the enrollment of Aby and Waxin Tiger as citizens of the Creek Nation.

Fancy Tiger, being duly sworn, testified as follows through her husband, Conzie Tiger, a sworn Euchee interpreter.

By Commission.

Q Ask her what is her name. A Fancy.
Q Is your name Frances or Fancy Tiger? A They spell it F a n c y Tiger.
Q How old are you? A Twentyeight years old. She doesn't know her age very well; she guesses twentysix or twentyeight. She is about twentyeight.

100

Q About twentyeight? A Yes, sir. They understood it that way.

Q And in the affidavit it is written that way? A Yes, sir.

Q You spell your name F a n c y? A Yes, sir.

Q She has two young children. What is the name of the oldest one? A Aby. There it is there. It's a girl.

Q Do you know how to spell the name of the other child? W a x i n.

Q In this affidavit you say Waxin and in another you say Woxin. Which is correct? A Waxin.

Q You say W a is correct? A Yes, sir.

Q Both of these children ar[sic] living? A Yes, sir.

Q Tell her we will have her make out new affidavits now to correct these mistakes? A Yes, sir.

I, J. Y. Miller, on oath state that as stenographer to the Commission to the Five Civilized Tribes. Five Civilized Tribes, I reported the above case and that this is a true, full and correct transcript of my stenographic notes in the same, as said notes appear in said report.

JY Miller

Subscribed and sworn to before me this 11 day of July 1906.

Edw C Griesel
Notary Public.

N.C. 22.

DEPARTMENT OF THE INTERIOR,
COMMISSION TO THE FIVE CIVILIZED TRIBES.
Muskogee, Ind. Ter., June 15, 1905.

In the matter of the application for the enrollment of Aby and Waxin Tiger as citizens of the Creek Nation.

Fancy Tiger, being duly sworn, testified as follows through her husband, Conzie Tiger, a sworn Euchee interpreter.

By Commission.

Q Ask her what is her name. A Fancy.

Q Is your name Frances or Fancy Tiger? A They spell it F a n c y Tiger.

Q How old are you? A Twentyeight years old. She doesn't know her age very well; she guesses twentysix or twentyeight. She is about twentyeight.

Q About twentyeight? A Yes, sir. I don't know how old she is.

Q We have affidavits here executed by her and signed by mark. In one place it is written Frances and another place Fancy. Is that the same one? A Yes, sir. They understood it that way.

Q And in the affidavit it is written that way? A Yes, sir.

Q You spell her name F a n c y? A Yes, sir.

Q She has two young children. What is the name of the oldest one? A Aby. There it is there. It's a girl.
Q Do you know how to spell the name of the other child? W a x i n.
Q In this affidavit you say Waxin and in another you say Woxin. Which is correct? A Waxin.
Q You say W a is correct? A Yes, sir.
Q Both of these children ar[sic] living? A Yes, sir.
Q Tell her we will have her make out new affidavits now to correct these mistakes? A Yes, sir.

I, J. Y. Miller, on oath state that as stenographer to the Commission to the Five Civilized Tribes. Five Civilized Tribes, I reported the above case and that this is a true, full and correct transcript of my stenographic notes in the same, as said notes appear in said report.

JY Miller

Subscribed and sworn to before me this 11 day of July 1906.

Edw C Griesel
Notary Public.

BIRTH AFFIDAVIT.

DEPARTMENT OF THE INTERIOR.

COMMISSION TO THE FIVE CIVILIZED TRIBES.

IN RE APPLICATION FOR ENROLLMENT, as a citizen of the Creek Nation, of Aby Tiger, born on the 12 day of January, 1902

Name of Father: Conzie Tiger	a citizen of the Creek	Nation.
Name of Mother: Frances Tiger	a citizen of the Creek	Nation.

Postoffice   Sapulpa I.T.

AFFIDAVIT OF MOTHER.

UNITED STATES OF AMERICA, Indian Territory, ⎤
      Western   DISTRICT. ⎦

I, Frances Tiger, on oath state that I am 28 years of age and a citizen by blood, of the Creek Nation; that I am the lawful wife of Conzie Tiger, who is a citizen, by blood, of the Creek Nation; that a female child was born to me on 12 day of January , 1902, that said child has been named Aby Tiger , and was living March 4, 1905.

her
Frances x Tiger
mark

102

Applications for Enrollment of Creek Newborn
Act of 1905   Volume I

Witnesses To Mark:
{ J.J. Jones
{ A.M. Parker

Subscribed and sworn to before me this 20 day of May, 1905.

Wm P Rook
Notary Public.

AFFIDAVIT OF ATTENDING PHYSICIAN OR MID-WIFE.

UNITED STATES OF AMERICA, Indian Territory, ⎤
     Western   DISTRICT. ⎰

I, Arluquing Pickett, a mid-wife, on oath state that I attended on Mrs. Frances Tiger, wife of Conzie Tiger on the 12 day of January , 1902 ; that there was born to her on said date a female child; that said child was living March 4, 1905, and is said to have been named Aby Tiger.
her
Arluquing x Pickett
mark

Witnesses To Mark:
{ J J Jones
{ AM Parker
Subscribed and sworn to before me this 20 day of May, 1905.

Wm P Rook
Notary Public.

BIRTH AFFIDAVIT.
DEPARTMENT OF THE INTERIOR.
COMMISSION TO THE FIVE CIVILIZED TRIBES.

IN RE APPLICATION FOR ENROLLMENT, as a citizen of the Creek Nation, of Aby Tiger, born on the 12 day of January, 1902

Name of Father: Conzie Tiger	a citizen of the Creek	Nation.
Name of Mother: Fancy "	a citizen of the "	Nation.

Postoffice   Sapulpa

Applications for Enrollment of Creek Newborn
Act of 1905   Volume I

(child present)

AFFIDAVIT OF MOTHER.

UNITED STATES OF AMERICA, Indian Territory,
Western   DISTRICT.

I, Fancy Tiger, on oath state that I am 26 years of age and a citizen by blood, of the Creek Nation; that I am the lawful wife of Conzie Tiger, who is a citizen, by blood, of the Creek Nation; that a female child was born to me on 12 day of January , 1902, that said child has been named Aby Tiger , and was living March 4, 1905.

her
Fancy x Tiger
mark

Witnesses To Mark:
{ JY Miller
  EC Griesel

Subscribed and sworn to before me this 14 day of March, 1905.

Edw C Griesel
Notary Public.

---

father
AFFIDAVIT OF ATTENDING PHYSICIAN OR MID-WIFE.

UNITED STATES OF AMERICA, Indian Territory,
Western   DISTRICT.

I, Conzie Tiger, a na, ~~on oath state that I attended on Mrs. (blank), wife~~ husband of Fancy Tiger on the 12 day of January , 1902 ; that there was born to her on said date a female child; that said child was living March 4, 1905, and is said to have been named Aby Tiger.

Conzie Tiger

Witnesses To Mark:

{

Subscribed and sworn to before me this 14 day of March, 1905.

Edw C Griesel
Notary Public.

Applications for Enrollment of Creek Newborn
Act of 1905   Volume I

BIRTH AFFIDAVIT.

DEPARTMENT OF THE INTERIOR.
COMMISSION TO THE FIVE CIVILIZED TRIBES.

IN RE APPLICATION FOR ENROLLMENT, as a citizen of the Creek Nation, of Aby Tiger, born on the 12" day of Jany, 1902

Name of Father: Conzie Tiger   a citizen of the   Creek   Nation.
Name of Mother: Fancy Tiger   a citizen of the   "   Nation.

Postoffice   Sapulpa

AFFIDAVIT OF MOTHER.

UNITED STATES OF AMERICA, Indian Territory,⎫
     Western   DISTRICT.⎰

     I, Fancy Tiger, on oath state that I am about 28 years of age and a citizen by blood, of the Creek Nation; that I am the lawful wife of Conzie Tiger, who is a citizen, by blood, of the Creek Nation; that a female child was born to me on 12" day of January , 1902, that said child has been named Aby Tiger , and was living March 4, 1905.

her
Fancy x Tiger
mark

Witnesses To Mark:
    ⎰ H.G. Harris
    ⎱ Irwin Donovan

     Subscribed and sworn to before me this 15" day of June, 1905.

Henry G. Harris
Notary Public.

BIRTH AFFIDAVIT.

DEPARTMENT OF THE INTERIOR.
COMMISSION TO THE FIVE CIVILIZED TRIBES.

IN RE APPLICATION FOR ENROLLMENT, as a citizen of the Creek Nation, of Woxin Tiger, born on the 20 day of Dec., 1903

Name of Father: Conzie Tiger   a citizen of the   Creek   Nation.
Name of Mother: Fancy   "   a citizen of the   "   Nation.

Postoffice   Sapulpa

Applications for Enrollment of Creek Newborn
Act of 1905 Volume I

(child present - Gr)

AFFIDAVIT OF MOTHER.

UNITED STATES OF AMERICA, Indian Territory,⎫
   Western   DISTRICT.⎰

    I, Fancy Tiger, on oath state that I am 26 years of age and a citizen by blood, of the Creek Nation; that I am the lawful wife of Conzie Tiger, who is a citizen, by blood, of the Creek Nation; that a male child was born to me on 20 day of Dec., 1903, that said child has been named Woxin Tiger , and was living March 4, 1905.

her
Fancy x Tiger
mark

Witnesses To Mark:
  ⎰ JY Miller
  ⎱ EC Griesel

    Subscribed and sworn to before me this 14 day of March, 1905.

Edw C Griesel
Notary Public.

---

father
AFFIDAVIT OF ATTENDING PHYSICIAN OR MID-WIFE.

UNITED STATES OF AMERICA, Indian Territory,⎫
   Western   DISTRICT.⎰

    I, Conzie Tiger, a m[sic], on oath state that I ~~attended on Mrs. (blank), wife~~ husband of Fancy Tiger on the 20 day of Dec. , 1903 ; that there was born to her on said date a male child; that said child was living March 4, 1905, and is said to have been named Woxin Tiger.

Conzie Tiger

Witnesses To Mark:
⎰

    Subscribed and sworn to before me this 14 day of March, 1905.

Edw C Griesel
Notary Public.

BIRTH AFFIDAVIT.

DEPARTMENT OF THE INTERIOR.
COMMISSION TO THE FIVE CIVILIZED TRIBES.

IN RE APPLICATION FOR ENROLLMENT, as a citizen of the Creek Nation, of Waxin Tiger, born on the 20 day of Dec., 1903

Name of Father: Conzie Tiger	a citizen of the Creek	Nation.
Name of Mother: Fancy "	a citizen of the "	Nation.

Postoffice   Sapulpa I.T.

AFFIDAVIT OF MOTHER.

UNITED STATES OF AMERICA, Indian Territory,⎤
    Western   DISTRICT. ⎦

I, Fancy Tiger, on oath state that I am about 28 years of age and a citizen by blood, of the Creek Nation; that I am the lawful wife of Conzie Tiger, who is a citizen, by blood, of the Creek Nation; that a male child was born to me on 20 day of Dec., 1903, that said child has been named Waxin Tiger , and was living March 4, 1905.

her
Fancy x Tiger
mark

Witnesses To Mark:
⎰ H.G. Harris
⎱ Irwin Donovan

Subscribed and sworn to before me this 15" day of June, 1905.

Henry G Harris
Notary Public.

---

father
AFFIDAVIT OF ATTENDING PHYSICIAN OR MID-WIFE.

UNITED STATES OF AMERICA, Indian Territory,⎤
    Western   DISTRICT. ⎦

I, Conzie Tiger, a *(blank)* , on oath state that ~~I attended on~~ Mrs. Fancy Tiger, wife of myself on the 20" day of Dec. , 1903 ; that there was born to her on said date a male child; that said child was living March 4, 1905, and is said to have been named Waxin Tiger.

Conzie Tiger

Witnesses To Mark:

{

107

Applications for Enrollment of Creek Newborn
Act of 1905 Volume I

Subscribed and sworn to before me this 15" day of June, 1905.

Henry G. Harris
Notary Public.

———————

Department of the Interior,
Commission to the Five Civilized Tribes.

In re Application for enrollment as a citizen of the Creek Nation of Waxin Tiger born on the 20th day of December, 1903.

Name of Father	Conzie Tiger,	a citizen of the	Creek	Nation.
Name of Mother	Frances Tiger,	a citizen of the	Creek	Nation.

Postoffice   Sapulpa, I.T

Affidavit of mother.

United States of America, Western District, Indian Territory. SS.

I Frances Tiger on oath state that I am 28 years of age and a citizen by and a citizen by blood of the Creek Nation; that I am the lawful wife of lawful wife of Conzie Tiger who is a citizen by blood of the Creek Nation; that on December 20th 1903 a male child was born to me; that said child has been named Waxin Tiger; that said child was living march, 4, 1905.

Witnesses to mark.
J.J. Jones
A.M. Parker

her
Frances x Tiger
mark

Subscribed and sworn to before me this 20 day of May, 1905.

Wm P Rook

Affidavit of Mid wife.

United States, Indian Territory, Western District. SS.

I, Arluquing Pickett a mid-wife on oath state that I attended on Mrs. Frances Tiger wife of Conzie Tiger on the 20th day of December, 1903; that there was born to her on said date a male child; that said child was living March 4, 1905, and is said to have been named Waxin Tiger.

Witnesses to mark.
J.J. Jones
AM Parker

her
Arluquing x Pickett
mark

Subscribed and sworn to before me this 20th day of May, 1905.

Wm P Rook
Notary Public.

My Commission as Notary expires October 21, 1906.

NC 23.

Muskogee, Indian Territory, January 16, 190?.

Bessie Wayman,
    c/o Eugene Wayman,
        Muskogee, Indian Territory.

Dear Madam:

There is herewith enclosed one copy of the Statement and Order of the Commissioner to the Five Civilized Tribes, dated January 15, 190?, dismissing the application made by you *(illegible)* the enrollment of your minor child, Eugene T. Wayman, deceased, as a citizen by blood of the Creek Nation.

Respectfully,

IM-71.   Commissioner.

BIRTH AFFIDAVIT.

DEPARTMENT OF THE INTERIOR.
COMMISSION TO THE FIVE CIVILIZED TRIBES.

IN RE APPLICATION FOR ENROLLMENT, as a citizen of the Creek Nation, of Eugene T. Wayman, born on the 26 day of Nov , 1904

Name of Father: Eugene Wayman	a citizen of the	U.S.	Nation.
Name of Mother: Bessie Wayman	a citizen of the	Creek	Nation.

Postoffice   Muskogee, IT

Applications for Enrollment of Creek Newborn
Act of 1905 Volume I

AFFIDAVIT OF ~~MOTHER~~. father

UNITED STATES OF AMERICA, Indian Territory, ⎫
    Western   DISTRICT. ⎰

I, Eugene Wayman, on oath state that I am 29 years of age and a citizen by ----- of the U.S. Nation; that I am the lawful ~~wife~~ husband of Bessie Wayman, who is a citizen, by blood, of the Creek Nation; that a male child was born to me on 26" day of November, 1904, that said child has been named Eugene T. Wayman, and ~~was living March 4, 1905~~ only lived a few minutes, dying the same day.

Witnesses To Mark:

⎰
⎱   (Seal)

Subscribed and sworn to before me this 6" day of March, 1905.

Edw C Griesel
Notary Public.

BIRTH AFFIDAVIT.

DEPARTMENT OF THE INTERIOR.
COMMISSION TO THE FIVE CIVILIZED TRIBES.

IN RE APPLICATION FOR ENROLLMENT, as a citizen of the Creek Nation, of Eugene T. Wayman, born on the 26 day of Nov , 1904

Name of Father: Eugene Wayman	a citizen of the	U.S.	Nation.
Name of Mother: Bessie Wayman	a citizen of the	Creek	Nation.

Postoffice   Muskogee, IT

AFFIDAVIT OF ~~MOTHER~~. father

UNITED STATES OF AMERICA, Indian Territory, ⎫
    Western   DISTRICT. ⎰

I, Eugene Wayman, on oath state that I am 29 years of age and a citizen by ----- of the U.S. Nation; that I am the lawful ~~wife~~ husband of Bessie Wayman, who is a citizen, by blood, of the Creek Nation; that a male child was born to me on 26 day of November, 1904, that said child has been named Eugene T. Wayman, and ~~is now living.~~ only lived a few minutes, dying the same day.

Witnesses To Mark:

⎰
⎱

Subscribed and sworn to before me this 6 day of March, 1905.

Edw C Griesel
Notary Public.

NC 23   JLD

DEPARTMENT OF THE INTERIOR,
COMMISSIONER TO THE FIVE CIVILIZED TRIBES.

In the matter of the application for the enrollment of Eugene T. Wayman, deceased, as a citizen of the Creek Nation.

. . . .

STATEMENT AND ORDER.

The record in this case shows that on March 6, 1905, application was made, in affidavit form, for the enrollment of Eugene T. Wayman, deceased, as a citizen by blood of the Creek Nation, under the provisions of the act of Congress approved March 3, 1905.

It appears from the affidavit filed in this matter that said Eugene T. Wayman, deceased, was born November 26, 1904, and died November 26, 1904.

The act of Congress approved March 3, 1905, (33 Stats., 1048), provides:

"That the Commission to the Five Civilized Tribes is authorized for sixty days after the date of the approval of this act to receive and consider applications for enrollment of children born subsequent to May twenty-fifth, nineteen hundred and one, and prior to march fourth, nineteen hundred and five, and living on said latter date, to citizens of the Creek tribe of Indians whose enrollment has been approved by the Secretary of the Interior prior to the approval of this act; and to enroll and make allotments to such children, to citizens of the Creek tribe of Indians whose enrollment has been approved by the Secretary of the Interior prior to the approval of this act; and to enroll and make allotments to such children."

It is, therefore, ordered that the application for the enrollment of said Eugene T. Wayman, deceased, as a citizen by blood of the Creek Nation, be, and the same is, hereby dismissed.

(Name Illegible)   Commissioner.

Muskogee, Indian Territory.
JAN 15 1907

Applications for Enrollment of Creek Newborn
Act of 1905   Volume I

DEPARTMENT OF THE INTERIOR,
COMMISSIONER TO THE FIVE CIVILIZED TRIBES.

REFER IN REPLY TO THE FOLLOWING:

N.C. -24.

Muskogee, Indian Territory, **August 4, 1905.**

Mary U. Saltsman,
    Care of Eugene F. Saltsman,
        Eufaula, Indian Territory.

Dear Madam:

You are hereby advised that on **July 28, 1905.** , the Secretary of the Interior approved the enrollment of your minor child, **Gordon P. Saltsman** , as a citizen by blood of the **Creek** Nation, and that the name of said child appears upon the roll of new born citizens of the **Creek** Nation as Number **16.**

The child is now entitled to an allotment, and application therefor should be made without delay at the Land Office for the Nation in which the prospective allotment is located.

An entire allotment for said child must be selected at the time of the original application.

Respectively,

Commissioner.

BIRTH AFFIDAVIT.

DEPARTMENT OF THE INTERIOR.
COMMISSION TO THE FIVE CIVILIZED TRIBES.

IN RE APPLICATION FOR ENROLLMENT, as a citizen of the Creek Nation, of Gordon P. Saltsman, born on the 9 day of Dec , 1904

Name of Father: Eugene F. Saltsman   a citizen of the   U.S.   Nation.
Name of Mother: Mary U.   "   a citizen of the   Creek   Nation.

Postoffice   Eufaula, I.T.

AFFIDAVIT OF ~~MOTHER~~. father

UNITED STATES OF AMERICA, Indian Territory, ⎱
    Western   DISTRICT. ⎰

I, Eugene F. Saltsman, on oath state that I am 25 years of age and a citizen by -----
of the U.S. Nation; that I am the lawful ~~wife~~ husband of Mary U. Saltsman, who is a

112

citizen, by blood, of the Creek Nation; that a male child was born to me on 9 day of Dec , 1904, that said child has been named Gordon P. Saltsman, and is now living.

E.F. Saltsman

Witnesses To Mark:

{

Subscribed and sworn to before me this 6 day of March, 1905.

Edw C Griesel
Notary Public.

Affidavit of Physician

State of Oklahoma
County of Oklahoma.

R. M. Counterman, a physician, being duly sworn on oath states that he attended on Mrs Mary U. Saltsman, wife of E. F. Saltsman, on the 9th day December 1904; that there was born unto her on said date a male child; that said child is now living and has been named Gordon Parker Saltsman.

R.M. Counterman

Sworn and subscribed to before me this *(illegible)* day of March 1905

(Illegible) G. Bedford
Notary Public

my commission expires May 15th 1907.

BIRTH AFFIDAVIT.

DEPARTMENT OF THE INTERIOR.
COMMISSION TO THE FIVE CIVILIZED TRIBES.

IN RE APPLICATION FOR ENROLLMENT, as a citizen of the Creek Nation, of Gordon Parker Saltsman, born on the 9 day of December, 1904

Name of Father: E. F. Saltsman   a citizen of the United States Nation.
Name of Mother: Mary Saltsman (nee Simpson) a citizen of the   Creek   Nation.
Tuckahatche Town.

Postoffice   Eufaula, I.T.

Applications for Enrollment of Creek Newborn
Act of 1905 Volume I

AFFIDAVIT OF MOTHER.   Child present.

UNITED STATES OF AMERICA, Indian Territory, ⎱
    Western   **DISTRICT.** ⎰

I, Mary Saltsman, on oath state that I am 24 years of age and a citizen by blood of the Creek Nation; that I am the lawful wife of E. F. Saltsman, who is a citizen, ~~by~~ *(blank)*, of the United States ~~Nation~~; that a male child was born to me on 9 day of December, 1904, that said child has been named Gordon Parker Saltsman, and was living March 4, 1905.

Mary Saltsman

Witnesses To Mark:

{

Subscribed and sworn to before me this 3 day of April, 1905.

Drennan C. Skaggs
Notary Public.

B.A. -35B.

DEPARTMENT OF THE INTERIOR,
COMMISSION TO THE FIVE CIVILIZED TRIBES.
MUSKOGEE, INDIAN TERRITORY, MARCH 6, 19o5[sic].

-ooOoo-

In the matter of the application for the enrollment of Ruby Rowley, deceased, as a citizen by blood of the Creek Nation.

CHARLEY ROWLEY, being duly sworn, testified as follows:

EXAMINATION BY COMMISSION:
Q What is your name? A Charley Rowley.
Q How old are you? A 44.
Q What is your postoffice address? A Okmulgee, I. T.
Q Have you any children? A Yes.
Q When was your last child born? A October 19.
Q What year was she born in? A One year old liking eight days.
Q I mean—what year was she born in? A Last year.
Q What year was that? A 1903.
Q What year did she die? A Liking eight days of being one year old when she died---that was in October.
Q When was that? A The same year in which she was born.
Q If it was born in October and died in October it must have been one year old? A Yes.
Q What was last year? A 1904, and this is 1905 now.

114

Applications for Enrollment of Creek Newborn
Act of 1905   Volume I

Q Was there any one present at the birth of that child? A Yes, my mother-in-law was present.
Q Was there any Doctor present at its birth? A Not then but afterwards.
Q How soon afterwards? A Two days.
Q What is the name of that doctor? A R. W. Young.
Q What is his postoffice address? A He is in Louisiana now, but he was here then.
Q Did you have a mid-wife in attendance at the child's birth? A My mother-in-law.
Q What is her name? A Adelia Stevens.
Q Are you a citizen of the Creek Nation? A Yes.
Q Is your wife a citizen? A No.

Witness identified as Charles Rowley on Creek Indian Card, Field Number 295, and his name is contained in the partial list of Creek citizens by blood, approved by the Secretary of the Interior March 13, 1903, Roll Number 980.
Q Was there any doctor present when this child died? A There was three present.
Q Name them? A Dr. Thomas was one.
Q What is his postoffice address? A Ft. Smith, Arkansas.
Q The other doctor? A Dr. Stevenson.
Q What is his postoffice address? A Same place--Ft. Smith
Q What other doctor? A Dr. Harrison.
Q Have you any record of the birth and death of this child? A Yes.
Q What is it in? A A Bible.
Q Did you look at that record before you came up here? A No, I never thought of it.
Q Then, how do you remember the dates so well? A I know when she was born.

Witness is advised that it will be necessary
for his wife, the mother of Ruby Rowley, to appear before the Commission for the purpose of giving testimony
in this case, and to bring with her the book containing
the dates of birth and death of said child.

Zera Ellen Parrish, being sworn, on her oath states that as stenographer for the Commission to the Five Civilized Tribes. Five Civilized Tribes she reported the above case and that th is[sic] is a full, true and correct transcript of her stenographic notes in same.

Zera Ellen Parrish

Subscribed and sworn to before me
th is[sic] 11th day of March, 1905.   Edw C Griesel
                                                         Notary Public.

B.A. -35B.

DEPARTMENT OF THE INTERIOR,
COMMISSION TO THE FIVE CIVILIZED TRIBES.
MUSKOGEE, INDIAN TERRITORY, MARCH 6, 19o5[sic].

-ooOoo-

In the matter of the application for the enrollment of Ruby Rowley, deceased, as a citizen by blood of the Creek Nation.

CHARLEY ROWLEY, being duly sworn, testified as follows:

EXAMINATION BY COMMISSION:

Q What is your name? A Charley Rowley.
Q How old are you? A 44.
Q What is your postoffice address? A Okmulgee, I. T.
Q Have you any children? A Yes.
Q When was your last child born? A October 19.
Q What is its name? A Ruby Rowley.
Q What year was she born in? A One year old liking eight days.
Q I mean—what year was she born in? A Last year.
Q What year was that? A 1903.
Q What year did she die? A Liking eight days of being one year old when she died--- that was in October.
Q When was that? A The same year in which she was born.
Q If it was born in October and died in October it must have been one year old? A Yes.
Q What was last year? A 1904, and this is 1905 now.
Q Was there any one present at the birth of that child? A Yes, my mother-in-law was present.
Q Was there any Doctor present at its birth? A Not then but afterwards.
Q How soon afterwards? A Two days.
Q What is the name of that doctor? A R. W. Young.
Q What is his postoffice address? A He is in Louisiana now, but he was here then.
Q Did you have a mid-wife in attendance at the child's birth? A My mother-in-law.
Q What is her name? A Adelia Stevens.
Q Are you a citizen of the Creek Nation? A Yes.
Q Is your wife a citizen? A No.

Witness identified as Charles Rowley on Creek Indian Card, Field Number 295, and his name is contained in the partial list of Creek citizens by blood, approved by the Secretary of the Interior March 13, 1903, Roll Number 980.

Q Was there any doctor present when this child died? A There was three present.
Q Name them? A Dr. Thomas was one.
Q What is his postoffice address? A Ft. Smith, Arkansas.
Q The other doctor? A Dr. Stevenson.
Q What is his postoffice address? A Same place--Ft. Smith

Applications for Enrollment of Creek Newborn
Act of 1905   Volume I

Q What other doctor? A Dr. Harrison.
Q Have you any record of the birth and death of this child? A Yes.
Q What is it in? A A Bible.
Q Did you look at that record before you came up here? A No, I never thought of it.
Q Then, how do you remember the dates so well? A I know when he was born.

> Witness is advised that it will be necessary
> for his wife, the mother of Ruby Rowley, to appear be-
> fore the Commission for the purpose of giving testimony
> in this case, and to bring with her the book containing
> the dates of birth and death of said child.

Zera Ellen Parrish, being sworn, on her oath states that as stenographer for the Commission to the Five Civilized Tribes. Five Civilized Tribes she reported the above case and that th is[sic] is a full, true and correct transcript of her stenographic notes in same.

Zera Ellen Parrish

Subscribed and sworn to before me
th is[sic] 11th day of March, 1905.   Edw C Griesel
Notary Public.

N.C. 26.

Muskogee, Indian Territory, August 3, 1905.

Charles Rowley,
    1614 W. 11th Street,
        Fort Smith, Arkansas.

Dear Sir:

Receipt is acknowledged of your letter of July 28, 1905, relative to the application for enrollment of your minor child, Ruby Rowley, deceased.

In reply you are advised that there are on file in this office affidavits from which it appears that said Ruby Rowley was born October 19, 1903, and died October 11, 1904. You are further advised that a child who was born and died on said dates is not entitled to enrollment as a citizen of the Creek Nation.

Respectfully,

Commissioner.

DCS.

(The above letter was copied again.)

117

REFER IN REPLY TO THE FOLLOWING:

N.C. 26

DEPARTMENT OF THE INTERIOR,
COMMISSIONER TO THE FIVE CIVILIZED TRIBES.

Muskogee, Indian Territory, November 17, 1905.

Charles Rowley,
　　Okmulgee, Indian Territory.

Dear Sir:

　　There is herewith enclosed one copy of the Order of the Commissioner to the Five Civilized Tribes, dated November 14, 1905, dismissing the application made by you for the enrollment of your minor child, Ruby Rowley, deceased, as a citizen by blood of the Creek Nation.

　　　　　　　　　　Respectfully,

　　　　　　　　　　　　(Name Illegible)

　　　　　　　　　　　　　　Commissioner.

AG-26

N.C. 26　　　　　　　　　　　　　　　　　　　　I.D.

DEPARTMENT OF THE INTERIOR,
COMMISSIONER TO THE FIVE CIVILIZED TRIBES.

　　In the matter of the application for the enrollment of Ruby Rowley, deceased, as a citizen by blood of the Creek Nation.

ORDER

　　The record in this case shows that on March 6, 1905, Charles Rowley appeared before the Commission to the Five Civilized Tribes and made application for the enrollment of his minor child, Ruby Rowley, deceased, as a citizen by blood of the Creek Nation.

　　The evidence shows that said Ruby Rowley, deceased, was born October 19, 1903, and that she died October 11, 1904.

　　The act of Congress of March 3, 1905 (Public No. 212), provides:

　　　　"That the Commission to the Five Civilized Tribes is authorized for sixty days after the date of the approval of this set to receive and consider application

Applications for Enrollment of Creek Newborn
Act of 1905   Volume I

for enrollment of children born subsequent to May twenty-five, nineteen hundred and five, and living on said latter date, to citizens of the Creek tribe of Indians whose enrollment has been approved by the Secretary of the Interior prior to the date of the approval of this act; and to enroll and make allotments to such children."

It is, therefore, ordered that there is no authority of law for the enrollment of said Ruby Rowley, deceased, as a citizen by blood of the Creek Nation, and that the application for her enrollment as such should be and the same is hereby dismissed.

Tams Bixby.
Commissioner.

Muskogee, Indian Territory.
NOV 14 1905

BIRTH AFFIDAVIT.   Copy
DEPARTMENT OF THE INTERIOR.
COMMISSION TO THE FIVE CIVILIZED TRIBES.

IN RE APPLICATION FOR ENROLLMENT, as a citizen of the Creek Nation, of Ruby Rowley, born on the 19 day of October , 1903

Name of Father: Charley Rowley	a citizen of the Creek	Nation.
Name of Mother: Anna Rowley	a citizen of the U. S.	Nation.

Postoffice   Okmulgee I.T.

Copy
AFFIDAVIT OF MOTHER.

UNITED STATES OF AMERICA, Indian Territory,
    State of Arkansas
    Sebastian County   DISTRICT.

I, Anna Rowley, on oath state that I am 36 years of age and a citizen ~~by~~ ----- of the United States Nation; that I am the lawful wife of Charley Rowley, who is a citizen, by blood, of the Creek Nation; that a female child was born to me on 19 day of October, 1903, that said child has been named Ruby Rowley, and ~~was living March 4, 1905~~. died Oct 10, 1904.

(Signed)   Anna Rowley

Witnesses To Mark:
  { James Dodson
  { Joe Dodson

Applications for Enrollment of Creek Newborn
Act of 1905   Volume I

(Seal)   Subscribed and sworn to before me this 7th day of March, 1905.

Sam'l Edmondson
Notary Public.

Copy
AFFIDAVIT OF ATTENDING PHYSICIAN OR MID-WIFE.

UNITED STATES OF AMERICA, Indian Territory,
State of Louisiana
Rapides Parrish   **DISTRICT.**

I, Isaac W. Young, a physician, on oath state that I attended on Mrs. Anna Rowley, wife of Charley Rowley on the 19" day of October, 1903; that there was born to her on said date a *(blank)* child; that said child was living March 4, 1905, and is said to have been named Ruby Rowley.

Isaac W. Young M.D.

Witnesses To Mark:
Chas M Calrit
Lee Wash

Subscribed and sworn to before me this 13 day of March, 1905.

W.J. Calrit Dy[sic] Clk
ex off   Notary Public.

BIRTH AFFIDAVIT.
DEPARTMENT OF THE INTERIOR.
COMMISSION TO THE FIVE CIVILIZED TRIBES.
Copy

IN RE APPLICATION FOR ENROLLMENT, as a citizen of the Creek Nation, of Ruby Rowley, born on the 19 day of Oct, 1903

Name of Father: Charles Rowley   a citizen of the   Creek   Nation.
Name of Mother: Anna Roley   a citizen of the U S   Nation.

Postoffice   Okmulgee I.T.

120

Applications for Enrollment of Creek Newborn
Act of 1905   Volume I

Copy

AFFIDAVIT OF ~~MOTHER~~. father

UNITED STATES OF AMERICA, Indian Territory, ⎫
   Western   **DISTRICT.** ⎰

I, Charles Rowley, on oath state that I am 44 years of age and a citizen by blood, of the Creek Nation; that I am the lawful ~~wife~~ husband of Anna Rowley, who is a citizen, by ----- of the U.S. Nation; that a female child was born to ~~me~~ her on 19 day of Oct, 1903, that said child has been named Ruby Rowley, and ~~was living March 4, 1905~~ died Oct 11-1904.

(Signed)   Charley Rowley

Witnesses To Mark:

{

Seal   Subscribed and sworn to before me this 6 day of March, 1905.

Edw C Griesel
Notary Public.

BA-73-74-B

DEPARTMENT OF THE INTERIOR,
COMMISSION TO THE FIVE CIVILIZED TRIBES.

Muskogee, Indian Territory, March 7, 1905.

In the matter of the application for the enrollment of Albert and Jessie King as Creeks.

Johnson King, being duly sworn, testified as follows:

EXAMINATION BY THE COMMISSION:
Q What is your name? A Johnson King.
Q What is your age? A I am 32 years old.
Q What is your postoffice? A Eufaula.
Q You are a citizen of the Creek Nation? A Yes sir.
Q Millie King is your wife? A Yes sir.
Q She is also a citizen of the Creek Nation? A Yes sir.
Q You have several new-borns have you not? A Yes sir.
Q What are the names of your minor children? A One named Jessie and one Albert.
Q Both living? A One is living; one dead.
Q Jessie is living? A Yes sir.
Q When was Jessie born? A born in 1902. November.
Q Do you know the day? A Yes sir.
Q What date? A 28.

Applications for Enrollment of Creek Newborn
Act of 1905   Volume I

Q You have 27. A I think it was 27.

Q That child is living? A Yes, sir.

Q You have another child named Albert? A Yes sir.

Q When was Albert born? A 1904.

Q What year, month and day? A November.

Q Do you remember the day? A 7th, I think.

Q When did the child die? A 19th of January, 1905.

Q You remember the day? A Wednesday morning.

Q Do you know what day of the month it was? A 7th or 8th, I forget.which.[sic]

Q Who was present at the (date of the) death of the child? A A lot of them.

Q Who were they? A Lewis Collins—Frank Turke.

Q Was there any physician there—did you have a doctor? A I had a doctor, but he was not present.

Q How old was that child, about, when he died? A Two months and six days, I believe.

Q Did you make any record of it in a book? A I have a record at home.

Q What kind of a book have you got it in? A In an album like. You can find it Tahly's store; they sent for a coffin.

Q At Eufaula? A Yes sir.

Q How soon after the death did you put down the date? A The same day when I went after the coffin.

Q Did you have a midwife at the time Albert was born? A No sir, I am a midwife myself.

Q Did not have a doctor? A No sir.

THE COMMISSIONER: You are requested to bring that record of the dates of the birth and death, of both your children. We would like to have your wife come in.

THE WITNESS: She will be in.

INDIAN TERRITORY, Western District.

I, J. Y. Miller a stenographer to the Commission to the Five Civilized Tribes, do hereby certify that the above and foregoing is a true and complete translation of my notes as same appear in my stenographic report of this case.

JY Miller

Sworn to and subscribed
before me this the
6 day of April,
1905.

Edw C Griesel
Notary Public.

BIRTH AFFIDAVIT.

DEPARTMENT OF THE INTERIOR.
COMMISSION TO THE FIVE CIVILIZED TRIBES.

IN RE APPLICATION FOR ENROLLMENT, as a citizen of the Creek Nation, of Jessie King, born on the 27 day of November, 1902

Name of Father: Johnson King	a citizen of the	Creek	Nation.
Name of Mother: Millie King	a citizen of the	Creek	Nation.

Postoffice   Eufaula

AFFIDAVIT OF MOTHER.

UNITED STATES OF AMERICA, Indian Territory,⎫
      Western   DISTRICT. ⎭

I, Johnson King, on oath state that I am 32 years of age and a citizen by blood, of the Creek Nation; that I am the lawful ~~wife~~ husband of Millie King, who is a citizen, by blood, of the Creek Nation; that a male child was born to ~~me~~ her on 27 day of November, 1902, that said child has been named Jessie King, and is now living.

Johnson King

Witnesses To Mark:

⎰
⎱ Subscribed and sworn to before me this 7 day of March, 1905.

Edw C Griesel
Notary Public.

N.C. 27

DEPARTMENT OF THE INTERIOR,
COMMISSION TO THE FIVE CIVILIZED TRIBES.
Muskogee, Indian Territory, March 7, 1905.

In the matter of the application for the enrollment of Jessie King as a citizen of the Creek Nation.

Millie King, being duly sworn, testified as follows:

By Commissioner.
Q What is your name? A Millie King.
Q How old are you? A About thirty two
Q What is your post office address? A Eufaula.

Q You are a citizen of the Creek Nation? A Yes sir.
Q What was the name of your father? A George Washington.
Q What was the name of your mother? A Nancy Washington.
Q Have you a child named Jessie King? A Yes, sir.
Q When was Jessie born? A November 7th
Q How old will he be next November 7th? A Will be three years old.
Q Born November 7, 1902 was he? A Yes, sir
Q Is he living? A Yes, there he is
Q Did you have a midwife or doctor when he was born? A No, sir, just my husband.
Q Jessie is a boy is he? A Yes, sir.

Johnson King, being duly sworn, testified as follows:
Q What is your name? A Johnson King.
Q How old are you? A About thirty two.
Q What is your post office address? A Eufaula.
Q Are you a citizen of the Creek Nation? A Yes, sir.
Q When was this child Jessie born? A November 7th
Q What year? A 1902
Q Are you sure of that now? A Yes, sir.
Q Once before you made out an affidavit saying the 7th and one affidavit saying the 27th and you gave testimony here and said the 27th, you were mistaken in that were you? A Yes, sir.
Q You are sure that this child Jessie was born November 7th? A Yes, sir

The parents of this child, the two witnesses present, are told that in the absence of a midwife at the birth of this child, this office requires the affidavit of two disinterested persons to the birth of said child.

I, Anna Garrigues, on oath state the above and foregoing is a true and correct copy of my stenographic notes taken in said cause on said date.

Anna Garrigues

Subscribed and sworn to before me this 8th day of July 1905.

Edw C Griesel
Notary Public.

BIRTH AFFIDAVIT.

DEPARTMENT OF THE INTERIOR.
COMMISSION TO THE FIVE CIVILIZED TRIBES.

IN RE APPLICATION FOR ENROLLMENT, as a citizen of the Creek Nation, of Jessie King, born on the 7 day of November, 1902

Name of Father: Johnson King   a citizen of the   Creek   Nation.
               Tuskegee
Name of Mother: Millie Washington nee   a citizen of the   Creek   Nation.
                     King
                   Postoffice   Eufaula

AFFIDAVIT OF MOTHER.

UNITED STATES OF AMERICA, Indian Territory,
      Western   **DISTRICT.**   Child present

I, Millie Washington nee King, on oath state that I am 32 years of age and a citizen by Blood, of the Creek Nation; that I am the lawful wife of Johnson King, who is a citizen, by Blood, of the Creek Nation; that a male child was born to me on seventh day of November, 1902, that said child has been named Jessie King, and was living March 4, 1905.

                                Millie Washington nee King
Witnesses To Mark:

Subscribed and sworn to before me this 13 day of June, 1905.

My commission   Preston *(Illegible)*
Expires May 19-1908   Notary Public.

AFFIDAVIT OF ATTENDING PHYSICIAN OR MID-WIFE.

UNITED STATES OF AMERICA, Indian Territory,
      Western   **DISTRICT.**

I, Johnson King, a Husband, on oath state that I attended on Mrs. Millie Washington nee King, wife of My wife on the 7 day of November, 1902; that there was born to her on said date a male child; that said child was living March 4, 1905, and is said to have been named Jessie King.

                                Johnson King
Witnesses To Mark:

Subscribed and sworn to before me this 13 day of June, 1905.

My Commission   Preston *(Illegible)*
Expires May 19-1908   Notary Public.

BA 73 B.

Muskogee, Indian Territory, May 15, 1905.

Johnson King,
    Eufaula, Indian Territory.

Dear Sir:

    There is on file with the Commission an affidavit relative to the birth of your minor child, Jessie King. The affidavit of the mother of said child and of the midwife or physician in attendance at its birth should be supplied.

    There is herewith enclosed a blank form of birth affidavit, and in executing same care should be exercised to see that all blanks are properly filled, all names written in full and in the event that either of the persons signing the affidavit is unable to write, signatures by mark must be attested by two witnesses. Each affidavit must be executed before a Notary Public and the notarial seal and signature of the officer must be attached to each separate affidavit.

Respectfully,

BC.   Chairman.

NC 27.

Muskogee, Indian Territory, June 22, 1905.

Millie King,
    Eufaula, Indian Territory.

Dear Madam:

    There are on file with the Commission affidavits relative to the enrollment of your minor child, Jessie King as a citizen of the Creek Nation, in which the date of its birth is given as November 27 and November 7, 1902.

    You will be allowed ten days from date within which to appear before the Commission at its office in Muskogee, Indian Territory, for the purpose of correcting this discrepancy in the date of birth.

126

Applications for Enrollment of Creek Newborn
Act of 1905   Volume I

Respectfully,

Chairman.

_____

DEPARTMENT OF THE INTERIOR.
COMMISSION TO THE FIVE CIVILIZED TRIBES.

_____

IN RE APPLICATION FOR ENROLLMENT, as a citizen of the Creek Nation, of Albert King, born on the 7 day of November, 1904

Name of Father: Johnson King	a citizen of the	Creek	Nation.
Name of Mother: Millie King	a citizen of the	Creek	Nation.

Postoffice   Eufaula

_____

AFFIDAVIT OF MOTHER.

UNITED STATES OF AMERICA, Indian Territory, ⎤
  Western   **DISTRICT.** ⎰

I, Johnson King, on oath state that I am 32 years of age and a citizen by blood, of the Creek Nation; that I am the lawful ~~wife~~ husband of Millie King, who is a citizen, by blood, of the Creek Nation; that a male child was born to ~~me~~ her on 7 day of November, 1904, that said child has been named Albert King, and ~~is now living~~. died January 28, 1905

Johnson King

Witnesses To Mark:

{

Subscribed and sworn to before me this 7 day of March, 1905.

Edw C Griesel
Notary Public.

_____

DEPARTMENT OF THE INTERIOR.
COMMISSION TO THE FIVE CIVILIZED TRIBES.

_____

IN RE APPLICATION FOR ENROLLMENT, as a citizen of the Creek Nation, of Jessie
                or about
King, born on ^ the 7" day of November , 1902

Name of Father: Johnson King   a citizen of the   Creek   Nation.
Name of Mother: Millie   "   a citizen of the   "   Nation.

Postoffice   Eufaula I.T.

AFFIDAVIT OF MOTHER. acquaintance

UNITED STATES OF AMERICA, Indian Territory, ⎫
    Western   **DISTRICT.** ⎰

I, L. G. Stidham, on oath state that I am 50 years of age and a citizen by blood, of
acquainted with Millie King
the Creek Nation; that I am ^ the lawful wife of Johnson King, who is a citizen by blood,
of the Creek Nation; that a male child was born to ~~me~~ them on or about 7" day of
November, 1902, that said child has been named Jessie King, and was living March 4,
1905. & I have no interest in this case.

                     L G Stidham

Witnesses To Mark:
    { ~~L G Stidham~~
      ~~L M Greenwood~~

Subscribed and sworn to before me this 8th day of July, 1905.

               (Name Illegible)
                   Notary Public.

Witness
AFFIDAVIT OF ATTENDING PHYSICIAN OR MID-WIFE.

UNITED STATES OF AMERICA, Indian Territory, ⎫
    Western   **DISTRICT.** ⎰

I, L.M. Greenwood, ~~a~~ *(blank)*, on oath state that I ~~attended on~~ know Mrs. Millie
or about
King, wife of Johnson King on ^ the 7" day of Nov., 1902; that there was born to her on
said date a male child; that said child was living March 4, 1905, and is said to have been
named Jessie King. & further I have no interest herein.

               L.M. Greenwood

Witnesses To Mark:
    { ~~L G Stidham~~
      ~~L M Greenwood~~

Subscribed and sworn to before me this 8th day of July, 1905.

               (Name Illegible)
                   Notary Public.

DEPARTMENT OF THE INTERIOR,
COMMISSIONER TO THE FIVE CIVILIZED TRIBES.

Muskogee, Indian Territory, January 18, 1907.

Millie King,
 c/o Johnson King,
  Eufaula, Indian Territory.
Dear Madam:

   There is herewith enclosed one copy of the Statement and Order of the Commissioner to the Five Civilized Tribes, dated January 18, 1907, dismissing the application made by you for the enrollment of your minor child, Albert King, deceased, as a citizen of the Creek Nation.

           Respectfully,

             (Name Illegible)

                  Commissioner.

LM-201.

N.C. 27.   J.L.De.

DEPARTMENT OF THE INTERIOR,
COMMISSIONER TO THE FIVE CIVILIZED TRIBES.

   In the matter of the application for the enrollment of Albert King, as a citizen by blood of the Creek Nation.

STATEMENT AND ORDER.

   The record in this case shows that on March 7, 1905, application was made, in affidavit form, supplemented by sworn testimony, for the enrollment of Albert King, deceased, as a citizen by blood of the Creek Nation, under the provisions of the act of Congress approved March 3, 1905.

   It appears from the weight of the evidence filed in this matter that said Albert King was born November 7, 1904, and died January 28, 1905.

   The act of Congress approved March 3, 1905, (33 Stats., 1048), in part provides:

   "That the Commission to the Five Civilized Tribes is authorized for sixty days after the date of the approval of this Act to receive and consider applications for enrollments of children born subsequent to May twenty five, nineteen hundred and one, and prior to March fourth, nineteen hundred and five, and living on said latter date, to citizens of the Creek tribe of Indians whose enrollment has been approved by the Secretary of the Interior prior to the date of approval of this Act; and to enroll and make allotments to such children."

Applications for Enrollment of Creek Newborn
Act of 1905   Volume I

It is therefore, ordered that the application for the enrollment of said Albert King, deceased, as a citizen by blood of the Creek Nation, be and the same is, hereby dismissed.

Muskogee, Indian Territory   *(Name Illegible)*   COMMISSIONER.
JAN 18 1907

REFER IN REPLY TO THE FOLLOWING:

DEPARTMENT OF THE INTERIOR,
COMMISSIONER TO THE FIVE CIVILIZED TRIBES.   N.C. -28.

Muskogee, Indian Territory, **August 4, 1905.**

William McCombs, Jr.,
    Eufaula, Indian Territory.

Dear Sir:

You are hereby advised that on **July 28, 1905.**   , the Secretary of the Interior approved the enrollment of your minor child, **Nathaniel H. McCombs** , as a citizen by blood of the **Creek** Nation, and that the name of said child appears upon the roll of new born citizens of the **Creek** Nation as Number **17.**

The child is now entitled to an allotment, and application therefor should be made without delay at the Land Office for the Nation in which the prospective allotment is located.

An entire allotment for said child must be selected at the time of the original application.

Respectively,

Commissioner.

Commission to the Five Civilized Tribes

In Re Application for enrollment of Nathaniel H. McCombs, born on 15th. day of December 1904. Name of father William McCombs Jr, a citizen by blood of the Creek Nation. Name of mother Alice L. McCombs, a citizen by blood of the Creek Nation. Post Office Eufaula, Indian Territory.

Affidavit of mother.

Alice L. McCombs, being duly sworn on oath, states that I am 25 years of age, a citizen by blood of the Creek Nation; that I am the lawful wife of William McCombs Jr; that on the 15th day of December 1904 there was born unto me a male child; that said child is now living and has been named Nathaniel H. McCombs.

130

Alice L. McCombs

Sworn and subscribed to before me this 6th day of march 1905

My Commission expires July 8-1906.   *(Name Illegible)*
                                                        Notary Public

Affidavit of Physician

Indian Territory
Western District

W. A. Tolleson, a physician, being duly sworn on oath, states that I attended on Mrs Alice L. McCombs, wife of William McCombs Jr on the 15th day of December 1904; that there was born unto her on the said date a male child; that said child is now living and has been named Nathaniel H. McCombs.

W.A. Tolleson

Sworn and subscribed to before me this 6th day of March 1905.

My Commission expires July 8-1906.   *(Name Illegible)*
                                                        Notary Public

---

BIRTH AFFIDAVIT.

DEPARTMENT OF THE INTERIOR.
COMMISSION TO THE FIVE CIVILIZED TRIBES.

IN RE APPLICATION FOR ENROLLMENT, as a citizen of the Creek Nation, of Bertie Haikey, born on the 29 day of April , 1904

Name of Father: Ben Haikey Jr.   a citizen of the   Creek   Nation.
Name of Mother: Louisa Haikey   a citizen of the   Creek   Nation.

Postoffice   Fry, Ind Ter

AFFIDAVIT OF MOTHER.

UNITED STATES OF AMERICA, Indian Territory, ⎫
        Western   DISTRICT. ⎰

I, Louisa Haikey, on oath state that I am 26 years of age and a citizen by Blood, of the Creek Nation; that I am the lawful wife of Ben Haikey Jr., who is a citizen, by Blood, of the Creek Nation; that a female child was born to me on 29 day of April, 1904, that said child has been named Bertie Haikey , and was living March 4, 1905.

her

Applications for Enrollment of Creek Newborn
Act of 1905 Volume I

Louisa x Haikey

Witnesses To Mark: mark
{ Howard Collins
{ Frank Jackson

Subscribed and sworn to before me this 17 day of June, 1905.

Willard ? McCullough

My Commission Expires March 21-1908.   Notary Public.

BA-41-B.

DEPARTMENT OF THE INTERIOR,
COMMISSION TO THE FIVE CIVILIZED TRIBES.

Muskogee, Indian Territory, March 6, 1905.

In the matter of the application for the enrollment of Bertha Haikey as a citizen by blood of the Creek Nation.

Ben Haikey, being duly sworn, testified as follows:

EXAMINATION BY THE COMMISSION:
Q What is your name? A Ben Haikey, Jr.
Q What is your age? A About 30 years, I guess.
Q What is your postoffice? A Fry.
Q Are you a citizen of the Creek Nation? A Yes, sir.

The witness is identified as Ben Haikey, Jr. on Creek Indian card, Field No. 285, and his name is contained in the partial list of Creek Indians approved by the Secretary of the Interior March 12, 1902, Roll No. 497.

Q Have you any children? A No; I had one three year old; died two months ago, named Mamie Haike[sic].
Q When was she born? A May 2, 1901.
Q Is she enrolled? A Yes, sir.
Q What is the name of your youngest child? A That's the youngest.
Q What is the name of this young child living with you? A Bertha.
Q When was Bertha born? A April 29.
Q What year? A 1904.
Q Is Bertha living? A Yes, sir.
Q What is the name of the other young child? A Birdie.
Q Is Birdie living? A No sir.
Q What date did she die? A June 18.
Q What year? A 1904.
Q When was she born? A April 29, 1904
Q Were Bertha and Birdie twins? A Yes, sir.

132

Applications for Enrollment of Creek Newborn
Act of 1905   Volume I

Q Who was present at the birth of these children? A My wife's cousin.
Q What is her name? A Nancy Davis.
Q Anyone else? A No sir; Nancy davis[sic], she was to come, but the train left her.
Q Was there a doctor present? A One doctor came there after the baby was born, about the next day.
Q What is the name? A Dr. Cokes.
Q Where does he live? A At Inola now.
Q Was there anyone present when Birdie died—any doctor? A Yes, sir., Dr. Broomfield.
Q Where does he live? A His residence is Broken Arrow but is in Missouri now.
Q Gone to Missouri to live or visit? A To live; he has a place at Broken Arrow.

Louisa Haikey, being duly sworn, testified as follows (through Jesse McDermott, Official Interpreter).

EXAMINATION BY THE COMMISSION:
Q What is your name? A Louisa Haikey.
Q Are you the wife of Ben Haikey, Jr.? A Yes, sir.
Q What was your name before you married him? A Chisholm.

Witness is identified as Louisa Chisholm on Creek Indian card, field No. 289, and her name appears upon the partial list of Creek citizens by blood approved by the Secretary of the Interior March 13, 1903, Roll No. 956.

Q Have you any children? A That's the only one that we have
Q Did you ever have any more? A I have only one.
Q Ask her did she have any other children? A This one and other one; twice I lost a girl.
Q Was the girl's name Mamie Chisholm? A Mamie Chisholm Haikey.
Q What is the name of the child you have with you? A Bertha Haikey.
Q You say there was another child born at the same time as this one? A Yes, sir.
Q What was its name? A Birdie.
Q When were Birdie and Bertha Born? A Last of April.
Q What year? A 1904.

Bertha Haikey is present and appears to be as old as stated.

Q When did Birdie Haikey die? A About two months old when she died.
Q Who was the midwife when these children were born? A Nancy Davis.
Q Was there any doctor present when Birdie died? A Dr. Broomfield.
Q When did Birdie die? A About June.
Q Of the same year she was born? A Yes, sir.
Q Did you put down in a book or anywhere the dates of the birth and death (of these children)? A The father has them down.
Q Is that in a Bible or in what kind of a book? A In the Bible.

Applications for Enrollment of Creek Newborn
Act of 1905 Volume I

Ben Haikey Jr. is notified that the testimony of the midwife is required in this case, and when the midwife comes in, to send with her the record in the Bible of the birth of these children.

INDIAN TERRITORY, Western District.

I, J. Y. Miller, a stenographer to the Commission to the Five Civilized Tribes, do hereby certify that the above and foregoing is a true and complete translation of my notes as same appear in my stenographic report of this case.

JY Miller

Sworn to and subscribed
before me this the
20 day of March,
1905.

Edw C Griesel
Notary Public.

NC 29.

DEPARTMENT OF THE INTERIOR,
COMMISSION TO THE FIVE CIVILIZED TRIBES.
MUSKOGEE, I. T. JUNE 20, 1905.

In the matter of the application for the enrollment of Bertha Haikey, as a citizen by blood of the Creek Nation.

Ben Haikey, Jr., being duly sworn, testified as follows:

Examination by the Commission:
Q What is your name? A Ben Haikey, Jr.
Q What is your age? A About 30.
Q What is your post office address? A Fry.
Q You have any children born since the 25th of May, 1901? A Yes, two.
Q What are their names? A Bertha and Birdie Haikey.
Q Which one is dead? A Birdie.
Q And Bertha is still living A Yes, sir.
Q When did Birdie die? A June 18, 1904.
Q You have made out some affidavits here in which you call one of your children Bertie do you mean that for Birdie or Bertha? A Who made the affidavit.
Q Sworn out by you – before Mr. McClellan, a Notary Public? A Whoever wrote it down made a mistake.
Q Did you mean that for Bertha or Birdie the one that is dead? A For Birdie.
Q And Bertha is living? A Yes, sir.
Q Bertha is the correct name? A Yes, sir.
Q Do you know when Bertha was born? A April 29, 1904, they were twins.
Q As I understand you had two children born on April 29, 1904, one of them was called Birdie Haikey and Birdie is now dead, and the other one was called Bertha Haikey and Bertha is now living, is that correct? A Yes, sir.
Q And Birdie died June 18, 1904? A Yes, sir.

Applications for Enrollment of Creek Newborn
Act of 1905   Volume I

Lona Merrick

Lona Merrick, being duly sworn, states that the above and foregoing is a true and correct transcript of her stenographic notes as taken in said cause on said date.

Subscribed and sworn to before
me this 20th day of June, 1905.   Edw C Griesel

Notary Public.

(The above was copied again.)

Dec'd.
~~BIRTH AFFIDAVIT.~~

DEPARTMENT OF THE INTERIOR.
COMMISSION TO THE FIVE CIVILIZED TRIBES.

IN RE APPLICATION FOR ENROLLMENT, as a citizen of the Creek Nation, of Bertie Haikey, born on the 29" day of April , 1904

Name of Father: Ben Haikey, Jr.	a citizen of the Creek	Nation.
Name of Mother: Louisa Haikey	a citizen of the Creek	Nation.

Postoffice   Fry Ind Ter

AFFIDAVIT OF MOTHER.

UNITED STATES OF AMERICA, Indian Territory, ⎫
    Western Judicial   **DISTRICT.** ⎭

I, Louisa Haikey, on oath state that I am 26 years of age and a citizen by Blood, of the Creek Nation; that I am the lawful wife of Ben Haikey Jr., who is a citizen, by Blood, of the Creek Nation; that a Female child was born to me on 29 day of April, 1904, that said child has been named Bertha Haikey , and was ~~living March 4, 1905~~. Deceased

Louisa Haikey

Witnesses To Mark:

{

Subscribed and sworn to before me this 17" day of April, 1905.

Robert E Lynch
Com Ex 7/3/1906   Notary Public.

135

AFFIDAVIT OF ATTENDING PHYSICIAN OR MID-WIFE.

UNITED STATES OF AMERICA, Indian Territory,⎫
    Western Judicial   **DISTRICT.** ⎭

I, Nancy W. Davis, a Midwife, on oath state that I attended on Mrs. Louisa
Haikey, wife of Ben Haikey, Jr on the 29" day of April, 1904; that there was born to her
                                is dead
on said date a Female child; ~~that said child was living March 4, 1905~~, and is said to have
been named Bertie Haikey.

                                        Nancy W. Davis
Witnesses To Mark:

⎰
⎱   Subscribed and sworn to before me this 17 day of April, 1905.

                                    Robert E Lynch
    Com Ex 7/3/1906   Notary Public.

BIRTH AFFIDAVIT.
                        DEPARTMENT OF THE INTERIOR.
            COMMISSION TO THE FIVE CIVILIZED TRIBES.

IN RE APPLICATION FOR ENROLLMENT, as a citizen of the Creek Nation, of Bertha
Haikey, born on the 29" day of April , 1904

Name of Father: Ben Haikey, Jr.   a citizen of the   Creek   Nation.
Name of Mother: Louisa Haikey   a citizen of the   Creek   Nation.

                    Postoffice   Fry Ind Ter

AFFIDAVIT OF MOTHER.

UNITED STATES OF AMERICA, Indian Territory,   ⎫
        Western Judicial   **DISTRICT.** ⎭
    I, Louisa Haikey, on oath state that I am 26 years of age and a citizen by Blood, of
the Creek Nation; that I am the lawful wife of Ben Haikey Jr., who is a citizen, by Blood,
of the Creek Nation; that a Female child was born to me on 29 day of April, 1904, that
said child has been named Bertha Haikey , and was living March 4, 1905.
                                        her
                            Louisa x Haikey
Witnesses To Mark: mark
⎰
⎱
    Subscribed and sworn to before me this 17" day of April, 1905.

Applications for Enrollment of Creek Newborn
Act of 1905   Volume I

Com Ex 7/3/1906

Robert E Lynch
Notary Public.

AFFIDAVIT OF ATTENDING PHYSICIAN OR MID-WIFE.

UNITED STATES OF AMERICA, Indian Territory,⎫
Western Judicial   DISTRICT. ⎭

I, Nancy W. Davis, a Midwife, on oath state that I attended on Mrs. Louisa Haikey, wife of Ben Haikey, Jr on the 29" day of April, 1904; that there was born to her on said date a *(blank)* child; that said child was living March 4, 1905, and is said to have been named Bertha Haikey.

Nancy W. Davis

Witnesses To Mark:

{

Subscribed and sworn to before me this 17 day of April, 1905.

Com Ex 7/3/1906

Robert E Lynch
Notary Public.

BIRTH AFFIDAVIT.
DEPARTMENT OF THE INTERIOR.
COMMISSION TO THE FIVE CIVILIZED TRIBES.

IN RE APPLICATION FOR ENROLLMENT, as a citizen of the Creek Nation, of Bertha Haikey, born on the 29 day of April , 1904

Name of Father: Ben Haikey, Jr.	a citizen of the	Creek	Nation.
Name of Mother: Louisa "	a citizen of the	Creek	Nation.

Postoffice   Fry I.T.

(Child is present) *(Initials Illegible)*
AFFIDAVIT OF MOTHER.

UNITED STATES OF AMERICA, Indian Territory, ⎫
Western   DISTRICT. ⎭

I, Louisa Haikey, on oath state that I am 26 years of age and a citizen by blood, of the Creek Nation; that I am the lawful wife of Ben Haikey Jr., who is a citizen, by blood, of the Creek Nation; that a female child was born to me on 29 day of April, 1904, that said child has been named Bertha Haikey , and is now living.

Ben Haikey Jr

Applications for Enrollment of Creek Newborn
Act of 1905   Volume I

Witnesses To Mark:

{

Subscribed and sworn to before me this 6 day of March, 1905.

Edw C Griesel
Notary Public.

Louisa Haikey Wife of Ben Haikey Jr. Maiden name Louisa Chisholm Roll no on her deed 926.

COMMISSIONERS: TAMS BIXBY, THOMAS B. NEEDLES, C.R. BRECKINBRIDGE. WM. O. BEALL Secretary	**DEPARTMENT OF THE INTERIOR,** **COMMISSIONER TO THE FIVE CIVILIZED TRIBES.**	REFER IN REPLY TO THE FOLLOWING: —————————— **BA 40 B.**

ADDRESS ONLY THE
COMMISSION TO THE FIVE CIVILIZED TRIBES.

Muskogee, Indian Territory, April 29, 1905.

Ben Haikey, Jr.
Fry, Indian Territory.

Dear Sir:

The Commission is in receipt of an affidavit executed by your wife, Louisa Haikey, relating to the birth of your minor child, Bertie Haikey. Said affidavit has been filed with the Commission and is considered as an application for the enrollment of said Bertie Haikey as a citizen by blood of the Creek Nation. It is stated in said affidavit that said child is dead.

There is herewith enclosed a blank form of death affidavit, which you are requested to fill out and execute, giving the exact date of the death of your said minor child and return same to the Commission, in the enclosed envelope.

You are further requested in filling out said affidavit to state the maiden name of your wife, Louisa Haikey, and also her roll number as the same appears on her deed or her allotment certificate.

Respectfully,

(Name Illegible)

Register.   Chairman.
1 D A.

NC-29

Muskogee, Indian Territory, May 29, 1905.

Ben Haikee[sic], Jr.
Fry, Indian Territory.

Dear Sir:

There is on file with the Commission an affidavit relative to the birth of your minor child, Bertia Haikee, in which Louisa Haikee, the mother of said child, signed by mark; the signatures of two witnesses to said mark have been omitted.

There is herewith enclosed a blank form of birth affidavit and you are requested to have your wife, Louisa Haikee, execute same. Care should be taken to see that all blanks are properly filled, all names spelled in full, and in the event that the person signing the affidavit is unable to write, signature by mark must be attested by two witnesses.

Respectfully,

1 B A   Chairman.

DEPARTMENT OF THE INTERIOR,
COMMISSIONER TO THE FIVE CIVILIZED TRIBES.

REFER IN REPLY TO THE FOLLOWING:

N.C. 29.

Muskogee, Indian Territory, **August 4, 1905.**

Ben Haikey, Jr.,
Fry, Indian Territory.

Dear Sir:

You are hereby advised that on **July 28, 1905** , the Secretary of the Interior approved the enrollment of your minor child, **Bertha Haikey** , as a citizen by blood of the **Creek** Nation, and that the name of said child appears upon the roll of new born citizens of the **Creek** Nation as Number **18** .

The child is now entitled to an allotment, and application therefor should be made without delay at the Land Office for the Nation in which the prospective allotment is located.

An entire allotment for said child must be selected at the time of the original application.

Respectively,

Commissioner.

139

DEPARTMENT OF THE INTERIOR.
COMMISSION TO THE FIVE CIVILIZED TRIBES.

In the matter of the death of   Bertie Haikey   a citizen of the Creek Nation, who formerly resided at or near   Fry   , Ind. Ter., and died on the   18   day of   June   , 1904.

AFFIDAVIT OF RELATIVE.

UNITED STATES OF AMERICA, Indian Territory, ⎱
    Western   DISTRICT. ⎰

I,   Ben Haikey Jr.   , on oath state that I am   30   Nation and a citizen, by Blood   of the   Creek   Nation; Nation   Fry   , Ind. Ter.; that I am   Father   of Bertie Haikey   who was a citizen, by   Blood   , of the   Creek   Nation and that said   Bertie Haikey   died on the   18   day of   June   , 1904.

                           Ben Haikey Jr.

Witnesses To Mark:
⎰ Aves McCullough
⎱ WM McCullough

Subscribed and sworn to before me this 6 day of May, 1905.

                    Willard M. McCullough
                        Notary Public.
          My Commission expires March 21-1908.

AFFIDAVIT OF ACQUAINTANCE.

UNITED STATES OF AMERICA, Indian Territory, ⎱
    Western   DISTRICT. ⎰

I,   Rosa Chisholm   , on oath state that I am   34   Nation and a citizen by Blood   of the   Creek   Nation; Nation   Fry   , Ind. Ter.; that I am Nation   Bertie Haikey   who was a citizen, by   Blood   , of the   Creek   Nation and that said Bertie   died on the   18   day of June   , 1904.
her

                    Rosa x Chisholm
Witnesses To Mark: mark
⎰ Aves McCullough
⎱ W M McCullough

Applications for Enrollment of Creek Newborn
Act of 1905   Volume I

Subscribed and sworn to before me this 6 day of May, 1905.

Willard M. McCullough
Notary Public.
My Commission expires March 21-1908.

BIRTH AFFIDAVIT.

DEPARTMENT OF THE INTERIOR.
COMMISSION TO THE FIVE CIVILIZED TRIBES.

IN RE APPLICATION FOR ENROLLMENT, as a citizen of the Creek Nation, of Birdie Haikey, born on the 29 day of April , 1904

Name of Father: Ben Haikey, Jr.	a citizen of the	Creek	Nation.
Name of Mother: Louisa "	a citizen of the	Creek	Nation.

Postoffice   Fry I.T.

(Child is present) *(Initials Illegible)*

AFFIDAVIT OF MOTHER.

UNITED STATES OF AMERICA, Indian Territory,
 Western   **DISTRICT.**

I, Louisa Haikey, on oath state that I am 26 Nation and a citizen by blood, of the Creek Nation; Nation lawful wife of Ben Haikey Jr., who is a citizen, by blood, of the Creek Nation; Nation was born to me on 29 day of April, 1904, that said child has been named Birdie Haikey , and is now living. died June 18-1904

Ben Haikey Jr

Witnesses To Mark:

{

Subscribed and sworn to before me this 6 day of March, 1905.

Nation C Griesel
Notary Public.

NC 29   JLD

DEPARTMENT OF THE INTERIOR,
COMMISSIONER TO THE FIVE CIVILIZED TRIBES.

In the matter of the application of Birdie Haikey, deceased, as a citizen by blood of the Creek Nation.

141

. . . .

STATEMENT AND ORDER.

The record in this case shows that on March 6, 1905, application was made, in affidavit form, supplemented by sworn testimony taken on June 20, 1905, for the enrollment of Birdie Haikey, deceased, as a citizen by blood of the Creek Nation, under the provisions of Nation March 3, 1905.

It appears from the evidence filed in this matter that said Birdie Haikey, deceased, was born April 29, 1904, and died June 18, 1904.

The act of Congress approved March 3, 1905 (33 Stats., 1048), provides:

"That the Commission to the Five Civilized Tribes is authorized for sixty days after the date of the approval of this act to receive and consider applications for enrollments of children born subsequent to May twenty fifth, nineteen hundred and one, and prior to March fourth, nineteen hundred and five, and living on said latter date, to citizens of the Creek tribe of Indians whose enrollment has been approved by the Secretary of the Interior prior to the approval of this act; and to enroll Nation to such children."

It is therefore, ordered that the application for the enrollment of said Birdie Haikey, deceased, as a citizen by blood of the Creek Nation be, and the same is, hereby dismissed.

(Name Illegible) Commissioner.

Muskogee, Indian Territory.
JAN 15 1907

NC 29.

Muskogee, Indian Territory, January 17, 1907.

Louisa Haikey,
    c/o Ben Haikey,
        Fry, Indian Territory

Dear Madam:

There is herewith enclosed one copy of the Statement and Order of the Nation Five Civilized Tribes, dated January 15, 1907, dismissing the application made by you for the enrollment of your minor child, Birdie Haikey, deceased, as a citizen by blood of the Creek Nation.

Respectfully,

LN-79.

Commissioner.

Applications for Enrollment of Creek Newborn
Act of 1905   Volume I

DEPARTMENT OF THE INTERIOR,
COMMISSION TO THE FIVE CIVILIZED TRIBES.
MUSKOGEE, INDIAN TERRITORY, MARCH 7, 1905.

In the matter of the application for the enrollment of Barney Chissoe, as a citizen by blood of the Creek Nation.

ANNIE CHISSOE, being duly sworn, testified as follows:
EXAMINATION BY THE COMMISSION:
Q What is your name? A Annie Chissoe.
Q How old are you? A 21.
Q What is your postoffice address? A Coweta.
Q Have you a child born since May 25, 1901? A Yes, sir.
Q What is its name? A Barney Chissoe.
Q When was it born? June 17th.
Q What year?   A Last year, 1904.
Q Is that child living? A Dead.
Q When did it die? A Last, October.
Q Do you remember the day A Yes, sir.
Q What day? A thirteenth.
Q What year? A Last Year, 1904.
Q About how old was that child when it died? A About three months.
Q Did yu[sic] have a Doctor waiting on it when it died? A No, Indian Doctor ----- Susie Atkins.
Q Who else was there? A That was all.
Q Did you have a mid-wife at the time this child was born? A Yes.
Q Who? A White woman.
Q What as her name? A Mrs. Skinners.
Q Have you any record of the dates of birth and death of this child? A Have date of her death on record.
Q What kind of a record---in what kind of a book? A In little memorandum book.
Q How soon after the date of the death of this child did you enter that record?   A Morning of her death.
Q Is it written with a led pencil or ink? A Led pencil.

Witness is hereby advised that the Commission
desires her to bring in that record.

MAGGIE CHILDERS, being duly sworn, testified as follows,
partly through Jesse McDermott, Official Interpreter.

EXAMINATION BY COMMISSION:
Q What is your name? A Maggie Childers.
Q How old are you? A 43.
Q What is your postoffice address? A Coweta.
A[sic] Are you the mother of Annie Chissoe? A Yes.

Applications for Enrollment of Creek Newborn
Act of 1905   Volume I

Q Were you present at the birth of Barney Chissoe? A I was waiting on another daughter of mine and was not present.
Q Do you know when this child was born? A It was sometime in June, but I am uneducated and do not know the date exact.
Q Was it June of last year? A Yes.
Q When did that child die? A Last October.
Q About how old was that child when it died? A I do not know how old the child was but it was from June until October.
Q Were you present when that child died? A I had the child in my arms when it died.
Q Who also was there? A My mother was there, and the father of the child was also present.

The records of the Commission examined and the name of Justin Chissoe is found on Creek Indian Card, Field Number 89, opposite Roll Number 325, approved by the Secretary of the Interior March 13, 1902.
The name of Annie Chissoe is identified on Creek Indian Card, Field Number 175, opposite Roll Number 626, as Annie Bird, and is contained in the partial list of citizens by blood of the Creek Nation, approved by the Secretary of the Interior, March 13, 1902.

------oooOooo---

Zera Ellen Parrish, having been duly sworn, upon her oath states that as stenographer for the Commission to the Five Civilized Tribes she reported the proceedings in the above entitled case and that same is a full, true and correct transcript of her stenographic notes thereof.

Zera Ellen Parrish

Subscribed and sworn to
before me this 8th day of
March, 1905.

Edw C Griesel
Notary Public.

BA- 43 & 44-B

DEPARTMENT OF THE INTERIOR,
COMMISSION TO THE FIVE CIVILIZED TRIBES.

Muskogee, Indian Territory, March 6, 1905.

In the matter of the application for the enrollment of Wattie Haikey (deceased) and Sissie Haikey, as citizens by blood of the Creek Nation.

Louisa Haikey, being duly sworn, testified as follows:

Applications for Enrollment of Creek Newborn
Act of 1905   Volume I

EXAMINATION BY THE COMMISSION:
Q What is your name? A Louisa Haikey
Q What is your age? A 24.
Q What is your postoffice address? A Fry.
Q Are you the mother of Wattie Haikey and Sissie Haikey? A Yes, sir.
Q Which is the older of these two children? A Wattie.
Q When was Wattie born? A Born on September 16, 1902.
Q Is Wattie living? A No, dead.
Q When did she die? A In January.
Q What year? A 1903.
Q Who was present when Wattie Haikey was born—who was there? A Sookey Hains.
Q Was she the midwife? A Yes sir.
Q Did you have a doctor present when it was born? A Yes sir
Q Present when it died? A *(Illegible)*
Q Any doctor attending when sick? A Yes sir.
Q What doctor? A Dr. Broomfield.
Q Where does he live? A He used to live at Fry. I don't know where he lives now—in Missouri some wheres[sic].
Q Do you know some people who were present at the funeral of this child? A We did not have a funeral; no one present.
Q Who buried him? A Anderson Chisholm.
Q About how old was he when he died? A About three months old.
Q Did you put down in a Bible or bookd[sic] of any kind the dates of the birth and death of Wattie Haikey? A Put it down in a memorandum book.
Q Have you that book with you? No sir.
Q Did you write in Creek or English? A English.
Q Did you write it? A Yes sir.
Q Did you write it just after the child was born? A Yes sir.
Q Did you have a child named Sissie Haike[sic]? A Yes sir.
Q Is she with you? A Yes sir.
Q When was she born? A October 2, 1904.

The child appears to be as old as stated.

Q What is the name of the father of this child? A Ben Haike.

The father of Wattie and Sissie Haikey is identified as Ben Haikey on Creek Indian card, field No. 288, and his name is contained in the partial list of Creek citizens by blood approved by the Secretary of the Interior March 13, 1902. Roll No. 950

Ben Haikey, being duly sworn, testified as follows (through Jesse McDermott, Official Interpreter):

EXAMINATION BY THE COMMISSION:
Q What is your name? A Ben Haikey.
Q What is your age? A 54 years old.
Q What is your postoffice? A Fry.

Applications for Enrollment of Creek Newborn
Act of 1905 Volume I

Q Are you the husband of Louisa Haikey? A Yes sir.

Q Have you any children by her? A Yes sir.

Q What are their names? A One is Sissie and the other Wattie.

Q Is Wattie Haikey living? A He is dead.

Q When did he die? A I don't know about the year.

Q How old was he when he died? A About two months old.

Q Do you know what ear he was born? A I don't know.

Q Did you write down anywhere the date of the birth of that child? A No sir. I am uneducated and cannot write; therefore did not make any note of the dates.

Q When was Sissie born? A I don't know when Sissie was born, but the child is about five months old now.

Q Is that the child present there? A Yes sir.

Q Did you have a midwife present when Wattie was born? A Yes, sir.

Q What is her name? A Sookey Haike, sometimes known as Sookey Hains.

Q Where does she live? A Right near Fry.

Ben and Eliza Haikey are advised to have the midwife appear before the commission and give testimony, and to bring the record of the birth of the children.

(Louisa Haikey is identified (as Louisa Malone) on Creek Indian card, field No. 668, and her name is contained in the partial roll of Creek Indians approved by the Secretary of the Interior March 13, 1902, Roll No. 2197.)

INDIAN TERRITORY, Western District.

I, J. Y. Miller, a stenographer to the Commission to the Five Civilized Tribes, do hereby certify upon oath that the above and foregoing is a true and complete translation of my notes as same appear in my stenographic report of this case.

JY Miller

Sworn to and subscribed
before me this the
20 day of March,
1905.

Edw C Griesel
Notary Public.

BA-43 & 44-B

DEPARTMENT OF THE INTERIOR,
COMMISSION TO THE FIVE CIVILIZED TRIBES.

Muskogee, Indian Territory, March 6, 1905.

In the matter of the application for the enrollment of Wattie Haike[sic] (deceased) and Sissie Haike, as citizens by blood of the Creek Nation.

Louisa Haike, being duly sworn, testified as follows:

146

Applications for Enrollment of Creek Newborn
Act of 1905   Volume I

EXAMINATION BY THE COMMISSION:
Q What is your name? A Louisa Haike.
Q What is your age? 24
Q What is your postoffice address? A Fry.
Q Are you the mother of Wattie Haike and Sissie Haike? A Yes, sir.
Q Which is the older of these two children? A Wattie.
Q When was Wattie born? A Born on September 16, 1902.
Q Is Wattie living? A No, dead.
Q When did she die? A In January.
Q What year? A 1903.
Q Who was present when Wattie Haike was born—who was there? A Sookey Hains.
Q Was she the midwife? A Yes sir.
Q Did you have a doctor present when it was born? A Yes sir
Q Present when it died? A *(Illegible)*
Q Any doctor attending when sick? A Yes sir.
Q What doctor? A Dr. Broomfield.
Q Where does he live? A He used to live at Fry. I don't know where he lives now—in Missouri some wheres[sic].
Q Do you know some people who were present at the funeral of this child? A We did not have a funeral; no one present.
Q Who buried him? A Anderson Chisholm.
Q About how old was he when he died? A About three months old.
Q Did you put down in a Bible or bookd[sic] of any kind the dates of the birth and death of Wattie Haike? A Put it down in a memorandum book.
Q Have you that book with you? No sir.
Q Did you write in Creek or English? A English.
Q Did you write it? A Yes sir.
Q Did you write it just after the child was born? A Yes sir.
Q Did you have a child named Sissie Haike? A Yes sir.
Q Is she with you? A Yes sir.
Q When was she born? A October 2, 1904.

The child appears to be as old as stated.

Q What is the name of the father of this child? A Ben Haike.

The father of Wattie and Sissie Haike is identified as Ben Haike on Creek Indian card, field No. 288, and his name is contained in the partial list of Creek citizens by blood approved by the Secretary of the Interior March 13, 1902. Roll No. 950

Ben Haike, being duly sworn, testified as follows (through Jesse McDermott, Official Interpreter):

EXAMINATION BY THE COMMISSION:
Q What is your name? A Ben Haike.
Q What is your age? A 54 years old.
Q What is your postoffice? A Fry.

147

Applications for Enrollment of Creek Newborn
Act of 1905 Volume I

Q Are you the husband of Louisa Haike? A Yes sir.
Q Have you any children by her? A Yes sir.
Q What are their names? A One is Sissie and the other Wattie.
Q Is Wattie Haike living? A He is dead.
Q When did he die? A I don't know about the year.
Q How old was he when he died? A About two months old.
Q Do you know what ear he was born? A I don't know.
Q Did you write down anywhere the date of the birth of that child? A No sir. I am uneducated and cannot write; therefore did not make any note of the dates.
Q When was Sissie born? A I don't know when Sissie was born, but the child is about five months old now.
Q Is that the child present there? A Yes sir.
Q Did you have a midwife present when Wattie was born? A Yes, sir.
Q What is her name? A Sookey Haike, sometimes known as Sookey Hains.
Q Where does she live? A Right near Fry.

Ben and Eliza Haike are advised to have the midwife appear before the commission and give testimony, and to bring the record of the birth of the children.

(Louisa Haike is identified (as Louisa Malone) on Creek Indian card, field No. 668, and her name is contained in the partial roll of Creek Indians approved by the Secretary of the Interior March 13, 1902, Roll No. 2197.)

INDIAN TERRITORY, Western District.
I, J. Y. Miller, a stenographer to the Commission to the Five Civilized Tribes, do hereby certify upon oath that the above and foregoing is a true and complete translation of my notes as same appear in my stenographic report of this case.

JY Miller

Sworn to and subscribed
    before me this the
    20 day of March,
    1905.   Edw C Griesel
                                                    Notary Public.

AFFIDAVIT OF ATTENDING PHYSICIAN OR MID-WIFE.

UNITED STATES OF AMERICA, Indian Territory, ⎱
        Western   DISTRICT. ⎰

I,We, Charlie Boston, Ben Long, on oath state that I ~~attended on~~ they was present at the *(illegible)* of Ben Haikey where the child was born to Mrs. Louisa Haikey , wife of Ben Haikey on the 2nd day of October , 1904 ; that there was born to her on said date a Female child; that said child was living March 4, 1905, and is said to have been named Sissie Haikey.

Charles Boston

Applications for Enrollment of Creek Newborn
Act of 1905 Volume I

Witnesses To Mark: Ben Long

{

Subscribed and sworn to before me this 20 day of May, 1905.

W. G. Cooper
Notary Public.

BIRTH AFFIDAVIT.

DEPARTMENT OF THE INTERIOR.
COMMISSION TO THE FIVE CIVILIZED TRIBES.

IN RE APPLICATION FOR ENROLLMENT, as a citizen of the Creek Nation, of Sissie Haikey , born on the 2 day of October , 1904

Name of Father: Ben Haikey   a citizen of the Creek   Nation.
Name of Mother: Louisa "   a citizen of the   "   Nation.

Postoffice   Fry, I.T.

AFFIDAVIT OF MOTHER.

(Child present HGH)
UNITED STATES OF AMERICA, Indian Territory, ⎱
       Western   **DISTRICT.** ⎰

I, Louisa Haikey, on oath state that I am 24 years of age and a citizen by blood, of the Creek Nation; that I am the lawful wife of Ben Haikey, who is a citizen, by blood, of the Creek Nation; that a female child was born to me on 2 day of Oct, 1904, that said child has been named Sissie Haikey, and is now living.

Louisa Haikey
Witnesses To Mark:

{

Subscribed and sworn to before me this 6 day of March, 1905.

Edw C Griesel
Notary Public.

149

Applications for Enrollment of Creek Newborn
Act of 1905   Volume I

father
AFFIDAVIT OF ~~ATTENDING PHYSICIAN OR MID-WIFE~~.

UNITED STATES OF AMERICA, Indian Territory, ⎫
    Western   **DISTRICT.** ⎬

husband

I, Ben Haikey, Sr. a ----- on oath state that I ~~attended on Mrs. , wife~~ of Louisa Haikey on the 2 day of Oct , 1904 ; that there was born to her on said date a female child; that said child is now living, and is said to have been named Sissie Haikey.

his
Ben x Haikey Sr.
mark

Witnesses To Mark:
  ⎰ J. McDermott
  ⎱ ECGriesel

Subscribed and sworn to before me this 6 day of March, 1905.

Edw C Griesel
Notary Public.

BIRTH AFFIDAVIT.
DEPARTMENT OF THE INTERIOR.
COMMISSION TO THE FIVE CIVILIZED TRIBES.

IN RE APPLICATION FOR ENROLLMENT, as a citizen of the Creek Nation, of Wattie Haikey, born on the 16 day of Sept , 1902

Name of Father: Ben Haikey	a citizen of the Creek	Nation.
Name of Mother: Louisa "	a citizen of the "	Nation.

Postoffice   Fry, I.T.

AFFIDAVIT OF MOTHER.

UNITED STATES OF AMERICA, Indian Territory, ⎫
    Western   **DISTRICT.** ⎬

I, Louisa Haikey, on oath state that I am 24 years of age and a citizen by blood, of the Creek Nation; that I am the lawful wife of Ben Haikey, who is a citizen, by blood, of the Creek Nation; that a male child was born to me on 16 day of Sept, 1902, that said child has been named Wattie Haikey, and ~~is now living~~. died Jan. – 1903.

Louisa Haikey

Applications for Enrollment of Creek Newborn
Act of 1905   Volume I

Witnesses To Mark:

{

Subscribed and sworn to before me this 6 day of March, 1905.

Edw C Griesel
Notary Public.

---

father

AFFIDAVIT OF ~~ATTENDING PHYSICIAN OR MID-WIFE~~.

UNITED STATES OF AMERICA, Indian Territory, ⎫
    Western   **DISTRICT.** ⎬

husband

I, Ben Haikey, Sr. a ----- on oath state that I ~~attended on Mrs. , wife~~ of Louisa Haikey on the 16 day of Sept , 1902 ; that there was born to her on said date a   male child; that said child ~~is now living~~, and is said to have been named Sissie Haikey.

in January 1903   his

Ben x Haikey Sr.
mark

Witnesses To Mark:
{ J. McDermott
  ECGriesel

Subscribed and sworn to before me this 6 day of March, 1905.

Edw C Griesel
Notary Public.

NC 31   JLD

DEPARTMENT OF THE INTERIOR,
COMMISSIONER TO THE FIVE CIVILIZED TRIBES.

. . . .

In the matter of the application for the enrollment of Wattie Haikey, as a citizen by blood of the Creek Nation.

. . . .

STATEMENT AND ORDER.

The record in this case shows that on March 6, 1905, application was made, in affidavit form, supplemented by sworn testimony, for the enrollment of Wattie Haikey, deceased, as a citizen by blood of the Creek Nation, under the provisions of the act of Congress approved March 3, 1905.

It appears from the evidence filed in this matter that said Wattie Haikey, deceased, was born September 16, 1902, and died in the month of January, 1903.

The act of Congress approved March 3, 1905, (33 Stats., 1048), in part provides: "That the Commission to the Five Civilized Tribes is authorized for sixty days after the date of the approval of this act to receive and consider applications for enrollment, of children, born subsequent to May twenty-fifth, nineteen hundred and one, and prior to March fourth, nineteen hundred and five, and living on said latter date, to citizens of the Creek tribe of Indians whose enrollment has been approved by the Secretary of the Interior prior to the approval of this act; and to enroll and make allotments to such children."

It is therefore, ordered that the application for the enrollment of said Wattie Haikey, deceased, as a citizen by blood of the Creek Nation, be and the same is, hereby dismissed.

(Name Illegible) Commissioner.

Muskogee, Indian Territory.

BA 43 B.

Muskogee, Indian Territory, May 15, 1905.

Ben Haikey,
Fry, Indian Territory.

Dear Sir:

There is on file with the Commission an affidavit executed relative to the birth of your minor child, Sissie Haikey. You are advised that the affidavit of the midwife in attendance at the birth of said child is required.

There is herewith enclosed a blank form of birth affidavit, and in executing same care should be exercised to see that all the blanks are properly filled, all names written in full and in the event that the person signing the affidavit is unable to write, signature by mark must be attested by two witnesses. Each affidavit must be executed before a Notary Public and the notarial seal and signature of the officer must be attached to each separate affidavit.

Respectfully,

BC.   Chairman.

DEPARTMENT OF THE INTERIOR,
COMMISSIONER TO THE FIVE CIVILIZED TRIBES.

REFER IN REPLY TO THE FOLLOWING:
N/C.-31.

Muskogee, Indian Territory, **August 4, 1905.**

Ben Haikey,
        Fry, Indian Territory.

Dear Sir:

You are hereby advised that on **July 28, 1905**   , the Secretary of the Interior approved the enrollment of your minor child, **Sissie Haikey** , as a citizen by blood of the **Creek** Nation, and that the name of said child appears upon the roll of new born citizens of the **Creek** Nation as Number **19** .

The child is now entitled to an allotment, and application therefor should be made without delay at the Land Office for the Nation in which the prospective allotment is located.

An entire allotment for said child must be selected at the time of the original application.

Respectively,

Commissioner.

––––––––––

NC 31.

Muskogee, Indian Territory, January 17, 1907.

Louisa Haikey,
        c/o Ben Haikey,
                Fry, Indian Territory.

Dear Madam:

There is herewith enclosed one copy of the Statement and Order of the Commissioner to the Five Civilized Tribes, dated January ??, 1907, dismissing the application made by you for the enrollment of your minor child Wattie Haikey, deceased, as a citizen by blood of the Creek Nation.

Respectfully,

Commissioner.

LM-77.

Applications for Enrollment of Creek Newborn
Act of 1905 Volume I

BA 77 B.

Muskogee, Indian Territory, May 15, 1905.

Johnson Phillips,
Eufaula, Indian Territory.

Dear Sir:

There is on file with the Commission an affidavit executed by you relative to the birth of your minor child, Lydia Phillips. The affidavits of the mother and midwife or physician in attendance at the birth of said child must be furnished.

There is therewith enclosed a blank form of birth affidavit, and in executing same care should be exercised to see that all blanks are properly filled, all names written in full and in the event that either of the persons signing the affidavits is unable to write, signatures by mark must be attested by two witnesses. Each affidavit must be executed before a Notary Public and the notarial seal and signature of the officer must be attached to each separate affidavit.

Respectfully,

BC.   Chairman.

DEPARTMENT OF THE INTERIOR,
COMMISSIONER TO THE FIVE CIVILIZED TRIBES.

REFER IN REPLY TO THE FOLLOWING:
N.C. 32.

Muskogee, Indian Territory, **August 4, 1905.**

John Phillips,
    Eufaula, Indian Territory.

Dear Sir:

You are hereby advised that on **July 28, 1905** , the Secretary of the Interior approved the enrollment of your minor child, **Lydia Phillips** , as a citizen by blood of the **Creek** Nation, and that the name of said child appears upon the roll of new born citizens of the **Creek** Nation as Number **20** .

The child is now entitled to an allotment, and application therefor should be made without delay at the Land Office for the Nation in which the prospective allotment is located.

An entire allotment for said child must be selected at the time of the original application.

Applications for Enrollment of Creek Newborn
Act of 1905   Volume I

Respectively,

Commissioner.

BIRTH AFFIDAVIT.

DEPARTMENT OF THE INTERIOR.
COMMISSION TO THE FIVE CIVILIZED TRIBES.

IN RE APPLICATION FOR ENROLLMENT, as a citizen of the Creek Nation, of Lydia Phillips, born on the 3rd day of Jan , 1903

Name of Father: Johnson Phillips Tuskegee Town   a citizen of the   Creek   Nation.
Name of Mother: Hettie Phillips Quassoda Town No 1   a citizen of the   Creek   Nation.

Postoffice   Eufaula

AFFIDAVIT OF MOTHER.

UNITED STATES OF AMERICA, Indian Territory,
      Western   DISTRICT.

I, Hettie Phillips, on oath state that I am 25 years of age and a citizen by blood, of the Creek Nation; that I am the lawful wife of Johnson Phillips, who is a citizen, by blood, of the Creek Nation; that a female child was born to me on 3rd day of January, 1903, that said child has been named Lydia Phillips, and was living March 4, 1905.

                                                                     her
                                                  Hettie Phillips   x
Witnesses To Mark: mark
   ⎰ T L Boone
   ⎱ D.M. Whitaker

Subscribed and sworn to before me this 31st day of May, 1905.

Thos. F. *(Illegible)*
Notary Public.

AFFIDAVIT OF ATTENDING PHYSICIAN OR MID-WIFE.

UNITED STATES OF AMERICA, Indian Territory,
      Western   DISTRICT.

I, Betsy Phillips, a Midwife, on oath state that I attended on Mrs. Hettie Phillips, wife of Johnson Phillips on the 3rd day of Jan, 1903; that there was born to her on said

155

Applications for Enrollment of Creek Newborn
Act of 1905 Volume I

date a female child; that said child was living March 4, 1905, and is said to have been named Lydia Phillips.

her

Betsy Phillips   x

mark

Witnesses To Mark:

{ T L Boone
{ D.M. Whitaker

Subscribed and sworn to before me this 31st day of May, 1905.

Thos. F. *(Illegible)*
Notary Public.

BIRTH AFFIDAVIT.

DEPARTMENT OF THE INTERIOR.
COMMISSION TO THE FIVE CIVILIZED TRIBES.

IN RE APPLICATION FOR ENROLLMENT, as a citizen of the Creek Nation, of Lydia Phillips, born on the 3 day of January, 1903

Name of Father: Johnson Phillips	a citizen of the	Creek	Nation.
Name of Mother: Hettie Phillips	a citizen of the	Creek	Nation.

Postoffice   Eufaula

AFFIDAVIT OF ~~MOTHER~~. father

UNITED STATES OF AMERICA, Indian Territory, ⎫
    Western   DISTRICT. ⎭

I, Johnson Phillips, on oath state that I am 37 years of age and a citizen by blood, of the Creek Nation; that I am the lawful ~~wife~~ husb of Hettie Phillips, who is a citizen, by blood, of the Creek Nation; that a female child was born to me on 3 day of January, 1903, that said child has been named Lydia Phillips, and is now living.

Johnson Phillips

Witnesses To Mark:

{

Subscribed and sworn to before me this 7 day of March, 1905.

Edw C Griesel
Notary Public.

BA 334 B.

Muskogee, Indian Territory, May 16, 1905.

Mitchell C. Fields,
    Irene, Indian Territory.

Dear Sir:

The Commission is in receipt of an affidavit relative to the birth of your minor child, Legus Fields. It is stated in said affidavit that there was no midwife present at the birth of said child. The Commission requires your affidavit in the matter of the birth of said child and also the affidavits of two disinterested witnesses relative to the birth of said Legus Fields.

There are herewith enclosed two blank forms of birth affidavits, and in executing same care should be exercised to see that blanks are properly filled, all names written in full and in the event that the persons signing the affidavits is[sic] unable to write signatures by mark must be attested by two witnesses. Each affidavit must be executed before a Notary Public and the notarial seal and signature of the officer must be attached to each separate affidavit.

Respectfully,

BC.   Chairman.

N.C.33

Muskogee, Indian Territory, July 7, 1905.

Indy Fields,
    Irene, Indian Territory.

Dear Madam:

You are advised that there are on file at this office, affidavits of Saber Jackson and Emma Sams relative to the enrollment of your minor child, Legus Fields, in which the date of birth of said child has been omitted.

You are advised that this office requires the affidavits of two dis-interested persons relative to the birth of said child.

There re herewith enclosed two blank forms of birth affidavits. In having same executed, care should be taken that all blanks are properly filled, all names written in full, and in the event that the person signing the affidavit is unable to write, signature by mark must be attested by two witnesses.

Respectfully,

AG-4-7-7-   Commissioner.

33

Muskogee, Indian Territory, August 8, 1905.

Indy Fields,
    Care of Mitchell Fields,
        Irene, Indian Territory.

Dear Madam:
    In the matter of the application for the enrollment of your minor child, Legus Fields, as a citizen by blood of the Creek Nation, you are advised that this office cannot identify you as a citizen of said Nation.

    You are requested to state your maiden name, the names of your parents, the Creek Indian Town to which you claim to belong, and, if possible, your roll number as same appears on deeds to land in the Creek Nation, which will help identify you as a citizen thereof.

Respectfully,

Commissioner.

N.C.33

COPY

Okemah. I.T. August L91.1905

Hon. Daws[sic] Commission, for the Five Tribes.

Muskogee, I.T.

Sir:-.

    In answer to you letter of aug. 8th 1905. would state. that my maiden name was India Fixico. and my fathers name Afoloky Fixico. Band cief Tobe Hill.
Lucinda
India
Siah.
Dicey
Millie
the above is the family of which i am a member

yours truly,
her
India x Fixico
mark

158

Applications for Enrollment of Creek Newborn
Act of 1905 Volume I

Witness to mark
H. G. Malat
David Knight

(Note: Typed as shown on microfilm)

AFFIDAVIT OF ACQUAINTANCE.

UNITED STATES OF AMERICA, Indian Territory, ⎱
   Western Judicial   **DISTRICT.** ⎰

     I, Saber Jackson, on oath state that I am 33 years of age, and a citizen by blood of
        Emma Sands "   "   "   "   " " 31
the Creek Nation; that my postoffice address is Irene , Ind. Ter.; that I was personally
               "   "
acquainted with Legus who ~~was~~ is a citizen by blood, of the Creek Nation; and that said
Legus Field[sic] is now living.

                            Saber Jackson
Witnesses To Mark: her
   ⎰ *(Name Illegible)*   Emma x Sands
   ⎱ Tupper *(Illegible)*   mark

     Subscribed and sworn to before me this 1st day of July, 1905.

     My com. Exp. Aug 19-1908   Tupper *(Illegible)*
                                   Notary Public.

BIRTH AFFIDAVIT.

DEPARTMENT OF THE INTERIOR.
COMMISSION TO THE FIVE CIVILIZED TRIBES.

     IN RE APPLICATION FOR ENROLLMENT, as a citizen of the Creek Nation, of Legus Fields,
     or about
born on ^ the 6" day of March , 1902

Name of Father: Mitchell Fields   a citizen of the   Creek   Nation.
Name of Mother: Indy Fields   a citizen of the   Creek   Nation.

               Postoffice   Irene, Ind. Ter.

Applications for Enrollment of Creek Newborn
Act of 1905 Volume I

Witness
AFFIDAVIT OF ~~MOTHER~~.

UNITED STATES OF AMERICA, Indian Territory, ⎱
      Western   **DISTRICT.** ⎰

I, Nicey Knight, on oath state that I am 24 years of age and a citizen by Blood, of
                         acquainted with Indy Fields
the Creek Nation; that I am ^ the lawful wife of Mitchell Fields, who is a citizen, by
                                            them   or about
blood, of the Creek Nation; that a male child was born to ~~me~~ on ^ 6 day of March, 1902,
that said child has been named Legus Fields, and was living March 4, 1905.

                                      her
                              Nicey x Knight
Witnesses To Mark: mark
 ⎰ David Knight
 ⎱ HG Malot

Subscribed and sworn to before me this 4 day of August, 1905.

                         HG Malot
                              Notary Public.
                    My com exp 2 July 1906

Witness
AFFIDAVIT OF ~~ATTENDING PHYSICIAN OR MID-WIFE~~.

UNITED STATES OF AMERICA, Indian Territory, ⎱
      Western   **DISTRICT.** ⎰
                              am acquainted with
       I, David Knight, on oath state that I ~~attended on~~ Mrs. Indy Fields , wife of
                         about the
Mitchell Fields on ~~the~~ 6th day of March , 1902 ; that there was born to her on said date
a male child; that said child was living March 4, 1905, and is said to have been named
Legus Fields.
                              David Knight
Witnesses To Mark:
 ⎰

Subscribed and sworn to before me this ~~21~~[sic] day of August, 1905.

                         HG Malot
                              Notary Public.
                    My com exp 2 July 1906

160

Applications for Enrollment of Creek Newborn
Act of 1905   Volume I

BIRTH AFFIDAVIT.

DEPARTMENT OF THE INTERIOR.
COMMISSION TO THE FIVE CIVILIZED TRIBES.

IN RE APPLICATION FOR ENROLLMENT, as a citizen of the Creek Nation, of Legus Fields, born on the 6 day of March , 1902

Name of Father: Mitchell Fields	a citizen of the	Creek	Nation.
Name of Mother: Indy Fields	a citizen of the	Creek	Nation.

Postoffice   Irene, Indian Territory

AFFIDAVIT OF MOTHER.

UNITED STATES OF AMERICA, Indian Territory,
Western   DISTRICT.

I, Indy Fields, on oath state that I am about 23 years of age and a citizen by blood, of the Creek Nation; that I am the lawful wife of Mitchell Fields, who is a citizen, by blood, of the Creek Nation; that a male child was born to me on 6 day of March, 1902, that said child has been named Legus Fields, and was living March 4, 1905. That no one attended me as midwife or physician at the time the child was born.

her
Indy x Fields
mark

Witnesses To Mark:
    Alex Posey
    DC Skaggs

Subscribed and sworn to before me this 13" day of March, 1905.

Drennan C. Skaggs
Notary Public.

DEPARTMENT OF THE INTERIOR,
COMMISSIONER TO THE FIVE CIVILIZED TRIBES.

REFER IN REPLY TO THE FOLLOWING:
N.C. 34.

Muskogee, Indian Territory, **August 4, 1905.**

Maggie Arnett,
Care of Albert W. Arnett,
Checotah, Indian Territory.

Dear Sir:

You are hereby advised that on **July 28, 1905** , the Secretary of the Interior approved the enrollment of your minor child, **Abbie Lee Arnett**, as a citizen by blood of the **Creek** Nation, and that the name of said child appears upon the roll of new born citizens of the **Creek** Nation as Number **21** .

The child is now entitled to an allotment, and application therefor should be made without delay at the Land Office for the Nation in which the prospective allotment is located.

An entire allotment for said child must be selected at the time of the original application.

Respectively,

Commissioner.

Muskogee, Indian Territory, August 14, 1905.

Maggie Arnett,
        Checotah, Indian Territory.

Dear Madam:

Receipt is acknowledged of your letter of August 10, 1905, in which you state you have received a notice that you could file for your minor child, Abbie Lee Arnett and you ask if it would be better for you to wait until the enrollment of your minor child, Iola Arnett, has been approved and you can file for them both at once.

In reply you are advised that the name of said Iola Arnett is contained in a schedule of new-born Creeks now pending before the Department.

As this office cannot state positively when said schedule will be finally approved, you are again advised that application should be made without delay at the Creek Land Office for allotment of land for said Abbie Lee Arnett.

Applications for Enrollment of Creek Newborn
Act of 1905   Volume I

Respectively,

Acting Commissioner.

United States of America,   )

                           ;

Indian Territory,   ) ss

                           ;

Western District.   )

On this 13th day of March, A.D. 1905, personally appeared before me the undersigned Charles Buford, a Notary Public, for and in the Western District of the Indian Territory, duly commissioned and acting as such, D. M. Pate, M.D., who being by me first duly sworn on his oath deposes and says: My name is D.M. Pate, I am 39 years old, my residence is Checotah, Creek Nation, Indian Territory; during the year 1904 for and for[sic] about 10 years prior to the year 1904 I resided in Checotah, I.T. where I was engaged in the active practice of medicine; I am well acquainted with A.W. Arnett and Maggie Arnett, his wife; they have lived in Checotah for the last five years where I have been well acquainted with them both; Maggie Arnett, the wife of A.W. Arnett is a citizen by blood of the Creek Nation; on the 19th day of February, 1904 there was born unto A.W. Arnett and Maggie Arnett a female child; I attended in my professional capacity Mrs Maggie Arnett at the time she gave birth to this child; I was present when this child was born; the child was afterwards gives the name of Abbie Lee Arnett and is now living with its parents at Checotah, I.T. I am well acquainted with this child, Abbie Lee Arnett.

D.M. Pate M.D.

Subscribed and sworn to before me this 13th day of March, A.D. 1905.

Charles Buford

My commission expires July 3rd 1906.   Notary Public.

BIRTH AFFIDAVIT.
DEPARTMENT OF THE INTERIOR.
COMMISSION TO THE FIVE CIVILIZED TRIBES.

IN RE APPLICATION FOR ENROLLMENT, as a citizen of the Creek Nation, of Abbie Lee Arnett , born on the 19 day of Feb , 1904

Name of Father: Albert W Arnett   a citizen of the U.S.   Nation.
Name of Mother: Maggie Arnett   a citizen of the   Creek   Nation.

Postoffice   Checotah, I.T.

Applications for Enrollment of Creek Newborn
Act of 1905 Volume I

UNITED STATES OF AMERICA, Indian Territory, ⎱
Western   DISTRICT. ⎰

I, Albert W. Arnett, on oath state that I am 34 years of age and a citizen by ----- of the U.S. Nation; that I am the lawful ~~wife~~ husb of Maggie Arnett, who is a citizen, by blood, of the Creek Nation; that a female child was born to me on 19 day of Feb , 1904, that said child has been named Abbie Lee Arnett , and is now living.

Albert W. Arnett

Witnesses To Mark:
{

Subscribed and sworn to before me this 7 day of March, 1905.

Edw C Griesel
Notary Public.

BIRTH AFFIDAVIT.

DEPARTMENT OF THE INTERIOR.
COMMISSION TO THE FIVE CIVILIZED TRIBES.

IN RE APPLICATION FOR ENROLLMENT, as a citizen of the Creek Nation, of Abbie Lee Arnett , born on the 19th day of February , 1904

Name of Father: A W Arnett   a citizen of the United States Nation.
Name of Mother: Maggie Arnett   a citizen of the   Creek   Nation.

Postoffice   Checotah, Ind. Ter.

AFFIDAVIT OF MOTHER.

UNITED STATES OF AMERICA, Indian Territory, ⎱
Western   DISTRICT. ⎰

I, Maggie Arnett, on oath state that I am 28 years of age and a citizen by Blood, of the Creek Nation; that I am the lawful wife of A.W. Arnett, who is a citizen, by *(blank)*, of the United States Nation; that a female child was born to me on day of , 190, that said child has been named , and was living March 4, 1905. was born to me on 19th day of February, 1904 that said child has been named Abbie Lee Arnett, and was living March 4, 1905.

Maggie Arnett

Witnesses To Mark:
{

164

Applications for Enrollment of Creek Newborn
Act of 1905   Volume I

Subscribed and sworn to before me this 13th day of March, 1905.

JB Morrow
Notary Public.

DEPARTMENT OF THE INTERIOR,
COMMISSIONER TO THE FIVE CIVILIZED TRIBES.

REFER IN REPLY TO THE FOLLOWING:

N.C. 35.

Muskogee, Indian Territory, **August 4, 1905.**

Benjamin Marshall,
Clarksville, Indian Territory.

Dear Sir:

You are hereby advised that on **July 28, 1905** , the Secretary of the Interior approved the enrollment of your minor child, **Benjamin Marshall, Jr.,** , as a citizen by blood of the **Creek** Nation, and that the name of said child appears upon the roll of new born citizens of the **Creek** Nation as Number **22** .

The child is now entitled to an allotment, and application therefor should be made without delay at the Land Office for the Nation in which the prospective allotment is located.

An entire allotment for said child must be selected at the time of the original application.

Respectively,

Commissioner.

DEPARTMENT OF THE INTERIOR,
COMMISSIONER TO THE FIVE CIVILIZED TRIBES.

REFER IN REPLY TO THE FOLLOWING:

N.C. 35.

Muskogee, Indian Territory, **August 4, 1905.**

Benjamin Marshall,
Clarksville, Indian Territory.

Dear Sir:

You are hereby advised that on **July 28, 1905** , the Secretary of the Interior approved the enrollment of your minor child, **George Freeman Marshall** , as a citizen by blood of the **Creek** Nation, and that the name of said child appears upon the roll of new born citizens of the **Creek** Nation as Number **23** .

165

Applications for Enrollment of Creek Newborn
Act of 1905   Volume I

      The child is now entitled to an allotment, and application therefor should be made without delay at the Land Office for the Nation in which the prospective allotment is located.

      An entire allotment for said child must be selected at the time of the original application.

Respectively,

Commissioner.

BIRTH AFFIDAVIT.

DEPARTMENT OF THE INTERIOR.
COMMISSION TO THE FIVE CIVILIZED TRIBES.

IN RE APPLICATION FOR ENROLLMENT, as a citizen of the Creek Nation, of George Freeman Marshall , born on the 1 day of Sept , 1904

Name of Father:	Benjamin Marshall	a citizen of the Creek	Nation.
Name of Mother:	Lizzie B Marshall	a citizen of the U S	Nation.

Postoffice   Clarksville

Child Present

AFFIDAVIT OF MOTHER.

UNITED STATES OF AMERICA, Indian Territory, ⎤
     Western   DISTRICT. ⎦

      I, Lizzie B. Marshall, on oath state that I am 31 years of age and a citizen by ----- of the U.S. Nation; that I am the lawful wife of Benjamin Marshall, who is a citizen, by blood, of the Creek Nation; that a male child was born to me on 1 day of Sept, 1904; that said child has been named George Freeman Marshall, and is now living.

Lizzie B. Marshall

Witnesses To Mark:

   {

    Subscribed and sworn to before me this 11 day of March, 1905.

Edw C Griesel
Notary Public.

166

Applications for Enrollment of Creek Newborn
Act of 1905   Volume I

AFFIDAVIT OF ATTENDING PHYSICIAN OR MID-WIFE.

UNITED STATES OF AMERICA, Indian Territory, ⎫
    Western   DISTRICT. ⎰

I, Mrs. Nora Briscoe, a Midwife, on oath state that I attended on Mrs. Lizzie B. Marshall , wife of Benjamin Marshall on the 1 day of Sept , 1904 ; that there was born to her on said date a male child; that said child is now living, and is said to have been named George Freeman Marshall.

                                        Mrs. Nora Briscoe

Witnesses To Mark:

{

Subscribed and sworn to before me this 11 day of March, 1905.

                                 Edw C Griesel
                                     Notary Public.

BIRTH AFFIDAVIT.

DEPARTMENT OF THE INTERIOR.
COMMISSION TO THE FIVE CIVILIZED TRIBES.

IN RE APPLICATION FOR ENROLLMENT, as a citizen of the **Creek**. Nation, of George Freeman Marshall , born on the 1 day of Sept , 1904

Name of Father: Benjamin Marshall   a citizen of the   Creek   Nation.
Name of Mother: Lizzie B   "   a citizen of the   U S   Nation.

                      Postoffice   Clarksville I.T.

AFFIDAVIT OF ~~MOTHER~~. father

UNITED STATES OF AMERICA, Indian Territory, ⎫
    Western   DISTRICT. ⎰

I, Benjamin Marshall, on oath state that I am 39 years of age and a citizen by blood, of the Creek Nation; that I am the lawful ~~wife~~ husb of Lizzie B. Marshall, who is a citizen, by ----- of the U.S. Nation; that a boy child was born to her on 1 day of Sept., 1904; that said child has been named George Freeman Marshall, and is now living.

                                 Benjamin Marshall

Witnesses To Mark:

{

Subscribed and sworn to before me this 7 day of March, 1905.

Applications for Enrollment of Creek Newborn
Act of 1905   Volume I

Edw C Griesel
Notary Public.

DEPARTMENT OF THE INTERIOR.
COMMISSION TO THE FIVE CIVILIZED TRIBES.

IN RE APPLICATION FOR ENROLLMENT, as a citizen of the Creek Nation, of Benjamin Marshall, Jr. born on the 29 day of Aug , 1902

Name of Father: Benjamin Marshall   a citizen of the   Creek   Nation.
Name of Mother: Lizzie B   "   a citizen of the   U S   Nation.

Postoffice   Clarksville

Child Present

AFFIDAVIT OF MOTHER.

UNITED STATES OF AMERICA, Indian Territory, ⎱
    Western   DISTRICT. ⎰

    I, Lizzie B. Marshall, on oath state that I am 31 years of age and a citizen by -----
of the U.S. Nation; that I am the lawful wife of Benjamin Marshall, who is a citizen, by blood, of the Creek Nation; that a male child was born to me on 29 day of Aug, 1902; that said child has been named Benjamin Marshall, Jr, and is now living.

Lizzie B. Marshall

Witnesses To Mark:

⎰

Subscribed and sworn to before me this 11 day of March, 1905.

Edw C Griesel
Notary Public.

AFFIDAVIT OF ATTENDING PHYSICIAN OR MID-WIFE.

UNITED STATES OF AMERICA, Indian Territory, ⎱
    Western   DISTRICT. ⎰

    I, Mrs. M. M. Freeman, a Midwife, on oath state that I attended on Mrs. Benj. Marshall , wife of Benjamin Marshall on the 29 day of Aug , 1902 ; that there was born to her on said date a male child; that said child is now living, and is said to have been named Benjamin Marshall, Jr.

Mrs. M. M. Freeman

Witnesses To Mark:

{

Subscribed and sworn to before me this 11 day of March, 1905.

Edw C Griesel
Notary Public.

BIRTH AFFIDAVIT.

DEPARTMENT OF THE INTERIOR.
COMMISSION TO THE FIVE CIVILIZED TRIBES.

IN RE APPLICATION FOR ENROLLMENT, as a citizen of the **Creek**. Nation, of Benjamin Marshall Jr , born on the 2̶8̶ 29 day of J̶u̶n̶e̶ Aug, 1902

Name of Father: Benjamin Marshall	a citizen of the	Creek	Nation.
Name of Mother: Lizzie B "	a citizen of the	U S	Nation.

Postoffice   Clarksville I.T.

AFFIDAVIT OF M̶O̶T̶H̶E̶R̶. father

UNITED STATES OF AMERICA, Indian Territory,
      Western   DISTRICT.

I, Benjamin Marshall, on oath state that I am 39 years of age and a citizen by blood, of the Creek Nation; that I am the lawful w̶i̶f̶e̶ husb of Lizzie B. Marshall, who is a citizen, by ----- of the U.S. Nation; that a boy child was born to her on 2̶8̶ 29 day of J̶u̶n̶e̶, Sept 1902; that said child has been named Benjamin Marshall, and is now living.

Benjamin Marshall

Witnesses To Mark:

{

Subscribed and sworn to before me this 7 day of March, 1905.

Edw C Griesel
Notary Public.

Applications for Enrollment of Creek Newborn
Act of 1905   Volume I

N.C.-36.

DEPARTMENT OF THE INTERIOR,
COMMISSIONER TO THE FIVE CIVILIZED TRIBES.
Muskogee, I.T., February 8, 1905.

In the matter of the application for the enrollment of Panuggee Ceasar as a citizen by blood of the Creek Nation.

SUMKA, being duly sworn, testified as follows:

Through Alex Posey official interpreter:

BY THE COMMISSIONER:

Q What is your name? A Sumka.

Q How old are you? A About thirty.

Q What is your post office address? A Paden.

Q Do you know Sissie Ceasar and London Harjo? A Yes, sir.

Q Are you any kin to Sissie Ceasar? A She is my full sister.

Q For what purpose do you now appear here? A I appear here in answer to a letter to my sister, Sissie, demanding the joint affidavit of her and London Harjo, electing in which Nation, Creek or Seminole, they desire to have Panuggee enrolled. Sissie is very sick and can't come in and they have delegated me and impowered[sic] me to come in and make that election for them.

Q Sissie is not married to London Harjo is she? A The husband of Sissie is Calarney Harjo, but London Harjo is the father of the child London is a Seminole. The child was named after the mother.

Q Has London Harjo, the Seminole father of this child, told you to elect for it in the Creek Nation? A I have never seen London.

Q How does Sissie's name come to be Ceasar? A She is married to Calarney Harjo but still goes by the name of Ceasar. Ceasar was her maiden name.

Q When was your sister, Sissie, married to Carlarney[sic] Harjo? A Last December a year ago.

Q After Panuggee was born? A Yes, sir.

Q She didn't name this child after its father London Harjo, nor her present husband, Calarney Harjo, but named it after herself, Ceasar, did she? A Yes, sir, she named it after herself.

Q All you came in to-day for is that your sister, Sissie, has told you that she wants this child enrolled in the Creek Nation? A Yes, sir.

The witness is handed a blank form for the joint affidavit
of London Harjo and Sissie Harjo, with the advise[sic] that he
should have them execute same at an early date and ⇢return[sic]
it to this office.

Q Is Panuggee living? A Yes, sir.

---ooo OOO ooo---

I, D. C. Skaggs, on oath state that the above and foregoing is a full and true transcript of my stenographic notes as taken in said cause on said date.

DC Skaggs

Subscribed and sworn to before me this 5th day of February, 1906.

J McDermott
Notary Public.

NC 36.

DEPARTMENT OF THE INTERIOR,
COMMISSIONER TO THE FIVE CIVILIZED TRIBES.
Paden, Indian Territory, October 13, 1906.

In the matter of the application for the enrollment of Panuggee Caeser[sic] as a citizen by blood of the Creek Nation.

SISSIE HARJO, being duly sworn, testified as follows through Jesse McDermott official interpreter:

BY COMMISSIONER:

Q What is your name? A Sissie Caeser[sic] was my name but it is now Sissie Harjo since I married to Carlarney Harjo.
Q What is your age? A About 23.
Q What is your postoffice address? A Paden.
Q Do you know London Harjo? A Yes.
Q Is he a Creek citizen? A No, he is a Seminole.
Q Did you have a child by him? A Yes.
Q What is the name of the child? A Panuggie[sic].
Q When was Panuggie born? A In December.
Q What day of the month? A About the 28th I think.
Q Do you know the year? A No.
Q How old will he be next December? A He will be four years old.
Q Is the father a fullblood Seminole? A I don't know.
Q Are you living with London Harjo now? A No; he is down near Sasakwa.
Q Does the father contribute anything toward the support of this child? A No.
Q Did you have a midwife? A Yes, a woman by the name of Cinda is the midwife but she lives near Sasakwa.
Q Is Panuggie living? A Yes. (The child is present) .[sic]

---oooOOOooo---

I, Jesse McDermott, on oath state that the above and foregoing is a full and true transcript of my notes as taken in said cause on said date.

Jesse McDermott

Subscribed and sworn to before me this 10th day of December, 1906.

(Name Illegible)
Notary Public.

NC 36

DEPARTMENT OF THE INTERIOR,
COMMISSIONER TO THE FIVE CIVILIZED TRIBES.
Sasakwa, Indian Territory, October 23, 1906.

In the matter of the application for the enrollment of Panuggie Caeser[sic] as a citizen by blood of the Creek Nation.

LONDON HARJO, being duly sworn, testified as follows through Jesse McDermott official interpreter.

BY COMMISSIONER:

Q What is your name? A London Harjo.
Q What is your age? A About 22.
Q What is your postoffice address? A Sasakwa.
Q Are you a Creek citizen? A No, I am a Seminole.
Q Do you know Sissie Caeser[sic]? A Yes.
Q Did she have a child by you? A I was told that she said I was the father of the child.
Q Do you know that to be the truth? A Yes.
Q Had she lived in the neighborhood in which you live prior to the birth of the child? A Yes.
Q Did you ever go in accompany with her? A Yes.
Q Are you a fullblood Seminole? A Yes, I guess so.
Q Are you as the father of Paguggie[sic] willing for him to be enrolled in the Creek Nation? A Yes.

---oooOOOooo---

I, Jesse McDermott, on oath state that the above and foregoing is a full and true transcript of my notes as taken in said cause on said date.

Jesse McDermott

Subscribed and sworn to before me this 10th day of December, 1906.

(Name Illegible)
Notary Public.

Applications for Enrollment of Creek Newborn
Act of 1905   Volume I

BA 335 B.

Muskogee, Indian Territory, May 16, 1906.

London Harjo,
    Paden, Indian Territory.

Dear Sir:

The Commission is in receipt of an affidavit relative to the birth of your minor child, Panuggee Caesar[sic]. In said affidavit it is stated that you are a citizen of the Seminole Nation and that your wife is a Creek. It is also stated in said affidavit that there was no midwife present at the birth of said child.

You are advised that the Commission desires the evidence of two disinterested witnesses as to the birth of said child. You are further advised that you will be allowed reasonable time within which to appear before the Commission at its office in Muskogee, Indian Territory, for the purpose of electing in which nation[sic] you desire said child to have its allotment.

Respectfully,

Chairman.

NC.36.

Muskogee, Indian Territory, July 13, 1905.

Commissioner to the Five Civilized Tribes,
    Seminole Enrollment Division,
        Muskogee, Indian Territory.

Gentlemen:

March 13, 1905, application was made to the Commission to the Five Civilized Tribes for the enrollment of Panuggee Ceasar, born December 28, 1902, as a citizen by blood of the Creek Nation. It is stated in said application that the father of said child is London Harjo, a citizen by blood of the Seminole Nation, and that the mother is Sissie Ceasar, a citizen by blood of the Creek Nation.

You are requested to inform the Creek Enrollment Division as to whether an application was made for the enrollment of said Panuggee Ceasar, as a citizen of the Seminole Nation, and if so, what disposition has been made of the same.

Respectfully,

Commissioner.

(COPY)

AFFIDAVIT.

Personally appeared before ma as Notary Public on and for the Western District, S. B. Davis, and upon oath states that he is well acquainted with Sissie Ceasar, a Creek citizen and further states that on the 27th day of Dec 1902 their[sic] was born to her a child who was named Panuggee Ceasar, and that their[sic] was no midwife present at the birth of said child, and that the said child is now living.

I make this statement as a disinterested party, and have no claim in this matter whatever. I am a Creek citizen and 37 years of age and know the above facts to be true.

(Signed)   S. B. Davis

Subscribed and sworn to before me this the 11" day of October, 1905.

(SEAL)   (Signed) G. P. Lawfenton.

Notary Public.

My commission expires Apr 16, 1909.

NC-36

DEPARTMENT OF THE INTERIOR,
COMMISSIONER TO THE FIVE CIVILIZED TRIBES.

Muskogee, Indian Territory, July 14, 1905.

Clerk in Charge,
    Creek Enrollment Division.

Dear Sir:

Receipt is acknowledge of your communication of July 13, 1905, requesting to be advised as to whether or not an application was made to the Commission to the Five Civilized Tribes for enrollment as a citizen of the Seminole Nation of Panuggee Caesar, born December 28, 1902, child of London Harjo, a citizen by blood of the Seminole Nation, and Sissie Caesar, a citizen by blood of the Creek Nation.

In reply to your letter you are advised that it does not appear from an examination of the records of this office that any application was ever made to the Commission to the Five Civilized Tribes for the enrollment of the said Panuggee Caesar as a citizen of the Seminole Nation.

Respectfully.

(Name Illegible) Commissioner.

174

NC 36

Muskogee, I T July 31, 1905

Sissie Caesar
                Paden I T

Dear Madam:

There is on file at this office an affidavit executed by you relative to the birth of your minor child, Panuggee Caesar as a citizen of the Creek Nation, in which it is stated that the father of said child is a citizen of the Seminole Nation, that you are a citizen of the Creek Nation, and that there was no midwife present at the birth of said child.

You are advised that the affidavits of two disinterested witnesses as to the birth of said child are required.

You are further advised that you will be given a reasonable time within which to appear at the office of the Commissioner to the Five Civilized Tribes in Muskogee, I T for the purpose of electing in which nation[sic] you desire said child to be enrolled.

Respectfully,

Commissioner

NC 36.

Muskogee, Indian Territory, November 20, 1905.

Sissie Caesar,
        c/o London Harjo,
                Paden, Indian Territory.

Dear Madam:

In the matter of the application for the enrollment of Panuggee Caesar, you are advised that it will be necessary for you and your husband London Harjo to file your joint affidavit electing whether you will have said child enrolled as a citizen of the Creek Nation or Seminole Nation.

This matter should have your immediate attention.

Respectfully,

Acting Commissioner.

Applications for Enrollment of Creek Newborn
Act of 1905   Volume I

NC 36.

Muskogee, Indian Territory, December 11, 1905.

Sissie Caesar,
    Care of London Harjo,
        Paden, Indian Territory.

Dear Madam:

In the matter of the application for the enrollment of your minor child, Panuggie Caesar, as a citizen by blood of the Creek Nation, you are advised that this office requires the joint affidavit of yourself and London Harjo, the Seminole father of said child, electing in which Nation, Creek or Seminole, you desire to have said child enrolled.

This matter should receive your immediate attention.

Respectfully,

Acting Commissioner.

———————

NC 36.

Muskogee, Indian Territory, March 1, 1907.

Sissie Harjo (or Caesar),
    c/o London Harjo,
        Paden, Indian Territory.

Dear Madam:

You are hereby advised that on February 15, 1907, the Secretary of the Interior approved the enrollment of your minor child, Panuggee Caesar, as a citizen by blood of the Creek Nation, and that the name of said child appears upon the roll of New Born citizens by blood of the Creek Nation, enrolled under the act of Congress approved March 3, 1905, as number 1130.

This child is now entitled to allotment, and application therefor should be made without delay of the Creek Land Office, Muskogee, Indian Territory.

Respectfully,

Commissioner.

———————

AFFIDAVIT.

Personall[sic] appeared before me a Notary Public on and for the Western District, SB Davis and upon oath states that he is well acquainted with Sissie Caesar, a Creek citizen and further state that on the 27th day of De 1902 their[sic] was born to her a child who was named Panuggee Caesar, and that their[sic] was no midwife present at the birth of said child, and that the said child is now Living. I make this statement as a disinterested party, and have no claim in this matter whatever.

I am a Creek citizen and 37 years of age and know the above facts to be true.

S.B. Davis

Subscribed and sworn to before me this the 11 day of October, 1905.

(Name Illegible)
Notary Public.

My Commission Expires Apr 26. 1907

_____

_____   _____

AFFIDAVIT.

(Name

Personall[sic] appeared before me a Notary Public on and for the Western District, SB
Illegible)
Davis and upon oath states that he is well acquainted with Sissie Caesar, a Creek citizen and further state that on the 27th day of De 1902 their[sic] was born to her a child who was named Panuggee Caesar, and that their[sic] was no midwife present at the birth of said child, and that the said child is now Living. I make this statement as a disinterested party, and have no claim in this matter whatever.

I am a Creek citizen and 37 years of age and know the above facts to be true.

(Name Illegible)
S.B. Davis

Subscribed and sworn to before me this the 11 day of October, 1905.

(Name Illegible)
Notary Public.

My Commission Expires Apr 26. 1907

Witness_____

_____   _____

Applications for Enrollment of Creek Newborn
Act of 1905   Volume I

Indian Territory,I
  I ss:
Western District,I

We, the undersigned, do hereby elect to have our child, <u>Panuggee Caesar</u>, born on the <u>28</u> day of <u>December</u>, <u>1902</u>, enrolled as a citizen of the <u>Creek</u> Nation, and to have said child receive <u>an</u> allotment of land and distribution of moneys in said Nation.

	His
Witnesses to mark:	*(Illegible)* x Harjo
J. L Bruce	mark
	Her
Mrs J D Lewis	*(Illegible)* x Harjo
	mark

Subscribed and sworn to before me this <u>12</u> day of <u>Feby</u>, 1906.

J. L. Bruce
Notary Public.

Indian Territory, I
  I ss:
Western District, I

We, the undersigned, do hereby elect to have our child, <u>Panuggee Caesar</u>, born on the <u>28</u> day of <u>December</u>, <u>1902</u>, enrolled as a citizen of the <u>Creek</u> Nation, and to have said child receive <u>his</u> allotment of land and distribution of moneys in said Nation.

	His
Witnesses to mark:	*(Illegible)* x Harjo
J L Bruce	mark
	Her
Mrs J D Lewis	*(Illegible)* x Harjo
	mark

Subscribed and sworn to before me this <u>12</u> day of <u>Feby</u>, 1906.

J. L. Bruce
Notary Public.

Indian Territory, I
  I ss:
Western District, I
  I   my
  ~~We~~, the undersigned, do hereby elect to have ~~our~~ child, <u>Panuggee Caesar</u>, born on the <u>28</u> day of <u>December</u>, <u>1902</u>, enrolled as a citizen of the <u>Creek</u> Nation, and to have said child receive <u>his</u> allotment of land and distribution of moneys in said Nation.

178

	her
Witnesses to mark:	Sissie x Caesar
J McDermott	mark
Mary Foiles	

Subscribed and sworn to before me this 13 day of Oct, 1906.

My commission	J McDermott
expires July 25" 1907	Notary Public.

Indian Territory, I
     I ss:
Western District, I
     I   my

~~We~~, the undersigned, do hereby elect to have ~~our~~ child, Panuggee Caesar, born on the 28 day of December, 1902, enrolled as a citizen of the Creek Nation, and to have said child take its allotment of land and distribution of money in said nation[sic].

Witnesses to mark:	London Harjo

Subscribed and sworn to before me this 28 day of Oct, 1906.

My Commission	J McDermott
Expires July 25" 1907	Notary Public.

BIRTH AFFIDAVIT.

DEPARTMENT OF THE INTERIOR.
COMMISSION TO THE FIVE CIVILIZED TRIBES.

IN RE APPLICATION FOR ENROLLMENT, as a citizen of the Creek Nation, of Panuggee Caeser[sic] , born on the 28" day of December , 1902

Name of Father: London Harjo	a citizen of the	Seminole	Nation.
Name of Mother: Sissy Caeser[sic]	a citizen of the	Creek	Nation.

Postoffice   Paden, Indian Territory

AFFIDAVIT OF MOTHER.

UNITED STATES OF AMERICA, Indian Territory, ⎫
    Western   **DISTRICT.** ⎰

I, Sissy Caeser[sic], on oath state that I am 22 years of age and a citizen by blood, not of the Creek Nation; that I am ^ the lawful wife of London Harjo, who is a citizen, by blood, of the Seminole Nation; that a male child was born to me on 28" day of December,

was

1902, that said child has been named Panuggee Caeser , and ~~is now~~ living. March 4, 1905.   That no one attended on me as midwife or physician at the time the child was born.

her
Sissy x Caeser
mark

Witnesses To Mark:

{ Alex Posey
{ DC Skaggs

Subscribed and sworn to before me this 13" day of March, 1905.

(Seal)

Drennan C Skaggs
Notary Public.

(The above form was repeated)

BIRTH AFFIDAVIT.

DEPARTMENT OF THE INTERIOR.
COMMISSION TO THE FIVE CIVILIZED TRIBES.

IN RE APPLICATION FOR ENROLLMENT, as a citizen of the Creek Nation, of Panuggee Caesar , born on the 28" day of December , 1902

Name of Father: Londo[sic] Harjo	a citizen of the	Seminole	Nation.
Name of Mother: Sissie Caesar	a citizen of the	Creek	Nation.

Postoffice   Paden, IT

AFFIDAVIT OF ATTENDING PHYSICIAN OR MID-WIFE.

UNITED STATES OF AMERICA, Indian Territory, }
          Western   DISTRICT. }

I, Cinda Puntka, a midwife, on oath state that I attended on ~~Mrs~~. Sissie Caesar, not the wife of Londo Harjo on the 28 day of Dec , 1902 ; that there was born to her on said date a male child; that said child was living March 4, 1905, and is said to have been named Panuggee Caesar.

her
Cinda x Harjo
mark

Applications for Enrollment of Creek Newborn
Act of 1905   Volume I

Witnesses To Mark:
{ J McDermott
{ J S P Weeden

Subscribed and sworn to before me this 23" day of October, 1906

My Commission   J McDermott
Expires July 25" 1907   Notary Public.

Cr BA-52-B

DEPARTMENT OF THE INTERIOR,
COMMISSION TO THE FIVE CIVILIZED TRIBES.

Muskogee, Indian Territory, March 6, 1905.

In the matter of the application for the enrollment of Maple Chisholm ag[sic] a citizen by blood of the Creek Nation.

Mose Chisholm, being duly sworn, testified as follows (through Jesse McDermott, Official Interpreter).

EXAMINATION BY THE COMMISSION:
Q What is your name? A Mose Chisholm
Q What is your age? A 29 years old.
Q What is your postoffice address? A Weer.
Q Are you married? A No sir.
Q Have you any young children? A Just one.
Q What is its name? A Maple Chisholm
Q Is she living or dead? A Living.

The witness is identified as Mose Chisholm on Creek Indian card, field No. 410, and his name is contained in the partial list of Creek Indians approved by the Secretary of the Interior March 13, 1902, Roll No. 1325.

Q Who is the mother of maple Chisholm? A Nettie Castelo.
Q Do you live with Nettie? A No sir.
When was maple Chisholm Born? A Sometime in December.
Q What year? A 1903.
Q Were you living with Nettie at that time? A We were not married according to the United States law, but we were living together.
Q How long did you live with her before this child was born? A About eight months.
Q You say you have been living with her six or eight months before this child was born? A Live with her about eight months and was away when the child was born.
Q Is Nettie living? A Yes sir.

Q Do you live with her now? A No sir.

Q Did anyone else live with her about that time? There was no one living with her at the time the child was born but Annie Kelly and soon after the birth of the child a white man under the name of George Castelo lived with her.

Q Are you sure that this white man did not have anything to do with her at the time you were going with her? A They were married—they had been married. They had separated about two years when I went with her.

Q Was he living in the neighborhood at the time you were living with her? A He was within nine miles of where the child's mother lived.

Q Did you live in the same house continuously with her for eight months? A Yes sir.

Q Is Nettie a citizen of the Creek Nation? A Yes sir.

Q What was her name before she married? A Nettie Wiley.

The mother of the child is identified as Nettie Wiley on Creek Indian card, Field No. 172, and her name is contained in the partial list of Creek citizens by blood, approved by the Secretary of the Interior March 13, 1902, Roll No. 610.

Q Does she acknowledge that you are the father of this child? A Yes sir.

Q Is this child living? A Yes sir.

Annie Kelley, being duly sworn, testified as follows:

EXAMINATION BY THE COMMISSION:

Q What is your name? A Annie Kelley.

Q What is your age? A I don't know; about 50.

Q What is your postoffice address? A Weer.

Q Do you know Nettie Castelo? A Yes sir.

Q Was she ever named Nettie Wiley? A Yes sir, that was her name before.

Q Do you know a child of hers named Maple? A Yes sir.

Q Was she living with any man about the time this child was born? A She was living with her husband.

Q What is her husband's name? A George Castello[sic].

Q Was she living with him when Maple was born? A Yes sir.

Q How long before Maple was born was she living with George Castelo? A I don't know; about two months.

Q Who lived with her before Castelo? A She was living with him.

Q Any man live with her before Castelo? A There was no one lived with her.

Q Did Mose Chisholm ever live with her? A They lived together before she went and lived with this white man.

Q How long before Maple was born did Mose Chisholm start living with her? A I don't know for certain how long it was.

Q Well, about how long? A About one year.

Q Did Nettie ever tell you who is the father of Maple? A She told me that Mose Chisholm was her father.

Q When was Maple Chisholm born? A Sometime in the fall of the year, but I don't know the name of the month.

Q What year? A I don't know.

Applications for Enrollment of Creek Newborn
Act of 1905 Volume I

Q Was it as much as two years ago? A It is over one year, a year (or two?)

Mose Chisholm is advised that it will be necessary for the mother of the child to appear before the Commission and give testimony about its birth and that it is advisable for him to have the child present.

INDIAN TERRITORY, Western District.

I, J. Y. Miller, a stenographer to the Commission to the Five Civilized Tribes, do hereby certify that the above and foregoing is a true and complete translation of my notes as same appear in my stenographic report of this case.

JY Miller

Sworn to and subscribed before me this ? day of March, 1905.

Edw C Griesel

Notary Public.

Copy

BIRTH AFFIDAVIT.

DEPARTMENT OF THE INTERIOR.
COMMISSION TO THE FIVE CIVILIZED TRIBES.

IN RE APPLICATION FOR ENROLLMENT, as a citizen of the Creek Nation, of Maple Chisholm , born on the ----- day of Dec , 1903

Name of Father: Mose Chisholm   a citizen of the Creek   Nation.
Name of Mother: Nettie Castello   a citizen of the   Creek   Nation.

Postoffice   Weer, I.T.

AFFIDAVIT OF ~~MOTHER~~. father

UNITED STATES OF AMERICA, Indian Territory, ⎤
       Western   **DISTRICT.** ⎦

I, Mose Chisholm, on oath state that I am 29 years of age and a citizen by blood,
not married
of the Creek Nation; that I am ~~the lawful wife of~~ to Nettie Castello, who is a citizen, by blood, of the Creek Nation; that a female child was born to me on ----- day of Dec, 1903,
is now
that said child has been named Maple Chisholm , and ~~was~~ living ~~March 4, 1905~~.

Mose Chisholm

Witnesses To Mark:

{

183

Applications for Enrollment of Creek Newborn
Act of 1905   Volume I

Subscribed and sworn to before me this 6 day of March, 1905.

Edw C Griesel
Notary Public.

Copy
AFFIDAVIT OF ATTENDING PHYSICIAN OR MID-WIFE.

UNITED STATES OF AMERICA, Indian Territory, ⎱
     Western   DISTRICT. ⎰

I, Annie Kelly, a midwife, on oath state that I attended on Mrs. Nettie Castello , ~~wife of~~ *(blank)* on the ----- day of December , 1903; that there was born to her on said
is now
date a female child; that said child ~~was~~ living ~~March 4, 1905~~, and is said to have been named Maple Chisholm.

Annie Kelly

Witnesses To Mark:
  { J McDermott
    EDGriesel

Subscribed and sworn to before me this 6 day of Mar, 1905.

Edw C Griesel
Notary Public.

BIRTH AFFIDAVIT.

DEPARTMENT OF THE INTERIOR.   Corrected by
COMMISSION TO THE FIVE CIVILIZED TRIBES. letter

Sept 23- 1903

IN RE APPLICATION FOR ENROLLMENT, as a citizen of the Creek Nation, of Maple Chisholm , born on the ----- day of Dec , 1903

Name of Father: Mose Chisholm	a citizen of the	Creek	Nation.
Name of Mother: Nettie Castello	a citizen of the	Creek	Nation.

Postoffice   Weer, I.T.

AFFIDAVIT OF ~~MOTHER.~~ father

UNITED STATES OF AMERICA, Indian Territory, ⎱
     Western   DISTRICT. ⎰

I, Mose Chisholm, on oath state that I am 29 years of age and a citizen by blood,
not married

184

of the Creek Nation; that I am ~~the lawful wife of~~ to Nettie Castello, who is a citizen, by blood, of the Creek Nation; that a female child was born to me on ----- day of Dec, 1903, that said child has been named Maple Chisholm , and is now living.

Mose Chisholm

Witnesses To Mark:

{

Subscribed and sworn to before me this 6 day of March, 1905.

Edw C Griesel
Notary Public.

AFFIDAVIT OF ATTENDING PHYSICIAN OR MID-WIFE.

UNITED STATES OF AMERICA, Indian Territory,
      Western   **DISTRICT.**

I, Annie Kelly, a midwife, on oath state that I attended on Mrs. Nettie Castello , ~~wife of~~ ----- on the ----- day of December , 1903; that there was born to her on said
                                        is now
date a female child; that said child ~~was~~ living ~~March 4, 1905~~, and is said to have been named Maple Chisholm.

Her
Annie x Kelly
Mark

Witnesses To Mark:
{ J McDermott
{ EDGriesel

Subscribed and sworn to before me this 6 day of Mar, 1905.

Edw C Griesel
Notary Public.

N C 37

Weer, Ind. Ter. 3/18 1905.

Hon. Tam Bixby, Chairman,
      of Dawes Commission.
            Muskogee, Ind. Te.

Dear Sir:

Applications for Enrollment of Creek Newborn
Act of 1905 Volume I

I was at you[sic] office a few days ago and made applictin to the enroolment of my Girl Maple Chisholm and forgot to insert the date of her birth she was Born September 23 1903 the affidavits is all rode excit this iff any the more needt let me know.

Moore Chisolm .

(The above letter copied exactly as on microfilm.)

BS 52 B.

Muskogee, Indian Territory, May 13, 1905.

Mose Chisholm,
    Weer, Indian Territory.

Dear Sir:

There is on file with the Commission an affidavit executed by you relative to the birth of your minor child, Maple Chisholm, The affidavit of the mother and midwife or physician in attendance at the birth of said child is required.

There is herewith enclosed a blank form of birth affidavit, and in executing same care should be exercised to see that all blanks are properly filled, all names written in full and in the event that either of the parties signing the affidavit is unable to write, signatures by mark must be attested by two witnesses. Each affidavit must be executed before a Notary Public and the notarial seal and signature of the officer must be attached to each separate affidavit.

Respectfully,

Chairman.

NC.37.

Muskogee, Indian Territory, July 13, 1905.

Mose Chisholm,
    Weer, Indian Territory.

Dear Sir:

There is on file at this office an affidavit executed by you relative to the birth of your minor child, Maple Chisholm, as a citizen of the Creek Nation. The affidavit of the mother and midwife or physician in attendance at the birth of said child should be supplied.

Applications for Enrollment of Creek Newborn
Act of 1905   Volume I

There is herewith enclosed a blank form of birth affidavit, and in executing same care should be exercised to see that all blanks are properly filled, all names written in full and in the event that either of the parties signing the affidavit is unable to write, signatures by mark must be attested by two witnesses. Each affidavit must be executed before a Notary Public and the notarial seal and signature of the officer must be attached to each separate affidavit.

Respectfully,

1 BA.   Commissioner.

N.C.37.

_____

Muskogee, Indian Territory, July 3, 1906.

Mose Chisholm,
　　Weer, Indian Territory.

Dear Sir:

In the matter of the application for the enrollment of your minor child, Maple Chisholm, born September 23, 1903, as a citizen of the Creek Nation, you have been repeatedly advised that this office requires the affidavit of the mother.

There is herewith inclosed[sic] blank form of birth affidavit and you should have same executed at once by Nettie Castello, the reputed mother of said child, and return it to this office in the inclosed[sic] envelope.

Respectfully,

BA   Commissioner.
Env.

N.C.37.

_____

Muskogee, Indian Territory, July 3, 1906.

Nettie Castello,
　　Care George Castello,
　　　　Weer, Indian Territory.

Dear Madam:

In the matter of the application for the enrollment of your minor child, Maple Chisholm, born September 23, 1903, as a citizen of the Creek Nation, you have been repeatedly advised that this office requires your affidavit.

187

There is herewith enclosed blank form of birth affidavit and you should execute at once and return to this office in the inclosed[sic] envelope.

Respectfully,

BA   Commissioner.
Env.

_____

N.C.37.

Muskogee, Indian Territory, January 13, 1907.

Nettie Castello,
    c/o Mose Chisholm,
        Weer, Indian Territory.

Dear Madam:

You are hereby advised that this office requires your affidavit in the matter of the birth of your minor child, Maple Chisholm, as a citizen of the Creek Nation, and a blank form of birth affidavit is herewith enclosed, which you should have properly executed and returned to this office within five days. Said affidavit is necessary before the rights of said child can be adjudicated and you are requested to five this matter your immediate attention.

Respectfully,

Commissioner.

1 BA

_____

BA 53 B.

Muskogee, Indian Territory, May 13, 1905.

William R. Harris,
    Muskogee, Indian Territory.

Dear Sir:

There is on file with the Commission an affidavit executed by you relative to the birth of your minor child, Mary J. Harris. The affidavit of the other of said child and of the midwife or physician in attendance at the birth of said child is required.

There is herewith enclosed a blank form of birth affidavit, and in executing same care should be exercised to see that all blanks are properly filled, all names written in full and in the event that either of the persons signing the affidavit is unable to write, signatures by mark must be attested by two witnesses. Each affidavit must be executed before a Notary Public and the notarial seal and signature of the officer must be attached to each separate affidavit.

Respectfully,

BC.   Chairman.

DEPARTMENT OF THE INTERIOR,
COMMISSIONER TO THE FIVE CIVILIZED TRIBES.

REFER IN REPLY TO THE FOLLOWING:
N.C. 38.

Muskogee, Indian Territory, **August 4, 1905.**

William R. Harris,
Muskogee, Indian Territory.

Dear Sir:

You are hereby advised that on **July 28, 1905.** , the Secretary of the Interior approved the enrollment of your minor child, **Mary J. Harris** , as a citizen by blood of the **Creek** Nation, and that the name of said child appears upon the roll of new born citizens of the **Creek** Nation as Number **24** .

The child is now entitled to an allotment, and application therefor should be made without delay at the Land Office for the Nation in which the prospective allotment is located.

An entire allotment for said child must be selected at the time of the original application.

Respectively,

Commissioner.

BIRTH AFFIDAVIT.

DEPARTMENT OF THE INTERIOR.
COMMISSION TO THE FIVE CIVILIZED TRIBES.

IN RE APPLICATION FOR ENROLLMENT, as a citizen of the Creek Nation, of Mary J Harris, born on the 11 day of Aug., 1904

Name of Father: W.J.R. Harris	a citizen of the	Creek	Nation.
Name of Mother: Lela Harris	a citizen of the	U.S.	Nation.

Applications for Enrollment of Creek Newborn
Act of 1905 Volume I

Postoffice   Muskogee, I.T.

_____

(Child appeared)

AFFIDAVIT OF MOTHER.

UNITED STATES OF AMERICA, Indian Territory, ⎱
Western   **DISTRICT.** ⎰

     I, WJR Harris, on oath state that I am 43 years of age and a citizen by blood, of the Creek Nation; that I am the lawful ~~wife~~ husband of Lela Harris, who is a citizen, by ----- of the U.S. Nation; that a *(blank)* child was born to me on 11 day of Aug. 1904; that said child has been named Mary J. Harris, and is now living.

A.V.R.[sic] Harris

Witnesses To Mark:

⎰

   Subscribed and sworn to before me this 6 day of March, 1905.

Edw C Griesel
Notary Public.

_____

(The above form typed again.)

_____

BIRTH AFFIDAVIT.

DEPARTMENT OF THE INTERIOR.
COMMISSION TO THE FIVE CIVILIZED TRIBES.

_____

    IN RE APPLICATION FOR ENROLLMENT, as a citizen of the Creek Nation, of Mary J. Harris, born on the 11th day of August , 1904

Name of Father: William R Harris   a citizen of the Creek   Nation.
Name of Mother: Lela C Harris   a citizen of the Creek   Nation.

Postoffice   Muskogee, Ind. Ty.

_____

AFFIDAVIT OF MOTHER.

UNITED STATES OF AMERICA, Indian Territory, ⎱
Western   **DISTRICT.** ⎰

    I, Lela C Harris, on oath state that I am 33 years of age and a citizen by adoption, of the Creek Nation; that I am the lawful wife of William R. Harris, who is a citizen by

190

birth, of the Creek Nation; that a female child was born to me on 11th day of August, 1904, that said child has been named Mary Jones Harris , and was living March 4, 1905.

Lela C Harris

Witnesses To Mark:

{

Subscribed and sworn to before me this 16th day of May, 1905.

WE Abney

My Commission Expires March 24, 1907   Notary Public.

AFFIDAVIT OF ATTENDING PHYSICIAN OR MID-WIFE.

UNITED STATES OF AMERICA, Indian Territory,
         Western   **DISTRICT.**

I, Nilla A Harris, a midwife, on oath state that I attended on Mrs. Lela C. Harris , wife of William R Harris on the 11th day of August , 1904 ; that there was born to her on said date a female child; that said child was living March 4, 1905, and is said to have been named Mary Jones Harris.

Nillia A Harris

Witnesses To Mark:

{

Subscribed and sworn to before me this 16th day of May, 1905.

My Commission Expires March 24, 1907   WE Abney
                                              Notary Public.

DEPARTMENT OF THE INTERIOR, **COMMISSIONER TO THE FIVE CIVILIZED TRIBES.**	REFER IN REPLY TO THE FOLLOWING: —————— **N.C. 39.**

Muskogee, Indian Territory, **August 4, 1905.**

J. Ewing Ross,
         Muskogee, Indian Territory.

Dear Sir:

You are hereby advised that on **July 28, 1905** , the Secretary of the Interior approved the enrollment of your minor child, **Lena M Ross** , as a citizen by blood of the **Creek** Nation, and that the name of said child appears upon the roll of new born citizens of the **Creek** Nation as Number **25** .

Applications for Enrollment of Creek Newborn
Act of 1905   Volume I

The child is now entitled to an allotment, and application therefor should be made without delay at the Land Office for the Nation in which the prospective allotment is located.

An entire allotment for said child must be selected at the time of the original application.

Respectively,

Commissioner.

BIRTH AFFIDAVIT.

DEPARTMENT OF THE INTERIOR.
COMMISSION TO THE FIVE CIVILIZED TRIBES.

IN RE APPLICATION FOR ENROLLMENT, as a citizen of the Creek Nation, of Lena M Ross , born on the 20 day of June , 1902

Name of Father: J. Ewing Ross	a citizen of the Creek	Nation.
Name of Mother: Nellie Ross	a citizen of the U.S.	Nation.

Postoffice   Muskogee

Child Brought in Mar 20-05

AFFIDAVIT OF ~~MOTHER~~. father

UNITED STATES OF AMERICA, Indian Territory, ⎱
      Western   **DISTRICT.** ⎰

I, J. Ewing Ross, on oath state that I am 28 years of age and a citizen by blood, of the Creek Nation; that I am the lawful ~~wife~~ husband of Nellie Ross, who is a citizen, by -- --- of the U.S. Nation; that a female child was born to me on 20 day of June, 1902 that said child has been named Lena M. Ross, and is now living.

J Ewing Ross

Witnesses To Mark:

{

Subscribed and sworn to before me this 6 day of March, 1905.

Edw C Griesel
Notary Public.

192

Applications for Enrollment of Creek Newborn
Act of 1905   Volume I

BIRTH AFFIDAVIT.

DEPARTMENT OF THE INTERIOR.
COMMISSION TO THE FIVE CIVILIZED TRIBES.

IN RE APPLICATION FOR ENROLLMENT, as a citizen of the Creek Nation, of Lena M Ross , born on the 20 day of June, 1902

Name of Father: J. Ewing Ross	a citizen of the	Creek	Nation.
Name of Mother: Nellie "	a citizen of the	U S.	Nation.

Postoffice   Muskogee

Child Present

AFFIDAVIT OF MOTHER.

UNITED STATES OF AMERICA, Indian Territory, ⎱
    Western   **DISTRICT.** ⎰

I, Nellie Ross, on oath state that I am 27 years of age and a citizen by ----- of the U.S. Nation; that I am the lawful wife of J. Ewing Ross, who is a citizen by blood, of the Creek Nation; that a female child was born to me on 20 day of June, 1902, that said child has been named Lena M Ross , and is now living.

Mrs. J.E. Ross

Witnesses To Mark:

{

Subscribed and sworn to before me this 20 day of March, 1905.

Edw C Griesel
Notary Public.

BIRTH AFFIDAVIT.

DEPARTMENT OF THE INTERIOR.
COMMISSION TO THE FIVE CIVILIZED TRIBES.

IN RE APPLICATION FOR ENROLLMENT, as a citizen of the Creek Nation, of Lena M Ross , born on the 20th day of June, 1902

Name of Father: J. Ewing Ross	a citizen of the	Creek	Nation.
Name of Mother: Nellie Ross	a citizen of the United States	Nation.	

Postoffice   Muskogee, Indian Territory

Applications for Enrollment of Creek Newborn
Act of 1905 Volume I

UNITED STATES OF AMERICA, Indian Territory, ⎫
Western   DISTRICT. ⎰

I, M.F. Williams, a Physician, on oath state that I attended on Mrs. Nellie Ross , wife of J Ewing Ross on the 20th day of June , 1902 ; that there was born to her on said date a Female child; that said child was living March 4, 1905, and is said to have been named Lena M Ross.

M.F. Williams, M.D.

Witnesses To Mark:

{

Subscribed and sworn to before me this 10th day of May, 1905.

My commission expires   Joshua Ross
July 2, 1906   Notary Public.

BA 81 B.

Muskogee, Indian Territory, May 15, 1905.

Charles Johnson,
        Checotah, Indian Territory.

Dear Sir:

The Commission is in receipt of affidavits relative to the birth of your minor child, Viola Johnson and of your step-child, Myrtle Mary Howard. The affidavits of the mother and midwife or physician in attendance at the birth of said child should be supplied.

There is therewith enclosed a blank form of birth affidavit, and in executing same care should be exercised to see that all blanks are properly filled out, all names written in full and in the event that either of the persons signing the affidavits is unable to write, signatures by mark must be attested by two witnesses. Each affidavit must be executed before a Notary Public and the notarial seal and signature of the officer must be attached to each separate affidavit.

Respectfully,

BC.   Chairman.

Applications for Enrollment of Creek Newborn
Act of 1905   Volume I

DEPARTMENT OF THE INTERIOR,
COMMISSIONER TO THE FIVE CIVILIZED TRIBES.

REFER IN REPLY TO THE FOLLOWING:

N.C. 40.

Muskogee, Indian Territory, **August 4, 1905.**

Abbie Lee Johnson,
    Care of Charles Johnson,
        Checotah, Indian Territory.

Dear Madam:

You are hereby advised that on **July 28, 1905** , the Secretary of the Interior approved the enrollment of your minor child, **Myrtle May Howard** , as a citizen by blood of the **Creek** Nation, and that the name of said child appears upon the roll of new born citizens of the **Creek** Nation as Number **26** .

The child is now entitled to an allotment, and application therefor should be made without delay at the Land Office for the Nation in which the prospective allotment is located.

An entire allotment for said child must be selected at the time of the original application.

Respectively,

Commissioner.

DEPARTMENT OF THE INTERIOR,
COMMISSIONER TO THE FIVE CIVILIZED TRIBES.

REFER IN REPLY TO THE FOLLOWING:

N.C. 40.

Muskogee, Indian Territory, **August 4, 1905.**

Abbie Lee Johnson,
    Care of Charles Johnson,
        Checotah, Indian Territory.

Dear Madam:

You are hereby advised that on **July 28, 1905**   , the Secretary of the Interior approved the enrollment of your minor child, **Viola Johnson** , as a citizen by blood of the **Creek** Nation, and that the name of said child appears upon the roll of new born citizens of the **Creek** Nation as Number **27** .

195

Applications for Enrollment of Creek Newborn
Act of 1905 Volume I

The child is now entitled to an allotment, and application therefor should be made without delay at the Land Office for the Nation in which the prospective allotment is located.

An entire allotment for said child must be selected at the time of the original application.

Respectively,

Commissioner.

BIRTH AFFIDAVIT.

DEPARTMENT OF THE INTERIOR.
COMMISSION TO THE FIVE CIVILIZED TRIBES.

IN RE APPLICATION FOR ENROLLMENT, as a citizen of the Creek Nation, of Myrtle May Howard , born on the 20 day of June, 1902

Name of Father: George Howard (D	a citizen of the U.S.	Nation.
Name of Mother: Abbie Lee Howard	a citizen of the U.S. Creek	Nation.

Postoffice   Checotah

AFFIDAVIT OF MOTHER. step-father

UNITED STATES OF AMERICA, Indian Territory, ⎱
    Western   DISTRICT. ⎰

I, Charles Johnson, on oath state that I am 36 years of age and a citizen by ----- of the U.S. Nation; that I am the lawful wife hus of Abbie Lee Howard, who is a citizen, by blood, of the Creek Nation; that a female child was born to me on 20 day of June, 1902, that said child has been named Myrtle May Howard , and is now living.

Charles Johnson

Witnesses To Mark:

{

Subscribed and sworn to before me this 7 day of March, 1905.

Edw C Griesel
Notary Public.

Applications for Enrollment of Creek Newborn
Act of 1905   Volume I

BIRTH AFFIDAVIT.

DEPARTMENT OF THE INTERIOR.
COMMISSION TO THE FIVE CIVILIZED TRIBES.

IN RE APPLICATION FOR ENROLLMENT, as a citizen of the Creek Nation, of Myrtle May Howard , born on the 20th day of June, 1902

Name of Father: George Howard   a citizen of the   non citizen   Nation.

Abbie Lee Howard

Name of Mother: Abbie Lee Johnson - nee ^   a citizen of the   Creek   Nation.

Postoffice   Checotah Ind Terry

AFFIDAVIT OF MOTHER.

UNITED STATES OF AMERICA, Indian Territory,
Western   DISTRICT.

I, Abbie Lee Johnson, nee Howard, on oath state that I am 25 years of age and a citizen by blood, of the Creek Nation; that I am the lawful wife of Charles Johnson, who is a citizen, by marriage, of the Creek Nation; that a female child was born to me on 20th day of June, 1902, that said child has been named Myrtle May Howard , and was living March 4, 1905.

Abbie Lee Johnson

Witnesses To Mark:

Subscribed and sworn to before me this 16th day of May, 1905.

J B Lucas
Notary Public.

AFFIDAVIT OF ATTENDING PHYSICIAN OR MID-WIFE.

UNITED STATES OF AMERICA, Indian Territory,
Western   DISTRICT.

I, Dr. William R Reid, a Physician, on oath state that I attended on Mrs. Abbie Lee Howard nee Abbie Lee Johnson , wife of Geo Howard now wife of Charles Johnson, on the 20th day of June , 1902 ; that there was born to her on said date a Female child; that said child was living March 4, 1905, and is said to have been named Myrtle May Howard.

William A Reid

Witnesses To Mark:

Applications for Enrollment of Creek Newborn
Act of 1905   Volume I

Subscribed and sworn to before me this 16th day of May, 1905.

J. B. Lucas
Notary Public.

BIRTH AFFIDAVIT.

DEPARTMENT OF THE INTERIOR.
COMMISSION TO THE FIVE CIVILIZED TRIBES.

IN RE APPLICATION FOR ENROLLMENT, as a citizen of the Creek Nation, of Viola Johnson, born on the 3rd day of October , 1904

Name of Father: Charlie Johnson   a citizen of the United States Nation.
Name of Mother: Abbie Lee Johnson   a citizen of the   Creek   Nation.

Postoffice   Checotah, Ind Ter.

AFFIDAVIT OF MOTHER.

UNITED STATES OF AMERICA, Indian Territory, ⎫
Western   DISTRICT. ⎰

I, Abbie Lee Johnson, on oath state that I am 25 years of age and a citizen by Blood, of the Creek Nation; that I am the lawful wife of Charlie Johnson, who is a citizen, ~~by~~ of the United States of America ~~blood of the   Nation~~; that a female child was born to me on 3rd day of October, 1904, that said child has been named Viola Johnson , and is now living.

Abbie Lee Johnson

Witnesses To Mark:

{

Subscribed and sworn to before me this 10th day of April, 1905.

J B Lucas
Notary Public.

AFFIDAVIT OF ATTENDING PHYSICIAN OR MID-WIFE.

UNITED STATES OF AMERICA, Indian Territory, ⎫
Western   DISTRICT. ⎰

I, Maggie Dickerson, a Midwife, on oath state that I attended on Mrs. Abbie Lee Johnson , wife of Charlie Johnson on the 3rd day of October , 1904; that there was born

198

to her on said date a Female child; that said child is now living, and is said to have been named Viola Johnson.

Maggie Dickson[sic]

Witnesses To Mark:
{ Chas R Freeman
J B Lucas

Subscribed and sworn to before me this 10th day of April, 1905.

J B Lucas
Notary Public.

BIRTH AFFIDAVIT.

DEPARTMENT OF THE INTERIOR.
COMMISSION TO THE FIVE CIVILIZED TRIBES.

IN RE APPLICATION FOR ENROLLMENT, as a citizen of the Creek Nation, of Viola Johnson, born on the 3 day of Oct, 1904

Name of Father: Charles Johnson	a citizen of the U.S.	Nation.
Name of Mother: Abbie Lee "	a citizen of the Creek	Nation.

Postoffice   Checotah

AFFIDAVIT OF ~~MOTHER~~. ~~Step~~-father

UNITED STATES OF AMERICA, Indian Territory,
Western   DISTRICT.

I, Charles Johnson, on oath state that I am 36 years of age and a citizen by ----- of the U.S. Nation; that I am the lawful ~~wife~~ hus of Abbie Lee Howard, who is a citizen, by blood, of the Creek Nation; that a female child was born to me on 3 day of Oct, 1904, that said child has been named Viola Johnson , and is now living.

Charles Johnson

Witnesses To Mark:
{

Subscribed and sworn to before me this 7 day of March, 1905.

Edw C Griesel
Notary Public.

BIRTH AFFIDAVIT.

DEPARTMENT OF THE INTERIOR.
COMMISSION TO THE FIVE CIVILIZED TRIBES.

IN RE APPLICATION FOR ENROLLMENT, as a citizen of the Creek Nation, of Viola Johnson, born on the 3ʳᵈ day of October , 1904

Name of Father: Charles Johnson   a citizen of the non citizen   Nation.

                                        Howard
Name of Mother: Abbie Lee Johnson nee ^   a citizen of the   Creek   Nation.

Postoffice   Checotah, Ind Ter.

AFFIDAVIT OF MOTHER.

UNITED STATES OF AMERICA, Indian Territory, ⎫
    Western   DISTRICT. ⎰

I, Abbie Lee Johnson, on oath state that I am 25 years of age and a citizen by blood, of the Creek Nation; that I am the lawful wife of Charles Johnson, who is a citizen, by marriage of the Creek Nation; that a Female child was born to me on 3rd day of October, 1904, that said child has been named Viola Johnson , and was living March 4, 1905.

Abbie Lee Johnson

Witnesses To Mark:

{

Subscribed and sworn to before me this 16ᵗʰ day of May, 1905.

J B Lucas
Notary Public.

AFFIDAVIT OF ATTENDING PHYSICIAN OR MID-WIFE.

UNITED STATES OF AMERICA, Indian Territory, ⎫
    Western   DISTRICT. ⎰

I, Maggie Dickson, a Midwife, on oath state that I attended on Mrs. Abbie Lee Johnson , wife of Charles Johnson on the 3rd day of October , 1904; that there was born to her on said date a Female child; that said child was living March 4, 1905, and is said to have been named Viola Johnson.

Maggie Dickson

Witnesses To Mark:

{

200

Applications for Enrollment of Creek Newborn
Act of 1905   Volume I

Subscribed and sworn to before me this 16th day of May, 1905.

J B Lucas
Notary Public.

BIRTH AFFIDAVIT.

DEPARTMENT OF THE INTERIOR.
COMMISSION TO THE FIVE CIVILIZED TRIBES.

IN RE APPLICATION FOR ENROLLMENT, as a citizen of the Creek Nation, of Myrtle May Howard , born on the 20 day of June , 1902

Name of Father: George Howard   a citizen of the United States Nation.
Name of Mother: Abbie Lee Howard   a citizen of the   Creek   Nation.

Postoffice   Checotah, Ind. Ter.

AFFIDAVIT OF MOTHER.

UNITED STATES OF AMERICA, Indian Territory, ⎤
    Western   **DISTRICT.** ⎦

I, I[sic] Abbie Lee Johnson (Nee Howard), on oath state that I am 25 years of age and a citizen by Blood, of the Creek Nation; that I am the lawful wife of Charlie Johnson, who is a citizen, by United States of America of the   *(blank)*   Nation; that a female child was born to me on 20 th[sic] day of June, 1902; that said child has been named Myrtle May Howard, and is now living.

Abbie Lee Johnson

Witnesses To Mark:

{

Subscribed and sworn to before me this 10th day of April, 1905.

J B Lucas
Notary Public.

AFFIDAVIT OF ATTENDING PHYSICIAN OR MID-WIFE.

UNITED STATES OF AMERICA, Indian Territory, ⎤
    Western   **DISTRICT.** ⎦

I, W.A. Ried[sic], a Physician, on oath state that I attended on Mrs. Abbie Lee Johnson (nee Howard) , wife of then wife of George Howard on the 20 day of June,

1902; that there was born to her on said date a Female child; that said child is now living, and is said to have been named Myrtle May Howard.

William A. Reid

Witnesses To Mark:

{

Subscribed and sworn to before me this 10th day of April, 1905.

J. B. Lucas
Notary Public.

BA-56-57-58-B

DEPARTMENT OF THE INTERIOR,
COMMISSION TO THE FIVE CIVILIZED TRIBES.

Muskogee, Indian Territory, March 6, 1905

In the matter of the application for the enrollment of Maggie E., Augusta V. and Nordeen Gaither as a citizen by blood of the Creek Nation.

Alice M. Gaither, being duly sworn, testified as follows:

EXAMINATION BY THE COMMISSION:
Q What is your name? A Alice M. Gaither.
Q What is your age? A 24.
Q What is your postoffice address? A Okmulgee.

The witness is identified as Alice M. Gaither, on Creek Indian card, field No. 48 and her name is contained in partial list of citizens by blood of the Creek Nation approved by the Secretary of the Interior March 13, 1902, Roll No. 177.

Q You have a child named Wolrey Gaither? A yes sir.
Q Is it enrolled? A Yes sir.
Q Have you any children born after Wolrey was born? A Yes sir.
Q What are their names? A Maggie Emily, Augusta Victoria and Nordine[sic] Victoria; the two last are twins.
Q When were Augusta Victoria and Nordeen born? A The 18th of June.
Q What year? A 1902.
Q They were twins, were they? A Yes sir.
Q Did you put down in a book anywhere the date of their birth? A Yes sir.
Q What kind of a book? A In a Bible.
Q Did you put it there yourself? A My husband did.

Q How long after they were born? A It was (not?) very long. We were all sick with small pox, and then we got able, he put it down.

Q How long did Augusta Victoria live? A About two days.

Q How long did Nordine live? A Three weeks and four or five days.

Q Did you put down in the Bible about the date of their death? A I think so; I think they have. I know the birth is there.

Q Who was present when these children were born? A My mother-in-law and Mrs. Rowe.

Q What is your mother's-in-law name? A Mrs. Gaither; I don't know her initials.

Q Was she the midwife? A No sir. Did not wait, she was sick at the time.

Q Who waited on you? A Dr. Hinsley.

Q What is his postoffice address? A Okmulgee.

Q When was Maggie Gaither?[sic] A Was born in 1904, June 7.

Q Is this Maggie that's with you? A Yes sir.

The child, Maggie, is present and appears to be of the age stated.

Q Is the father of these children a Creek citizen? A No sir.

Q Citizen of any Nation in Indian Territory? A Yes sir.

Q What Nation? A No sir; United States citizen.

W. J. Gaither, being duly sworn, testified as follows:

EXAMINATION BY THE COMMISSION:

Q What is your name? A W J Gaither.

Q What is your age? A 33.

Q What is your postoffice address? A Okmulgee.

Q Are you the husband of Alice M. Gaither? A Yes sir.

Q Have you any children by her? A Yes sir.

Name them. A Wolrey Gaither, Nordine and Augusta Victoria.

Q Any more? A Maggie E.

Q Wolrey is enrolled is he not? A Yes sir.

Q When was Augusta Victoria born? A In June, 1902.

Q When was Nordine born? A The same time; they were twins. I couldn't swear to dates, we were sick with smallpox.

Q How long did Nordine live? A I don't know; Nordine Victoria died first, one day— the second day after it was born; the other very near four weeks.

Q Did you put down in a book the date of the birth of these children? A Yes sir.

Q How long after? A Little while; assoon[sic] as I got up.

Q Did you put down the dates of their death? A One of them I put down the date it died.

Q You are sure that they were born alive? A Yes sir.

Q Did you have a doctor present when they were born? A Yes sir; Dr. Hinsley.

Q Was he present when they died? A Yes, one of them; the other he was there during the time it was sick and after it died.

Q When was Maggie born? A The 7th of June—that's the 9th. I made a mistake.

Q Maggie is living? A Yes sir.

Q Is that the child that your wife has? A Yes sir.

Applications for Enrollment of Creek Newborn
Act of 1905   Volume I

The witness is advised that it will be necessary for him to produce the Bible in which the entries of the birth and death of those children are recorded and it is also advisable for him to secure the testimony of Dr. Hinsley in this case and of Mrs. How[sic], the midwife.

INDIAN TERRITORY, Western District.

    I, J. Y. Miller, a stenographer to the Commission to the Five Civilized Tribes, do hereby certify upon oath that the above and foregoing is a true and complete translation of my notes as same appear in my stenographic report of this case.

J Y Miller

Sworn to and subscribed
  before me this the
  30th day of March,
  1905.   Edw C Griesel
                                   Notary Public.

BIRTH AFFIDAVIT.

DEPARTMENT OF THE INTERIOR.
COMMISSION TO THE FIVE CIVILIZED TRIBES.

IN RE APPLICATION FOR ENROLLMENT, as a citizen of the Creek Nation, of Maggie M. Gaither , born on the 7th day of June , 1904

Name of Father: Woollery Jackson Gaither	a citizen of the U.S.	Nation.
Name of Mother: Alice Maude Gaither	a citizen of the Creek	Nation.

Postoffice   Okmulgee, Ind. Ter.

AFFIDAVIT OF MOTHER.

UNITED STATES OF AMERICA, Indian Territory, ⎫
     Western   **DISTRICT.** ⎭

    I, Alice Maude Gaither, on oath state that I am 24 years of age and a citizen by blood, of the Creek Nation; that I am the lawful wife of Woollery Jackson Gaither, who is a citizen, by birth, of the U.S. Nation; that a female child was born to me on 7th day of June, 1904, that said child has been named Maggie M. Gaither , and was living March 4, 1905.

Alice Maud[sic] Gaither

Witnesses To Mark:
  {

    Subscribed and sworn to before me this 30th day of May, 1905.

204

Applications for Enrollment of Creek Newborn
Act of 1905   Volume I

W.E. Wood
Notary Public.

AFFIDAVIT OF ATTENDING PHYSICIAN OR MID-WIFE.

UNITED STATES OF AMERICA, Indian Territory, ⎤
    Western   DISTRICT. ⎦

I, Lin Alexander, a Physician, on oath state that I attended on Mrs. Alice Maude Gaither , wife of Woollery Jackson Gaither on the 7th day of June , 1904; that there was born to her on said date a female child; that said child was living March 4, 1905, and is said to have been named Maggie M. Gaither.

Lin Alexander MD

Witnesses To Mark:

{

Subscribed and sworn to before me this 30th day of May, 1905.

W.E. Wood
Notary Public.

BIRTH AFFIDAVIT.

DEPARTMENT OF THE INTERIOR.
COMMISSION TO THE FIVE CIVILIZED TRIBES.

IN RE APPLICATION FOR ENROLLMENT, as a citizen of the Creek Nation, of Maggie E. Gaither , born on the 9 day of June , 1904

Name of Father: W.J. Gaither   a citizen of the   U.S.   Nation.
Name of Mother: Alice M. Gaither   a citizen of the   Creek   Nation.

Postoffice   Okmulgee, I.T.

Child Present

AFFIDAVIT OF MOTHER.

UNITED STATES OF AMERICA, Indian Territory, ⎤
    Western   DISTRICT. ⎦

I, Alice M. Gaither, on oath state that I am 24 years of age and a citizen by blood, of the Creek Nation; that I am the lawful wife of W.J. Gaither, who is a citizen, by ----- of the U.S. Nation; that a female child was born to me on 9 day of June, 1904, that said child has been named Maggie E. Gaither , and is now living.

Alice M Gaither

Witnesses To Mark:

{

Subscribed and sworn to before me this 6 day of March, 1905.

Edw C Griesel
Notary Public.

BIRTH AFFIDAVIT.

DEPARTMENT OF THE INTERIOR.
COMMISSION TO THE FIVE CIVILIZED TRIBES.

IN RE APPLICATION FOR ENROLLMENT, as a citizen of the Creek Nation, of Lordeen Gaither , born on the 12 day of June , 1902

Name of Father: W.J. Gaither	a citizen of the U.S.	~~Nation~~.
Name of Mother: Alice M. Gaither	a citizen of the Creek	Nation.

Postoffice   Okmulgee, I.T.

AFFIDAVIT OF MOTHER.

UNITED STATES OF AMERICA, Indian Territory, ⎱
  Western   DISTRICT. ⎰

I, Alice M. Gaither, on oath state that I am 24 years of age and a citizen by blood, of the Creek Nation; that I am the lawful wife of W.J. Gaither, who is a citizen, by *(blank)*, of the U.S. ~~Nation~~; that a female child was born to me on 12 day of June, 1902, that said child has been named *(blank)* , ~~and is now living~~. and died about 3 weeks later

Alice M Gaither

Witnesses To Mark:

{

Subscribed and sworn to before me this 6 day of March, 1905.

Edw C Griesel
Notary Public.

BIRTH AFFIDAVIT.

DEPARTMENT OF THE INTERIOR.
COMMISSION TO THE FIVE CIVILIZED TRIBES.

IN RE APPLICATION FOR ENROLLMENT, as a citizen of the Creek Nation, of Augusta V
Gaither , born on the 12 day of June , 1902

Name of Father: W.J. Gaither	a citizen of the U.S.	Nation.
Name of Mother: Alice M. "	a citizen of the Creek	Nation.

Postoffice   Okmulgee

AFFIDAVIT OF MOTHER.

UNITED STATES OF AMERICA, Indian Territory, ⎱
    Western   DISTRICT. ⎰

I, Alice M. Gaither, on oath state that I am 24 years of age and a citizen by blood,
of the Creek Nation; that I am the lawful wife of W.J. Gaither, who is a citizen, by ----- of
the U.S. Nation; that a female child was born to me on 12 day of June, 1902, that said
child has been named Augusta V. Gaither , and is now living. died two days after born
birth

Alice M Gaither

Witnesses To Mark:

{

Subscribed and sworn to before me this 6 day of March, 1905.

Edw C Griesel
Notary Public.

N.C.41   J.L.De

DEPARTMENT OF THE INTERIOR,
COMMISSIONER TO THE FIVE CIVILIZED TRIBES.

In the matter of the application for the enrollment of Augusta V. Gaither,
deceased, and Nordeen Gaither, deceased , as citizens by blood of the Creek Nation.

STATEMENT AND ORDER.

The record in this case shows that on March 6, 1905, applications were made, in
affidavit form, supplemented by sworn testimony, for the enrollment of Augusta V.
Gaither, deceased, and Nordeen Gaither, deceased, as citizens by blood of the Creek
Nation, under the provisions of the act of Congress approved March 3, 1905.

Applications for Enrollment of Creek Newborn
Act of 1905   Volume I

It appears from the evidence filed in this matter that said Augusta V. Gaither and Nordeen Gaither were twins born on June 12, 1902; if further appears that said Augusta V. Gaither died two days after birth and said Nordeen Gaither died three weeks after birth.

The act of Congress approved March 3, 1905, (33 Stats., 1048), provides in part as follows:

"That the Commission to the Five Civilized Tribes is authorized for sixty days after the date of the approval of this act to receive and consider applications for enrollment, of children, born subsequent to May twenty-fifth, nineteen hundred and one, and prior to March fourth, nineteen hundred and five, and living on said latter date, to citizens of the Creek tribe of Indians whose enrollment has been approved by the Secretary of the Interior prior to the approval of this act; and to enroll and make allotments to such children."

It is, therefore, ordered that the applications for the enrollment of Augusta V. Gaither, deceased, and Nordeen Gaither, deceased, as citizens by blood of the Creek Nation, be, and the same are hereby dismissed.

(Name Illegible) Commissioner.

Muskogee, Indian Territory.
    JAN 18 1907

BA 56 B.

Muskogee, Indian Territory, May 13, 1905.

W. J. Gaither,
    Okmulgee, Indian Territory.

Dear Sir:

There is on file with the Commission an affidavit executed by you relative to the birth of your minor child, Maggie E. Gaither. The affidavit of the midwife or the physician in attendance at the birth of said child is required.

There is herewith enclosed a blank form of birth affidavit, and in executing same care should be exercised to see that all blanks are properly filled, all names written in full and in the event that either of the persons signing the affidavit is unable to write, signature by mark must be attested by two witnesses. Each affidavit must be executed before a Notary Public and the notarial seal and signature of the officer must be attached to each separate affidavit.

Respectfully,

BC.   Chairman.

(The above letter was copied again.)

___

NC 41.

Muskogee, Indian Territory, January 19, 1907.

Alice M. Gaither,
c/o W. J. Gaither,
Okmulgee, Indian Territory.

Dear Madam:

There is herewith enclosed one copy of the Statement and Order of the Commissioner to the Five Civilized Tribes, dated January 18[sic], 1907, dismissing the application made by you for the enrollment of your minor children, Augusta V. and Nordeen Gaither, both deceased, as citizens of the Creek Nation.

Respectfully,

Register.   Commissioner.
LM-1113.

___

DEPARTMENT OF THE INTERIOR,
COMMISSIONER TO THE FIVE CIVILIZED TRIBES.

REFER IN REPLY TO THE FOLLOWING:
_____
N.C. 42.

Muskogee, Indian Territory, **August 4, 1905.**

Emma Coppedge,
Care of Charles E. Coppedge,
Bixby, Indian Territory.
Dear Madam:

You are hereby advised that on **July 28, 1905** , the Secretary of the Interior approved the enrollment of your minor child, **Velma G. Coppedge** , as a citizen by blood of the **Creek** Nation, and that the name of said child appears upon the roll of new born citizens of the **Creek** Nation as Number **28** .

The child is now entitled to an allotment, and application therefor should be made without delay at the Land Office for the Nation in which the prospective allotment is located.

An entire allotment for said child must be selected at the time of the original application.

Applications for Enrollment of Creek Newborn
Act of 1905   Volume I

Respectively,

Commissioner.

DEPARTMENT OF THE INTERIOR.
COMMISSION TO THE FIVE CIVILIZED TRIBES.

IN RE APPLICATION FOR ENROLLMENT, as a citizen of the Creek Nation, of Velma G. Coppedge , born on the 30 day of July , 1902

Name of Father: Charles E. Coppedge	a citizen of the U. S.	Nation.
Name of Mother: Emma "	a citizen of the Creek	Nation.

Postoffice   Bixby

(Child present)

AFFIDAVIT OF MOTHER.

UNITED STATES OF AMERICA, Indian Territory, ⎫
      Western   DISTRICT. ⎰

I, Emma Coppedge, on oath state that I am 20 years of age and a citizen by blood, of the Creek Nation; that I am the lawful wife of Charles E. Coppedge, who is a citizen, by ----- of the U. S. Nation; that a female child was born to me on 30 day of July, 1902, that said child has been named Velma G. Coppedge, and is now living.

Emma Coppedge

Witnesses To Mark:

⎰

Subscribed and sworn to before me this 14 day of March, 1905.

Edw C Griesel
Notary Public.

AFFIDAVIT OF ATTENDING PHYSICIAN OR MID-WIFE.

UNITED STATES OF AMERICA, Indian Territory, ⎫
      Western   DISTRICT. ⎰

I, Charles E. Coppedge, a physician, on oath state that I attended on Mrs. Emma Coppedge my ~~wife of~~ wife on the 30 day of July , 1902 ; that there was born to her on said date a female child; that said child is now living, and is said to have been named Velma E. Coppedge.

Applications for Enrollment of Creek Newborn
Act of 1905   Volume I

Charles E. Coppedge

Witnesses To Mark:

{

Subscribed and sworn to before me this 14 day of March, 1905.

Edw C Griesel
Notary Public.

DEPARTMENT OF THE INTERIOR,
COMMISSION TO THE FIVE CIVILIZED TRIBES.   NC43.
MUSKOGEE, I. T. JUNE 29, 1905.

In the matter of the application for the enrollment of Johnnie Harjo, as a citizen by blood of the Creek Nation.

Jimmie Harjo, being duly sworn, testified as follows:
Through Official Interpreter Jesse McDermott.

Examination by the Commission.
Q What is your name? A Jimmie Harjo.
Q How old are you? A About 30.
Q What is your post office address? A Paden.
Q Of what Nation of the Five Tribes are you a citizen? A Seminole.
Q Have you a child named Johnnie Harjo? A yes sir.
Q Is it living A Yes sir.
Q About how old is it? A He will be two years old this coming July.
Q What is the name of the mother of this child? A Her name was Susie Chardy it is now Susie Harjo.
Q If it should be found that this child of yours Johnnie Harjo, has rights in both or either in the Creek or Seminole Nations, in which Nation do you elect to have him enrolled? A In the Creek Nation.

Lona Merrick, being duly sworn, states that the above and foregoing is a true and correct transcript of her stenographic notes taken in said case on said date.

Lona Merrick

Subscribed and sworn to before me this 30th day of June, 1905.

Edw C Griesel
Notary Public.

BIRTH AFFIDAVIT.

DEPARTMENT OF THE INTERIOR.
COMMISSION TO THE FIVE CIVILIZED TRIBES.

———————

IN RE APPLICATION FOR ENROLLMENT, as a citizen of the Creek Nation, of Johnnie Harjo, born on the 13 day of July , 1903

Name of Father: Jimmie Harjo   a citizen of the Seminole   Nation.
Name of Mother: Susie Harjo   a citizen of the   Creek   Nation.

Postoffice   Paden, Indian Territory

———————

AFFIDAVIT OF MOTHER.

UNITED STATES OF AMERICA, Indian Territory, ⎱
     Western   DISTRICT. ⎰

I, Susie Harjo, on oath state that I am 30 years of age and a citizen by blood, of the Creek Nation; that I am the lawful wife of Jimmie Harjo, who is a citizen, by blood, of the Seminole Nation; that a male child was born to me on 13 day of July, 1902, that said child has been named Johnnie Harjo , and was living March 4, 1905.

                           her
                Susie   x   Harjo
Witnesses To Mark: mark
  ⎰ Alex Posey
  ⎱ DC Skaggs

Subscribed and sworn to before me this 13" day of March, 1905.

                     Drennan C Skaggs
                     Notary Public.

———————

AFFIDAVIT OF ATTENDING PHYSICIAN OR MID-WIFE.

UNITED STATES OF AMERICA, Indian Territory, ⎱
     Western   DISTRICT. ⎰

I, Bessie Foster, a midwife, on oath state that I attended on Mrs. Susie Harjo, wife of Jimmie Harjo on the 13 day of July , 1903; that there was born to her on said date a male child; that said child was living March 4, 1905, and is said to have been named Johnnie Harjo.   her
                Bessie   x   Foster
Witnesses To Mark: mark
  ⎰ Alex Posey
  ⎱ DC Skaggs

Subscribed and sworn to before me this 13" day of March, 1905.

Drennan C Skaggs
Notary Public.

United States of America,
   Indian Territory,   } S.S.
West ern[sic] Judicial D istrict[sic].

Hon. Tams Bixby,

This is to certify that I, Jemmie[sic] Harjo, a Seminole by blood, is the father of Johnnie Harjo, and my certificate No. 2081, Seminole Roll No. 1314; and I further certify that Susie Chardy, a Creek Indian by blood is my wife, and that her Roll No. is q[sic] 8911, Commission No. 29616, and I further certify that the above Susie Chardy, is the mother of Johnnie Harjo,
   Johnnie Harjo will be two years old in July, 1905.

   This is to certify that I Susie Chardy, a Creek Indian By blood, is the mother of Johnnie Harjo, and that he, Johnnie Harjo, will be two years old in July, 1905.

(Signed)   Jemmie Harjo
          Father of Johnnie Harjo.
                  Her
(Signed)   Susie x Chardy
                mark
          Mother of Johnnie Harjo.

United States of America, }
Indian Territory,   } S.S.
Western Judicial District, }

Sworn and subscribed before me, a Notary Public, for the above named District, on this the 5th day of June, 1905.

                         JL Bruce
My Commission Expires, Feb., 19, 1907   Notary Public.

BA 336 B.

Muskogee, Indian Territory, May 15, 1905.

Jennie Harjo,
      Paden, Indian Territory.

Dear Madam:

Applications for Enrollment of Creek Newborn
Act of 1905   Volume I

The Commission is in receipt of an affidavit relative to the birth of your minor child, Johnnie Harjo, in which it is stated that you are a citizen of the Seminole Nation.

You are advised that it will be necessary for yourself and the mother of said child to appear before the Commission at its office in Muskogee, Indian Territory, at an early date, for the purpose of electing in which Nation you desire to select an allotment for said child.

Respectfully,

Chairman.

NC.43.

Muskogee, Indian Territory, July 13, 1905.

Commissioner to the Five Civilized Tribes,
   Seminole Enrollment Division,
     Muskogee, Indian Territory.

Gentlemen:

March 14, 1905, application was made to the Commission to the Five Civilized Tribes Five Civilized Tribes for the enrollment of Johnnie Harjo, born July 13, 1902, as a citizen of the Creek Nation. It is stated in said application that the father of said child is Jimmie Harjo, a citizen by blood of the Seminole Nation, and that the mother is Susie (sometimes known as Susie Chardy), a citizen of the Creek Nation.

You are requested to inform the Creek Enrollment Division as to whether an application was made for the enrollment of said Johnnie Harjo, as a citizen of the Seminole Nation, and if so, what disposition has been made of the same.

Respectfully,

Commissioner.

NC-43.

DEPARTMENT OF THE INTERIOR,
COMMISSIONER TO THE FIVE CIVILIZED TRIBES.

Muskogee, Indian Territory, July 15, 1905.

Clerk in Charge,
   Creek Enrollment Division.

Dear Sir:

214

Applications for Enrollment of Creek Newborn
Act of 1905   Volume I

Receipt is acknowledged of your letter of July 13, 1905 requesting to be advised as to whether an application was ever made to the Commission to the Five Civilized Tribes for the enrollment as a citizen of the Seminole Nation of Johnnie Harjo, born July 13, 1902, child of Jimmie Harjo, a citizen by blood of the Seminole Nation, and Susie (sometimes known as Susie Chardy), a citizen of the Creek Nation.

In reply to your letter you are advised that it does not appear from an examination of the records of this office that any application was ever made to the Commission to the Five Civilized Tribes for the enrollment of said Johnnie Harjo as a citizen of the Seminole Nation.

Respectfully,

(Name Illegible)   Commissioner.

NC-44

DEPARTMENT OF THE INTERIOR,
COMMISSION TO THE FIVE CIVILIZED TRIBES.

Muskogee, Indian Territory, June 15, 1905

In the matter of the application for the enrollment of Burney Haikey as a citizen of the Creek Nation.

Nicey Haikey, being duly sworn, yestified[sic] as follows (through Jesse McDermott, Official Interpreter).

EXAMINATION BY THE COMMISSION:
Q What is your name? A Nicey Haikey.
Q How old are you? A Nineteen or twenty-three; I don't know just what.
Q What is your postoffice address? A Fry.
Q Have you a child named Burney Haikey? A There he is.
Q How old is that child? A June 25th.
Q Is it June 25th or June 15th? On June 25th how old will it be? A It will be a year old this year.
Q It was born June 25, 1904? A Yes sir.

The child is present and appears to be one year old.

Q Nicey, we have two affidavits executed by you; in one you state that the child was born June 25, 1903, making the child two years old and the other June 25, 1904. The first one was a mistake was it? 1904 was correct and the other a mistake? A Yes sir.
Q Also there is a slight difference in the spelling of your name; it is given in the body of the affidavit as Nicy and signed Nicey; which is correct? A It ought to be spelled with an E, N i c e y.
Q You signed these two affidavits, didn't you? A Yes, sir; that's my writing.

215

Applications for Enrollment of Creek Newborn
Act of 1905 Volume I

Dave Haikey, being duly sworn, testified as follows:

EXAMINATION BY THE COMMISSIONER:
Q What is your name? A Dave Haikey.
Q How old are you? A About twenty-three.
Q What is your postoffice address? A Fry.
Q You made affidavit before the Commission in which the date of the birth of this child is given as June 25, 1903; is that correct? A It is 1904.
Q You made a mistake then, did you? A The first affidavit was a mistake.
Q You made out this one before a notary public of the Dawes Commission and you said the child was born in 1903; that would make the child two years? A It will be a year old the 25th of this June.
Q You got the wrong year in that affidavit? A Yes sir.
Q You are positive that it should be 1904 as your wife has testified and as the child appears to be? A Yes sir.
Q Do you know, Dave, who the midwife was when that child was born? A Kizzie Loler.

I, J. Y. Miller, a stenographer to the Commission to the Five Civilized Tribes, hereby certify that the foregoing is a true and complete translation of my notes as same appear in my stenographic report of this case.

JY Miller

Sworn to and subscribed before me this 17th day of June 1905.

Drennan C Skaggs
Notary Public.

BIRTH AFFIDAVIT.

DEPARTMENT OF THE INTERIOR.
COMMISSION TO THE FIVE CIVILIZED TRIBES.

IN RE APPLICATION FOR ENROLLMENT, as a citizen of the Creek Nation, of Burney Haikey , born on the 25 day of June, 1903

| Name of Father: Dave Haikey | a citizen of the Creek | Nation. |
| Name of Mother: Nicey Haikey | a citizen of the   " | Nation. |

Postoffice   Fry

216

(Child present)

AFFIDAVIT OF MOTHER.

UNITED STATES OF AMERICA, Indian Territory, ⎱
    Western   DISTRICT. ⎰

    I, Nicey Haikey, on oath state that I am 19 years of age and a citizen by blood, of the Creek Nation; that I am the lawful wife of Dave Haikey, who is a citizen, by blood, of the Creek Nation; that a male child was born to me on 25 day of June, 1903, that said child has been named Burney Haikey , and is now living.

Nicey Haikey

Witnesses To Mark:

{

    Subscribed and sworn to before me this 7 day of March, 1905.

Edw C Griesel
Notary Public.

BIRTH AFFIDAVIT.

DEPARTMENT OF THE INTERIOR.
COMMISSION TO THE FIVE CIVILIZED TRIBES.

    IN RE APPLICATION FOR ENROLLMENT, as a citizen of the Creek Nation, of Burney Haikey , born on the 25 day of June, 1903

Name of Father: Dave Haikey   a citizen of the   Creek   Nation.
Name of Mother: Nicey   "   a citizen of the   "   Nation.

Postoffice   Fry

(Child present)

AFFIDAVIT OF MOTHER.

UNITED STATES OF AMERICA, Indian Territory, ⎱
    Western   DISTRICT. ⎰

    I, Dave Haikey, on oath state that I am 23 years of age and a citizen by blood, of the Creek Nation; that I am the lawful wife of Nicey Haikey, who is a citizen, by blood, of the Creek Nation; that a male child was born to me on 25 day of June, 1903, that said child has been named Burney Haikey , and is now living.

Dave Haikey

Witnesses To Mark:

{

217

Subscribed and sworn to before me this 7 day of March, 1905.

Edw C Griesel
Notary Public.

_____

BIRTH AFFIDAVIT.

DEPARTMENT OF THE INTERIOR.
COMMISSION TO THE FIVE CIVILIZED TRIBES.

_____

IN RE APPLICATION FOR ENROLLMENT, as a citizen of the Creek Nation, of Burney Haikey , born on the 25 day of June, 1904

Name of Father: Dave Haikey	a citizen of the Creek	Nation.
Name of Mother: Nicy Haikey	a citizen of the Creek	Nation.

Postoffice   Fry Ind Ter

_____

AFFIDAVIT OF MOTHER.

UNITED STATES OF AMERICA, Indian Territory, ⎫
  Western   DISTRICT. ⎰

I, Nicy Haikey, on oath state that I am 22 years of age and a citizen by Blood, of the Creek Nation; that I am the lawful wife of Dave Haikey, who is a citizen, by Blood, of the Creek Nation; that a male child was born to me on 25 day of June, 1904, that said child has been named Burney Haikey , and was living March 4, 1905.

Nicey Haikey

Witnesses To Mark:
⎰ Anderson Chisholm
⎱ W.R. Craig

Subscribed and sworn to before me this 30 day of May, 1905.

Willard M McCullough
Notary Public.
My commission expires March 21-1908

_____

218

Applications for Enrollment of Creek Newborn
Act of 1905   Volume I

AFFIDAVIT OF ATTENDING PHYSICIAN OR MID-WIFE.

UNITED STATES OF AMERICA, Indian Territory, ⎱
      Western   DISTRICT. ⎰

    I, Kizzie Loler, a midwife, on oath state that I attended on Mrs. Nicy Haikey ,
wife of Dave Haikey on the 25 day of June , 1904; that there was born to her on said date
a male child; that said child was living March 4, 1905, and is said to have been named
Burney Haikey.

her
Kizzie x Loler
mark

Witnesses To Mark:
  ⎰ Anderson Chisholm
  ⎱ W.R. Craig

    Subscribed and sworn to before me this 30 day of May, 1905.

Willard M McCullough
Notary Public.
My commission expires March 21-1908

BA 84 B.

Muskogee, Indian Territory, May 15, 1905.

Dave Haikey,
    Fry, Indian Territory.

Dear Sir:

    There is on file with the Commission an affidavit relative to the birth of your
minor child, Burney Haikey. The affidavit of the midwife or physician in attendance at
the birth of said child must be furnished.

    There is herewith enclosed a blank form of birth affidavit, and in executing same
care should be exercised to see that all blanks are properly filled, all names written in full
and in the event that either of the persons signing the affidavit is unable to write,
signature by mark must be attested by two witnesses. Each affidavit must be executed
before a Notary Public and the notarial seal and signature of the officer must be attached
to each separate affidavit.

Respectfully,

BC.   Chairman.

Applications for Enrollment of Creek Newborn
Act of 1905 Volume I

NC44.

Muskogee, Indian Territory, June 3, 1905.

Nicey Haikey,
Fry, Indian Territory.

Dear Madam:

There are on file with the Commission affidavits executed by you relative to the birth of your minor child, Burney Haikey, in which affidavits the date is given as June 25, 1903 and June 25, 1904.

You are advised that you will be allowed fifteen days from date within which to appear before the Commission at the office in Muskogee, Indian Territory, for the purpose of correcting the error in the date of the birth of said child.

Respectfully,

Commissioner in Charge.

DEPARTMENT OF THE INTERIOR.
COMMISSION TO THE FIVE CIVILIZED TRIBES.

In the matter of the death of Mary Grant a citizen of the Creek Nation, who formerly resided at or near Paden , Ind. Ter., and died on the 8 day of December , 1904.

AFFIDAVIT OF RELATIVE.

UNITED STATES OF AMERICA, Indian Territory, ⎤
Western   DISTRICT. ⎦

I, Niffie Grant, on oath state that I am about 30 years of age and a citizen by blood, of the Creek Nation; that my postoffice address is Paden , Ind. Ter.; that I am husband of Mary Grant who was a citizen, by blood , of the Creek Nation and that said Mary Grant died on the 8 day of December , 1904.

                                    his
                              Niffie x Grant
Witnesses To Mark: mark
⎰ Alex Posey
⎱ DC Skaggs

220

Applications for Enrollment of Creek Newborn
Act of 1905   Volume I

Subscribed and sworn to before me this 13 day of March, 1905.

Drennan C Skaggs
Notary Public.

BIRTH AFFIDAVIT.

DEPARTMENT OF THE INTERIOR.
COMMISSION TO THE FIVE CIVILIZED TRIBES.

IN RE APPLICATION FOR ENROLLMENT, as a citizen of the Creek Nation, of Lena Grant , born on the 9th day of March , 1904

Name of Father: Niffey Grant	a citizen of the	Creek	Nation.
Name of Mother: Mary Grant	a citizen of the	Creek	Nation.

Postoffice   Paden, Ind., Ter.

AFFIDAVIT OF MOTHER.

UNITED STATES OF AMERICA, Indian Territory, ⎰
     Western   DISTRICT. ⎱

I,   *(blank)*   , on oath state that I am   *(blank)* years of age and a citizen by *(blank)* , of the   *(blank)*   Nation; that I am the lawful wife of   *(blank)*   , who is a
     The mother died the 8th of December, 1904.
citizen, by *(blank)*   of the *(blank)* Nation; that a *(blank)* child was born to me on *(blank)* day of *(blank)*   , 1*(blank)*; that said child has been named *(blank)*, and was living March 4, 1905.

(Blank)

Witnesses To Mark:

{

     Subscribed and sworn to before me this 28 day of March, 1905.

(Blank)

Notary Public.

AFFIDAVIT OF ATTENDING PHYSICIAN OR MID-WIFE.

UNITED STATES OF AMERICA, Indian Territory, ⎰
     Western   DISTRICT. ⎱

I, Annie Sands, a Mid-Wife, on oath state that I attended on Mrs. Mary Grant , wife of Niffey Grant on the 9th day of March , 1904; that there was born to her on said

221

Applications for Enrollment of Creek Newborn
Act of 1905   Volume I

date a girl child; that said child was living March 4, 1905, and is said to have been named Lena Grant.

Annie Sands

Witnesses To Mark:

{

Subscribed and sworn to before me this 30th day of June, 1905.

J.L. Bruce
Notary Public.

BIRTH AFFIDAVIT.

DEPARTMENT OF THE INTERIOR.

COMMISSION TO THE FIVE CIVILIZED TRIBES.

IN RE APPLICATION FOR ENROLLMENT, as a citizen of the Creek Nation, of Lena Grant , born on the 9 day of March , 1904

Name of Father: Niffie Grant	a citizen of the Creek	Nation.
Name of Mother: Mary Grant	a citizen of the Creek	Nation.

Postoffice   Paden, Indian Territory

AFFIDAVIT OF ~~MOTHER~~. father

UNITED STATES OF AMERICA, Indian Territory, ⎱
    Western   DISTRICT. ⎰

     I, Niffie Grant, on oath state that I am about 30 years of age and a citizen by blood of the Creek Nation; that I am the lawful ~~wife~~ husband of Mary Grant, who ~~is~~ was a citizen by blood, of the Creek Nation; that a female child was born to her ~~me~~ on 9 day of March, 1904, that said child has been named Lena Grant , and was living March 4, 1905. That I attended on my wife, who is now dead, at the time the child was born.

his
Niffie x Grant
mark

Witnesses To Mark:
{ DC Skaggs
  Alex Posey

Subscribed and sworn to before me this 13" day of March, 1905.

Drennan C. Skaggs
Notary Public.

Applications for Enrollment of Creek Newborn
Act of 1905   Volume I

United States of America,
   Indian Territory,
Westren[sic] Judicial District.

This is to certify that we Taylor and Annie Sands, citizens of the Creek nation[sic], Indian Territory, do know possitive[sic] that a female child was born to Niffie Grant and wife on the 9th day of March, 1904, and that said child is still living and is named Lena Grant.

And, we further certify that we are dis-interest[sic] parties in this matter of having Lena Grant[sic] name placed on the roll.

Taylor Sands

Annie Sands

United States of America,
   Indian Territory,
Western Judicial District.

Subscribed and sworn to before me this 28th day of July, 1905.

JL Bruce
Notary Public.

BA 337-338B.

Muskogee, Indian Territory, May 16, 1905.

Niffey Grant,
   Paden, Indian Territory.

Dear Sir:

The Commission is in receipt of an affidavit by you relative to the birth of your minor child, Lena Grant. In the affidavit it is stated that no midwife was present. You are advised that the Commission requires the affidavits of two disinterested parties as to the date of the birth of said child.

There are herewith enclosed two blank forms of birth affidavits, and in executing same care should be exercised to see that all blanks are properly filled, all names written in full and in the event that the persons signing the affidavits are unable to write, signatures by mark must be attested by two witnesses. Each affidavit must be executed before a Notary Public and the notarial seal and signature of the officer must be attached to each separate affidavit.

Respectfully,

BC.   Chairman.

N.C.45

Muskogee, Indian Territory, July ?, 1905.

Niffie Grant,
Paden, Indian Territory.

Dear Sir:

In the matter of the application for the enrollment of your minor child, Lena Grant, as a citizen of the Creek Nation, you are advised that this office requires the affidavits of two dis-interested witnesses relative to her birth.

There are herewith inclosed[sic] two blank forms of birth affidavits. In having same executed, care should be taken that all blanks are properly filled, all names written in full, and in the event that the person signing the affidavit is unable to write, signature by mark must be attested by two witnesses.

Respectfully,

2 B A   Commissioner.

N.C.46

DEPARTMENT OF THE INTERIOR,
COMMISSIONER TO THE FIVE CIVILIZED TRIBES.

Muskogee, Indian Territory, September 6, 1905.

In the matter of the application for the enrollment of Wilson Moffer, as a citizen by blood of the Creek Nation.

Waitie Moffer, being duly sworn, testified as follows through Jesse McDermott official interpreter.

Q What is your name? A Waitie Moffer.
Q Can you spell your last name? A Yes
Q How do you spell it? A W a i t i e M o f f e r.

Q We have here a couple of affidavits executed by your wife, who is the mother of Wilson, and the name is given as Moffit? A Yes
Q These were not signed by you and you do not appear to have executed any yourself, do you know how they happened to get this i t? A I was not present when the affidavits

224

Applications for Enrollment of Creek Newborn
Act of 1905   Volume I

were signed, the mother of the child was with her uncle and I suppose they called off the name and the person who made out the affidavit wrote it with an i t.

Q You are enrolled the way you give your name now M o f f er, that is the correct name and the i t which appears in these two affidavits which were signed by your wife by mark is incorrect? A Yes, it is a mistake.

Q The correct name of this minor child of yours is Wilson Moffer? A Yes, that is the right name.

Q What was the name of your wife before she married you? A Eliza Lowe

Q Is this child Wilson Moffer living? A Yes, he is living.

I, Anna Garrigues, state that the above is a true and correct transcript of my stenographic notes as taken in said cause on said date.

Anna Garrigues

Subscribed and sworn to
before me this 7th day of September 1905.

Henry G. Harris
Notary Public.

BIRTH AFFIDAVIT.
DEPARTMENT OF THE INTERIOR.
COMMISSION TO THE FIVE CIVILIZED TRIBES.

IN RE APPLICATION FOR ENROLLMENT, as a citizen of the Creek Nation, of Wilson Moffit, born on the 9 day of November , 1904

Name of Father: Watie Moffit   a citizen of the   Creek   Nation.
Name of Mother: Liza Moffit   a citizen of the   Creek   Nation.

Postoffice   Dustin, Ind. Ter.

AFFIDAVIT OF MOTHER.

UNITED STATES OF AMERICA, Indian Territory,
       Western   DISTRICT.

I, Liza Moffit, on oath state that I am about 23 years of age and a citizen by blood, of the Creek Nation; that I am the lawful wife of Watie Moffit, who is a citizen by blood, of the Creek Nation; that a male child was born to me on 9 day of November , 1904, that said child has been named Wilson Moffit , and was living March 4, 1905.

her
Liza x Moffit
mark

Witnesses To Mark:
  Alex Posey
  DC Skaggs

225

Applications for Enrollment of Creek Newborn
Act of 1905 Volume I

Subscribed and sworn to before me this 23 day of March, 1905.

Drennan C. Skaggs
Notary Public.

AFFIDAVIT OF ATTENDING PHYSICIAN OR MID-WIFE.

UNITED STATES OF AMERICA, Indian Territory, ⎱
    Western   DISTRICT. ⎰

    I, Cinda Harjo, a midwife, on oath state that I attended on Mrs. Liza Moffit , wife of Watie Moffit on the 9 day of November , 1904 ; that there was born to her on said date a male child; that said child was living March 4, 1905, and is said to have been named Wilson Moffit.

                                              her

                                 Cinda x Harjo
Witnesses To Mark: mark
    ⎰ Alex Posey
    ⎱ DC Skaggs

    Subscribed and sworn to before me this 23 day of March, 1905.

Drennan C. Skaggs
Notary Public.

BIRTH AFFIDAVIT.
DEPARTMENT OF THE INTERIOR.
COMMISSION TO THE FIVE CIVILIZED TRIBES.

    IN RE APPLICATION FOR ENROLLMENT, as a citizen of the Creek Nation, of Wilson Moffit, born on the 9 day of Nov. , 1904

Name of Father: Waitie Moffer   a citizen of the Creek   Nation.
Name of Mother: Eliza Moffer   a citizen of the   Creek   Nation.

                       Postoffice   Dustin, I T

AFFIDAVIT OF MOTHER.

UNITED STATES OF AMERICA, Indian Territory, ⎱
    Western   DISTRICT. ⎰

    I, Waitie Moffer, on oath state that I am 27 years of age and a citizen by blood, of the Creek Nation; that I am the lawful ~~wife~~ husband of Eliza Moffer, who is a citizen by

226

Applications for Enrollment of Creek Newborn
Act of 1905   Volume I

blood, of the Creek Nation; that a male child was born to ~~me~~ her on 9" day of Nov. , 1904, that said child has been named Wilson Moffer , and was living March 4, 1905.

I hereby certify that this is
my correct name.   Waitie Moffer

Witnesses To Mark:

{ Subscribed and sworn to before me this 6 day of Sept, 1905.

My Commission   J McDermott
Expires July 25" 05   Notary Public.

BIRTH AFFIDAVIT.

DEPARTMENT OF THE INTERIOR.
COMMISSION TO THE FIVE CIVILIZED TRIBES.

IN RE APPLICATION FOR ENROLLMENT, as a citizen of the Creek Nation, of Wilson Moffit, born on the 9 day of Nov. , 1904

Name of Father: Waitey Moffit   a citizen of the   Creek   Nation.
Name of Mother: Eliza   "   a citizen of the   Creek   Nation.

Postoffice   Dustin, I. T.

(Child Present)

AFFIDAVIT OF MOTHER.

UNITED STATES OF AMERICA, Indian Territory, ⎱
    Western   DISTRICT. ⎰

I, Eliza Moffit, on oath state that I am 23 years of age and a citizen by blood, of the Creek Nation; that I am the lawful wife of Waity Moffit, who is a citizen by blood, of the Creek Nation; that a boy child was born to me on 9 day of Nov. , 1904, that said child has been named Wilson Moffit , and is now living.

                                 her
                            Eliza x Moffit
Witnesses To Mark: mark
{ J McDermott
  ECGriesel

Subscribed and sworn to before me this 7 day of March, 1905.

Edw C Griesel
Notary Public.

227

N.C.46

Muskogee, Indian Territory, July 5, 1905.

Eliza Moffet, (of Moffer)
Dustin, I.T.

Dear Madam:

There are on file at this office affidavits executed by you relative to the birth of your minor child, Wilson Moffet.

It is stated that the father of said child is Waitie Moffet and that he is a citizen by blood of the Creek Nation.

The name of Waitie Moffet does not appear on the partial list of citizens by blood of the Creek Nation, approved by the Secretary of the Interior prior to March 3, 1905 but the name of Waitie Moffer does appear thereon.

You are hereby advised that it will be necessary for you to appear before the Commissioner to the Five Civilized Tribes, at his office in Muskogee, Indian Territory, with the father of said child for the purpose of being examined under oath relative to the correct name of said child and of its said father.

Respectfully,

Commissioner.

_____

46
N.C.~~40~~.

Muskogee, Indian Territory, July 20, 1905.

Eliza Moffet, (of Moffer)
Dustin, Indian Territory.

Dear Madam:

There are on file at this office affidavits executed by you relative to the birth of your minor child, Wilson Moffet. It is stated that the father of said child is Waitie Moffet and that he is a citizen by blood of the Creek Nation.

The name of Waitie Moffet does not appear on the partial list of citizens by blood of the Creek Nation, approved by the Secretary of the Interior prior to March 3, 1905 but the name of Waitie Moffer does appear thereon.

Applications for Enrollment of Creek Newborn
Act of 1905   Volume I

You are hereby advised that it will be necessary for you to appear before the Commissioner to the Five Civilized Tribes, at his office in Muskogee, Indian Territory, with the father of said child for the purpose of being examined under oath relative to the correct name of said child and of its said father.

Respectfully,

Commissioner.

N.C.47.

DEPARTMENT OF THE INTERIOR,
COMMISSIONER TO THE FIVE CIVILIZED TRIBES.

Muskogee, Indian Territory, August 3, 1905.

In the matter of the application for the enrollment of Winey Johnson as a citizen by blood of the Creek Nation.

John Yarbrough, being duly sworn, testified as follows through Jesse McDermott official interpreter:

By Commissioner.

Q What is your name? A John Yarbrough.
Q What is your age? A About 50
Q What is your post office address? A Paden.
Q Do you know Winey Johnson? A Yes, sir.
Q What is the name of her mother? A Betsey Yarbrough
Q Is Betsey your daughter? A Yes
Q What is the name of the father of Winey? Gilbert Johnson.
Q Is he a citizen of the Creek Nation? A No, sir, he is a Seminole
Q Were Gilbert and Betsey married? A No, sir, never married. There never did live together.
Q Is this child living today? A Yes, sir
Q With whom is it living, him or her? A The child and its mother live with me.
Q Do you know whether he and she have decided in which nation they want this child enrolled, Creek or Seminole? A No, sir. I don't but the child's mother tells me that she wants her enrolled in the Creek Nation and I have been looking at vacant land for it.

The witness, who is the grandfather, of said Winey, is advised that the parents will be required to make election for this child and h is requested to advise them again as they have been advised by letter that the joint affidavit of the parents of Winey electing which Nation they desire to have the child enrolled and alloted[sic] in, should be procured and filed in this case before Winey's rights can be finally determined.

229

Applications for Enrollment of Creek Newborn
Act of 1905 Volume I

Q Do you know when this child was born? A Yes
Q When? A The child was three years old the 10th of last July.

I, Anna Garrigues, on oath state that the above and foregoing is a true and correct copy of my stenographic notes taken in said cause on said date.

Anna Garrigues

Subscribed and sworn to before me this third day of August 1905.

Edw C Griesel
Notary Public.

BIRTH AFFIDAVIT.

DEPARTMENT OF THE INTERIOR.
COMMISSION TO THE FIVE CIVILIZED TRIBES.

IN RE APPLICATION FOR ENROLLMENT, as a citizen of the Creek Nation, of Winey Johnson , born on the 10th day of July , 1902

Name of Father: Gilbert Johnson   a citizen of the   Seminole   Nation.
Name of Mother: Betsey Yarbrough   a citizen of the   Creek   Nation.

Postoffice   Paden, I. T.

AFFIDAVIT OF MOTHER.

UNITED STATES OF AMERICA, Indian Territory, ⎫
    Western   DISTRICT. ⎭

I, Betsey Yarbrough, on oath state that I am 30 years of age and a citizen by blood, of the Creek Nation; that I am the lawful wife of Gilbert Johnson, who is a citizen by blood, of the Seminole Nation; that a female child was born to me on 10th day of July, 1902, that said child has been named Winey Johnson, and was living March 4, 1905.

Her
Betsey x Yarbrough
mark

Witnesses To Mark:
  ⎰ J L Bruce
  ⎱ (Name Illegible)

Subscribed and sworn to before me this 18th day of July, 1905.

J L Bruce
Notary Public.

230

BIRTH AFFIDAVIT.

DEPARTMENT OF THE INTERIOR.
COMMISSION TO THE FIVE CIVILIZED TRIBES.

———————

IN RE APPLICATION FOR ENROLLMENT, as a citizen of the Creek Nation, of Winey Johnson , born on the 10 day of July , 1902

Name of Father:	Gilbert Johnson	a citizen of the	Seminole	Nation.
Name of Mother:	Betsey Yarbrough	a citizen of the	Creek	Nation.

Postoffice   Paden, Indian Territory

———————

AFFIDAVIT OF MOTHER.

UNITED STATES OF AMERICA, Indian Territory, ⎫
      Western   **DISTRICT.** ⎬

I, Betsey Yarbrough, on oath state that I am about 22 years of age and a citizen by
                                                            not
blood, of the Creek Nation; that I am ^ the lawful wife of Gilbert Johnson, who is a citizen by blood, of the Seminole Nation; that a female child was born to me on 10 day of July, 1902, that said child has been named Winey Johnson, and was living March 4, 1905. That no one attended on me as mid wife or physician at the time my child was born.   Her

                                      Betsey x Yarbrough
Witnesses To Mark: mark
      ⎰ DC Skaggs
      ⎱ Alex Posey

Subscribed and sworn to before me this 13" day of March, 1905.

                                      Drennan C. Skaggs
                                      Notary Public.

———————

COMMISSIONERS:
TAMS BIXBY,
THOMAS B. NEEDLES,
C.R. BRECKINBRIDGE.

WM. O. BEALL
   Secretary

DEPARTMENT OF THE INTERIOR,
COMMISSIONER TO THE FIVE CIVILIZED TRIBES.

REFER IN REPLY TO THE FOLLOWING:
———————
BA 339 B.

            ADDRESS ONLY THE
   COMMISSION TO THE FIVE CIVILIZED TRIBES.

                        Muskogee, Indian Territory,

Gilbert Johnson,
            Paden, Indian Territory.

Applications for Enrollment of Creek Newborn
Act of 1905 Volume I

Dear Sir:

The Commission is in receipt of an affidavit relative to the birth of your minor child, Winey Johnson. Further evidence is necessary in the matter of your application for the enrollment of your said child. You and your wife Betsey Yarborough are required to appear before the Commission at an early date for the purpose of electing in which Nation you desire to select an allotment for said child.

Respectfully,

(Name Illegible)

Chairman.

NC 47.

Muskogee, Indian Territory, July 13, 1905.

Commissioner to the Five Civilized Tribes,
    Seminole Enrollment Division,
        Muskogee, Indian Territory.

Gentlemen:

March 14, 1905, application was made to the Commission to the Five Civilized Tribes for the enrollment of Winey Johnson, born July 10, 1902, as a citizen by blood of the Creek Nation. It is stated in said application that the father of said child is Gilbert Johnson, a citizen by blood of the Seminole Nation, and that the mother is Betsey Yarbrough, a citizen by blood of the Creek Nation.

You are requested to inform the Creek Enrollment Division as to whether an application was made for the enrollment of said Winey Johnson, as a citizen of the Seminole Nation, and if so, what disposition has been made of the same.

Respectfully,

Commissioner.

NC 47.

Muskogee, Indian Territory, July 13, 1905.

Betsey Yarbrough,
    Paden, Indian Territory.

Dear Madam:

Applications for Enrollment of Creek Newborn
Act of 1905   Volume I

There is on file at this office an affidavit executed by you relative to the birth of your minor child, Winey Johnson, as a citizen of the Creek Nation, in which it is stated that the father of said child is a citizen of the Seminole Nation.

You are advised that it will be necessary for you or the father of said minor child, to appear at the office of the Commissioner to the Five Civilized Tribes in Muskogee, Indian Territory, to elect in which Nation you desire said child to be enrolled.

You are further advised that the affidavits of two disinterested witnesses as to the birth of said child should be furnished.

There are herewith enclosed two blank forms of birth affidavit[sic], and in executing same care should be exercised to see that all blanks are properly filled, all names written in full and in the event that the persons signing the affidavits are unable to write, signatures by mark must be attested by two witnesses. Each affidavit must be executed before a Notary Public and the notarial seal and signature of the officer must be attached to each separate affidavit.

Respectfully,

2 BA   Commissioner.

DEPARTMENT OF THE INTERIOR.
COMMISSIONER TO THE FIVE CIVILIZED TRIBES.

Muskogee, Indian Territory, July 18, 1905.

Chief Clerk,
  Creek Enrollment Division.

Dear Sir:

Receipt is acknowledged of your letter of July 13, 1904 (NB-47) stating that an application was made to the Commission to the Five Civilized Tribes for the enrollment of Winey Johnson, born July 0, 1902, child of Gilbert Johnson, a citizen by blood of the Seminole Nation, and Betsey Yarbrough, a citizen by blood of the Creek Nation and requesting to be advised as to whether application has been made for the enrollment of said child as a citizen of the Seminole Nation.

In reply to your letter you are advised that is does not appear from an examination of the records of this office that any application was made to the Commission to the Five Civilized Tribes for the enrollment of said Winey Johnson as a citizen of the Seminole Nation.

Respectfully,

(Name Illegible) Commissioner.

Applications for Enrollment of Creek Newborn
Act of 1905   Volume I

A-F-F-I-D-A-V-I-T.

I, Betsey Yarbough[sic], On oath state that I am a citizen by blood of the Creek Nation, and that I am the mother of one Winey Johnson, a newborn, and that the father of said child is Gilbert Johnson a citizen of the Seminole Nation, and that I elect to have my said child, Winey Johnson, to be enrolled and receive her allotment in the Creek Nation.

Witnesses to her mark:
Jno. H. Phillips
John Yarbrough

her
Betsey x Yarbough
mark

Subscribed and sworn to before me
this 10 day of Oct. 1905.

John H. Phillips
Notary Public.

My Commission expires Sept. 6, 1906.

A-F-F-I-D-A-V-I-T.

United States of America,)
   Western District,   ) ss
   Indian Territory.

We, Jackson Knight and Mariah Larney, on oath state that we are personally acquainted with Betsey Yarbough, who is not the lawful wife of Gilbert Johnson; and that she a citizen of the Creek Nation and that he is the citizen of the Seminole Nation; and that there was born to her on or about the 10th day of July 1902; a female child and that the said child is said to have been named Winey Johnson and is now living.

Witnesses to mark:
Jno. H. Phillips

John Yarbrough

his
Jackson x Knight
mark
her
Mariah x Larney
mark

Subscribed and sworn to before me
this 10 day of Oct. 1905.

John H. Phillips
Notary Public.

My Commission expires Sept. 6, 1906.

| DEPARTMENT OF THE INTERIOR, | REFER IN REPLY TO THE FOLLOWING: |
| COMMISSIONER TO THE FIVE CIVILIZED TRIBES. | N.C. 48. |

Muskogee, Indian Territory, **August 4, 1905.**

Emma Nichols,
    Care of Steve F. Nichols,
        Paden, Indian Territory.

Dear Madam:

You are hereby advised that on **July 28, 1905** , the Secretary of the Interior approved the enrollment of your minor child, **Lee Carlton Nichols** , as a citizen by blood of the **Creek** Nation, and that the name of said child appears upon the roll of new born citizens of the **Creek** Nation as Number **30** .

The child is now entitled to an allotment, and application therefor should be made without delay at the Land Office for the Nation in which the prospective allotment is located.

An entire allotment for said child must be selected at the time of the original application.

Respectively,

Commissioner.

BIRTH AFFIDAVIT.

DEPARTMENT OF THE INTERIOR.
COMMISSION TO THE FIVE CIVILIZED TRIBES.

IN RE APPLICATION FOR ENROLLMENT, as a citizen of the Creek Nation, of Lee Carlton Nihols, born on the 23 day of March, 1903

Name of Father: Steve F. Nichols   a citizen of the United States Nation.
Name of Mother: Emma Nichols   a citizen of the   Creek   Nation.

Postoffice   Paden, Indian Territory

AFFIDAVIT OF MOTHER.

UNITED STATES OF AMERICA, Indian Territory, ⎤
    Western   DISTRICT. ⎦

I, Emma Nichols, on oath state that I am 26 years of age and a citizen by blood, of the Creek Nation; that I am the lawful wife of Steve F. Nichols, who is a citizen, by

Applications for Enrollment of Creek Newborn
Act of 1905   Volume I

(blank) of the United States Nation; that a male child was born to me on 23rd day of March, 1903, that said child has been named Lee Carlton Nichols , and was living March 4, 1905.

Emma Nichols

Witnesses To Mark:

{

Subscribed and sworn to before me this 13" day of March, 1905.

Drennan C. Skaggs
Notary Public.

AFFIDAVIT OF ATTENDING PHYSICIAN OR MID-WIFE.

UNITED STATES OF AMERICA, Indian Territory, ⎱
     Western   **DISTRICT.** ⎰

I, Mary J. Newton, a midwife, on oath state that I attended on Mrs. Emma Nichols, wife of Steve F. Nichols on or about the 23rd day of March , 1903; that there was born to her on said date a male child; that said child was living March 4, 1905, and is said to have been named Lee Carlton Nichols.

Mary J Newton

Witnesses To Mark:

{

Subscribed and sworn to before me this 13" day of March, 1905.

Drennan C. Skaggs
Notary Public.

DEPARTMENT OF THE INTERIOR,
COMMISSIONER TO THE FIVE CIVILIZED TRIBES.

REFER IN REPLY TO THE FOLLOWING:
N.C. 49.

Muskogee, Indian Territory, August 4, 1905.

Willie Skeeter,
    Mounds, Indian Territory.

Dear Sir:

You are hereby advised that on **July 28, 1905** , the Secretary of the Interior approved the enrollment of your minor child, **Fred Skeeter** , as a citizen by blood of the

236

Applications for Enrollment of Creek Newborn
Act of 1905   Volume I

Creek Nation, and that the name of said child appears upon the roll of new born citizens of the **Creek** Nation as Number **31** .

The child is now entitled to an allotment, and application therefor should be made without delay at the Land Office for the Nation in which the prospective allotment is located.

An entire allotment for said child must be selected at the time of the original application.

Respectively,

Commissioner.

See Duplicate Affidavit

BIRTH AFFIDAVIT.

DEPARTMENT OF THE INTERIOR.
COMMISSION TO THE FIVE CIVILIZED TRIBES.

IN RE APPLICATION FOR ENROLLMENT, as a citizen of the Creek Nation, of Fred Skeeter , born on the 23 day of July , 1904

Name of Father: Willie Skeeter	a citizen of the	Creek	Nation.
(Euchee)			
Name of Mother: Susannah Skeeter	a citizen of the	Creek	Nation.
(Euchee)			

Postoffice   Mounds

AFFIDAVIT OF MOTHER.

UNITED STATES OF AMERICA, Indian Territory, ⎱
     Western   **DISTRICT.** ⎰   Child Present

I, Susannah Skeeter, on oath state that I am 26 years of age and a citizen by blood, of the Creek   Nation; that I am the lawful wife of Willie Skeeter, who is a citizen, by blood of the Creek Nation; that a male child was born to me on 23   day of July , 1904, that said child has been named Fred Skeeter , and was living March 4, 1905.

her
Susannah x Skeeter
mark

Witnesses To Mark:
  ⎰ Davis Shelby
  ⎱ Jesse McDermott

Subscribed and sworn to before me this 25 day of April , 1905.

Applications for Enrollment of Creek Newborn
Act of 1905   Volume I

(Seal)   Edw C Griesel
                                           Notary Public.

AFFIDAVIT OF ATTENDING PHYSICIAN OR MID-WIFE.

UNITED STATES OF AMERICA, Indian Territory, ⎱
　　　Western　　　　　DISTRICT. ⎰

    I, Malinda Pickett, a Midwife, on oath state that I attended on Mrs. Susannah Skeeter , wife of Willie Skeeter on the 23 day of July , 1904 ; that there was born to her on said date a male child; that said child was living March 4, 1905, and is said to have been named Fred Skeeter.

	her
	Malinda x Pickett
Witnesses To Mark:	mark

    ⎰ Davis Shelby
    ⎱ Jesse McDermott

    Subscribed and sworn to before me this 25 day of April, 1905.

(Seal)   Edw C Griesel
                                           Notary Public.

BIRTH AFFIDAVIT.
DEPARTMENT OF THE INTERIOR.
COMMISSION TO THE FIVE CIVILIZED TRIBES.

IN RE APPLICATION FOR ENROLLMENT, as a citizen of the Creek Nation, of Fred Skeeter , born on the 23 day of July , 1904

Name of Father:	Willie Skeeter	a citizen of the	Creek	Nation.
Name of Mother:	Susanna "	a citizen of the	Creek	Nation.

Postoffice　　Mounds I.T.

AFFIDAVIT OF MOTHER.

UNITED STATES OF AMERICA, Indian Territory, ⎱　　　　Child Present
　　　Western　　　　　DISTRICT. ⎰

    I, Susanna Skeeter, on oath state that I am 26 years of age and a citizen by birth or blood, of the Creek or Muskogee Nation; that I am the lawful wife of Willie Skeeter, who is a citizen, by birth or blood of the Creek or Muskogee Nation; that a male child was born to me on 23rd day of July , 1904, that said child has been named Fred Skeeter , and is now living.

her
Susannah x Skeeter
mark

Witnesses To Mark:
{ Larry Brown
  Jennie Pickett

Subscribed and sworn to before me this 17 day of Mch , 1905.

L.S. Holcomb
Notary Public.

_____

AFFIDAVIT OF ATTENDING PHYSICIAN OR MID-WIFE.

UNITED STATES OF AMERICA, Indian Territory, }
Western **DISTRICT.** }

I, Malinda Pickett, a Midwife, on oath state that I attended on Mrs. Susanna Skeeter , wife of Willie Skeeter on the 23rd day of July , 1904 ; that there was born to her on said date a male child; that said child is now living, and is said to have been named Fred Skeeter.

her
Malinda x Pickett
mark

Witnesses To Mark:
{ Larry Brown
  Jennie Pickett

Subscribed and sworn to before me this 17 day of Mch , 1905.

L.S. Holcomb
Notary Public.

_____

BIRTH AFFIDAVIT.

DEPARTMENT OF THE INTERIOR.
COMMISSION TO THE FIVE CIVILIZED TRIBES.

_____

IN RE APPLICATION FOR ENROLLMENT, as a citizen of the Creek Nation, of Fred Skeeter , born on the 23 day of July , 1904

Name of Father:	Willie Skeeter	a citizen of the	Creek	Nation.
Name of Mother:	Susanna "	a citizen of the	"	Nation.

Postoffice   Mounds I.T.

_____

Applications for Enrollment of Creek Newborn
Act of 1905 Volume I

AFFIDAVIT OF MOTHER.

UNITED STATES OF AMERICA, Indian Territory, ⎱
    Western   DISTRICT. ⎰

I, Willie Skeeter , on oath state that I am 24 years of age and a citizen by blood , of the Creek Nation; that I am the lawful ~~wife~~ hus of Susanna Skeeter , who is a citizen, by blood of the Creek Nation; that a male child was born to me on 23 day of July , 1904 , that said child has been named Fred Skeeter , and is now living.

Willie Skeeter

Witnesses To Mark:

{

Subscribed and sworn to before me this 14 day of March , 1905.

Edw C Griesel
Notary Public.

| DEPARTMENT OF THE INTERIOR,
COMMISSIONER TO THE FIVE CIVILIZED TRIBES. | REFER IN REPLY TO THE FOLLOWING:
_____
N.C. 50. |

Muskogee, Indian Territory, August 4, 1905.

Mesulda Gray,
    Care of George C. Gray,
        Paden, Indian Territory.

Dear Madam:

You are hereby advised that on **July 28, 1905** , the Secretary of the Interior approved the enrollment of your minor child, **Johnson Gray** , as a citizen by blood of the **Creek** Nation, and that the name of said child appears upon the roll of new born citizens of the **Creek** Nation as Number **32** .

The child is now entitled to an allotment, and application therefor should be made without delay at the Land Office for the Nation in which the prospective allotment is located.

An entire allotment for said child must be selected at the time of the original application.

Respectively,

Commissioner.

Applications for Enrollment of Creek Newborn
Act of 1905   Volume I

BIRTH AFFIDAVIT.

DEPARTMENT OF THE INTERIOR.
COMMISSION TO THE FIVE CIVILIZED TRIBES.

IN RE APPLICATION FOR ENROLLMENT, as a citizen of the Creek Nation, of Johnson Gray , born on the 5 day of March , 1904

Name of Father: George C. Gray   a citizen of the United States Nation.
Name of Mother: Mesulda Gray (nee Long)   a citizen of the   Creek   Nation.

Postoffice   Paden, Indian Territory

AFFIDAVIT OF MOTHER.

UNITED STATES OF AMERICA, Indian Territory,⎫
    Western   DISTRICT. ⎭

I, Mesulda Gray , on oath state that I am about 20 years of age and a citizen by blood , of the Creek   Nation; that I am the lawful wife of George C. Gray , who is a citizen, ~~by~~ *(blank)* of the United States   Nation; that a male   child was born to me on 5 day of March , 1904 , that said child has been named Johnson Gray   , and was living March 4, 1905.

her
Mesulda x Gray
mark

Witnesses To Mark:
⎧ DC Skaggs
⎩ Alex Posey

Subscribed and sworn to before me this 13" day of March , 1905.

Drennan C. Skaggs
Notary Public.

AFFIDAVIT OF ATTENDING PHYSICIAN OR MID-WIFE.

UNITED STATES OF AMERICA, Indian Territory,⎫
    Western   DISTRICT. ⎭

I, Bessie Foster, a midwife, on oath state that I attended on Mrs. Mesulda Gray , wife of George C. Gray on the 5 day of March , 1904 ; that there was born to her on said date a *(blank)* child; that said child was living March 4, 1905, and is said to have been named Johnson Gray.

her
Bessie x Foster
mark

Witnesses To Mark:
⎧ DC Skaggs
⎩ Alex Posey

Subscribed and sworn to before me this 13" day of March, 1905.

Drennan C Skaggs
Notary Public.

NC-51

DEPARTMENT OF THE INTERIOR,
COMMISSIONER TO THE FIVE CIVILIZED TRIBES.

Muskogee, Indian Territory, August 8, 1905

In the matter of the application for the enrollment of Jimmie and Pearlie Futrell, as Creek citizens.

George C. Butte, being duly sworn, testified as follows:

EXAMINATION BY THE COMMISSIONER:
Q What is your name, age and postoffice? A George C. Butte; 28; Muskogee.
Q You are an attorney? A Yes sir.
Q State what you know about this case. A   I know the step-grandfather of these applicants. They talked with me about this matter, and he informed me that the correct spelling of the name of his grand-children is Futrell. I have also seen and have in my possession an instrument signed by the father of these children, Frank Futrell, in which he signs his own name and spells his surname, Futrell.
Q You have not it with you? A No sir; it is up in the office.

Thomas W. Jones, being duly sworn, testified as follows:

EXAMINATION BY THE COMMISSIONER:
Q What is your name, age and postoffice? A Thomas W. Jones; 34 Tulsa.
Q Are you any kin to these children? A Yes sir; my wife's grandchildren.
Q Do you know how your wife's son-in-law would spell that name? A Yes sir.
Q How? A Futrell.
Q What special circumstances, if any, affixes the spelling of that name—how do you know it? did you see any one sign it? A I have a power of attorney from her and her husband.
Q She does not sign her name, but he did? A Yes sir.
Q And you are sure he signed it Futrell? A Yes sir.

INDIAN TERRITORY, Western District.

I, J. Y. Miller, a stenographer to the Commissioner to the Five Civilized Tribes, do hereby certify that the above and foregoing is a true and complete translation of my notes as same appears in my stenographic report of this case.

JY Miller

Subscribed and sworn to before me
  this the 16 day of August, 1905   Edw C Griesel
                                                       Notary Public.

BIRTH AFFIDAVIT.

DEPARTMENT OF THE INTERIOR.
COMMISSION TO THE FIVE CIVILIZED TRIBES.

IN RE APPLICATION FOR ENROLLMENT, as a citizen of the Creek Nation, of Pearlie Futrell,
born on the 25 day of September , 1904

Name of Father: Frank Futrell   a citizen of the United States Nation.
Name of Mother: Alice Futrell   a citizen of the   Creek   Nation.

                    Postoffice   Tulsa Ind Ter

AFFIDAVIT OF MOTHER.

UNITED STATES OF AMERICA, Indian Territory, ⎤
       Western   DISTRICT. ⎦

I, Alice Futrell , on oath state that I am 18 years of age and a citizen by Birth   , of
the Creek   Nation; that I am the lawful wife of Frank Futrell   , who is a citizen, by
(blank) of the United States   Nation; that a Female   child was born to me on 25 day
of September , 1904 , that said child has been named Pearlie Futrell , and is now living.
                                                    Her
                                          Alice x Futrell
Witnesses To Mark: mark
  ⎰ R E Lynch
  ⎱ Mrs Elizabeth Dodge

Subscribed and sworn to before me this 8" day of March , 1905.

     Com Ex 7/3/1906   Robert E Lynch
                                                Notary Public.

AFFIDAVIT OF ATTENDING PHYSICIAN OR MID-WIFE.

UNITED STATES OF AMERICA, Indian Territory, ⎤
       Western   DISTRICT. ⎦

I, Elizabeth Gillis, a Midwife, on oath state that I attended on Mrs. Alice Futrell ,
wife of Frank Futrell on the 25 day of September , 1904 ; that there was born to her on

said date a Female child; that said child is now living, and is said to have been named Pearlie Futrell .

Her
Elizabeth x Gillis
mark

Witnesses To Mark:
{ R E Lynch
{ Mrs Elizabeth Dodge

Subscribed and sworn to before me this 8" day of March, 1905.

Com Ex 7/3/1906   Robert E Lynch
                             Notary Public.

BIRTH AFFIDAVIT.

DEPARTMENT OF THE INTERIOR.
COMMISSION TO THE FIVE CIVILIZED TRIBES.

IN RE APPLICATION FOR ENROLLMENT, as a citizen of the Creek Nation, of Pearlie Frutrell[sic], born on the 25 day of Sept , 1904

Name of Father: Frank Frutrell   a citizen of the   U S   Nation.
Name of Mother: Alice   "   a citizen of the   Creek Nation.

Postoffice   Tulsa I. T.

(Child Present)

AFFIDAVIT OF MOTHER.

UNITED STATES OF AMERICA, Indian Territory,⎫
    Western   DISTRICT. ⎬

I, Alice Frutrell , on oath state that I am 18 years of age and a citizen by blood , of the Creek   Nation; that I am the lawful wife of Frank Frutrell , who is a citizen, by ----- of the U. S. Nation; that a female   child was born to me on 25 day of Sept , 1904 , that said child has been named Pearlie Frutrell , and is now living.

Her
Alice x Frutrell
mark

Witnesses To Mark:
{ Frank Futrell
{ EC Griesel

Subscribed and sworn to before me this 7 day of March , 1905.

Edw C Griesel
Notary Public.

Applications for Enrollment of Creek Newborn
Act of 1905 Volume I

BIRTH AFFIDAVIT.

DEPARTMENT OF THE INTERIOR.
COMMISSION TO THE FIVE CIVILIZED TRIBES.

IN RE APPLICATION FOR ENROLLMENT, as a citizen of the Creek Nation, of Jimmie Frutrell[sic], born on the 12 day of March , 1902

Name of Father: Frank Frutrell	a citizen of the	U. S. Nation.
Name of Mother: Alice "	a citizen of the	Creek Nation.

Postoffice   Tulsa I. T.

(Child Present)

AFFIDAVIT OF MOTHER.

UNITED STATES OF AMERICA, Indian Territory,⎱
    Western   DISTRICT. ⎰

I, Alice Frutrell , on oath state that I am 18 years of age and a citizen by blood   , of the Creek   Nation; that I am the lawful wife of Frank Frutrell   , who is a citizen, by ----- of the U. S.   Nation; that a male   child was born to me on 12 day of March , 1902, that said child has been named Jimmie Frutrell , and is now living.

Her
Alice x Frutrell
Witnesses To Mark: mark
⎰ Frank Futrell
⎱ EC Griesel

Subscribed and sworn to before me this 7 day of March , 1905.

Edw C Griesel
Notary Public.

BIRTH AFFIDAVIT.

DEPARTMENT OF THE INTERIOR.
COMMISSION TO THE FIVE CIVILIZED TRIBES.

IN RE APPLICATION FOR ENROLLMENT, as a citizen of the Creek Nation, of Jimmie Futrell, born on the 12 day of March , 1902

Name of Father: Frank Futrell	a citizen of the	U. S. Nation.
Name of Mother: Alice Futrell	a citizen of the	Creek Nation.

Postoffice   Tulsa I.T.

Applications for Enrollment of Creek Newborn
Act of 1905 Volume I

AFFIDAVIT OF MOTHER.

UNITED STATES OF AMERICA, Indian Territory, ⎱
    Western   DISTRICT. ⎰

       I, Alice Futrell , on oath state that I am 18 years of age and a citizen by Birth , of the Creek Nation; that I am the lawful wife of Frank Futrell , who is a citizen, by *(blank)* of the United States Nation; that a male child was born to me on 12 day of March , 1902, that said child has been named Jimmie Futrell , and is now living.

Her
Alice x Frutrell
mark

Witnesses To Mark:
⎧ RE Lynch
⎨
⎩ Mrs Elizabeth Dodge

Subscribed and sworn to before me this 8 day of March , 1905.

Com Ex 7/3/1906   Robert E Lynch
                               Notary Public.

AFFIDAVIT OF ATTENDING PHYSICIAN OR MID-WIFE.

UNITED STATES OF AMERICA, Indian Territory, ⎱
    Western   DISTRICT. ⎰

       I, Mrs. Ada King, a Midwife, on oath state that I attended on Mrs. Alice Futrell , wife of Frank Futrell on the 12 day of March , 1905[sic] ; that there was born to her on said date a male child; that said child is now living, and is said to have been named Jimmie Futrell.

Mrs. Ada King

Witnesses To Mark:

⎧
⎨
⎩

Subscribed and sworn to before me this 8" day of March, 1905.

                            Robert E Lynch
                               Notary Public.

Com Ex 7/3/1906

Applications for Enrollment of Creek Newborn
Act of 1905 Volume I

NC 51.

Muskogee, Indian Territory, July 13, 1905.

Alice Futrell,
        Tulsa, Indian Territory.
Dear Madam:

There are on file at this office affidavits executed by you relative to the birth of your minor children, Pearlie and Jimmie Futrell, as citizens of the Creek Nation, in which you[sic] surname is spelled Futrell and Frutrell.

You are requested to state which is your correct name.

Respectfully,

Commissioner.

N.C.51   COPY

Tulsa, I.T. July 25" 05.

Dear Sir:-

We are requested by Mrs Alice Futrell to reply to yours of recent date with reference to her name.

The spelling Fretrell or Trutrell are both incorrect; her name if Futrell.

Yours respectfully.

U.S. Commissioner of Indian Affairs
    for Indian Territory.
        Muskogee, I.T.
Dic. C.C.M.Magee&[sic] Houck

COPY

N.C.51

Tulsa, Ind. Ter. August 9' 1905.

Hon. Tams Bixby,
        Commissioner to the Five Civilized Tribes,
            Muskogee, Ind. Ter.

Dear Sir:-

247

I find that you have enrolled my two children as "Frutrell" when in fact it is "Futrell", and I desire to have you correct the name.

Yours truly,

(Signed) Frank Futrell

DEPARTMENT OF THE INTERIOR,	REFER IN REPLY TO THE FOLLOWING:
COMMISSIONER TO THE FIVE CIVILIZED TRIBES.	N.C. 53.

Muskogee, Indian Territory, **August 4, 1905.**

Daniel Bigpond,
   Mounds, Indian Territory.

Dear Sir:

You are hereby advised that on **July 28, 1905** , the Secretary of the Interior approved the enrollment of your minor child, **Wilson Bigpond** , as a citizen by blood of the **Creek** Nation, and that the name of said child appears upon the roll of new born citizens of the **Creek** Nation as Number **33** .

The child is now entitled to an allotment, and application therefor should be made without delay at the Land Office for the Nation in which the prospective allotment is located.

An entire allotment for said child must be selected at the time of the original application.

Respectively,

Commissioner.

BIRTH AFFIDAVIT.

DEPARTMENT OF THE INTERIOR.
COMMISSION TO THE FIVE CIVILIZED TRIBES.

IN RE APPLICATION FOR ENROLLMENT, as a citizen of the Creek Nation, of Wilson Bigpond, - - - - - - - - , born on the 15th day of August, - - , 1902

Name of Father: Daniel Bigpond, - - - - - -   a citizen of the Creek, - - -   Nation.
Name of Mother: Nancy Bigpond, - - - - - -   a citizen of the Creek, - - - - - Nation.

Postoffice   Mounds, I.T.

Applications for Enrollment of Creek Newborn
Act of 1905   Volume I

AFFIDAVIT OF MOTHER.

UNITED STATES OF AMERICA, Indian Territory, ⎫
    Western   DISTRICT. ⎭

    I, Nancy Bigpond - - - - - - , on oath state that I am thirty six years of age and a citizen by Blood, - - - - , of the Creek, - - - - - - -   Nation; that I am the lawful wife of Daniel Bigpond, - - - - - - - - -   , who is a citizen, by Blood, - - - of the Creek, - - - - - - Nation; that a male   child was born to me on fifteenth, day of August, - - - - - , 1902 , that said child has been named Wilson Bigpond - - - - - - - - - , and is now living.

Nancy Bigpond

Witnesses To Mark:

    {

    Subscribed and sworn to before me this 15th day of March, - - - - - - , 1905.

(Name Illegible)
Notary Public.

My Commission expires Feb. 21, 1907

AFFIDAVIT OF ATTENDING PHYSICIAN OR MID-WIFE.

UNITED STATES OF AMERICA, Indian Territory, ⎫
    Western   DISTRICT. ⎭

    I, Millie Bighead - - - - - - - - - -, a Mid wife - -, on oath state that I attended on Mrs. Nancy Bigpond, - - - - - - - , wife of Daniel Bigpond, - - - - - on the 15th day of August , 1902 ; that there was born to her on said date a male child; that said child is now living, and is said to have been named Wilson Bigpond.

her
Millie x Bighead
mark

Witnesses To Mark:
  { Daniel Bigpond
    WR Casteel

Subscribed and sworn to before me this 15th day of March, 1905.

(Name Illegible)
Notary Public.

My Commission expires Feb. 21, 1907

249

Applications for Enrollment of Creek Newborn
Act of 1905   Volume I

BIRTH AFFIDAVIT.

DEPARTMENT OF THE INTERIOR.
COMMISSION TO THE FIVE CIVILIZED TRIBES.

IN RE APPLICATION FOR ENROLLMENT, as a citizen of the Creek Nation, of Wilson Bigpond , born on the 15th day of Aug , 1902

Name of Father:	Daniel Bigpond	a citizen of the	Creek	Nation.
Name of Mother:	Nancy "	a citizen of the	"	Nation.

Postoffice   Mounds

AFFIDAVIT OF MOTHER.

UNITED STATES OF AMERICA, Indian Territory,
Western   DISTRICT.

I, Daniel Bigpond , on oath state that I am 38 years of age and a citizen by blood, of the Creek   Nation; that I am the lawful ~~wife~~ hus of Nancy Bigpond   , who is a citizen, by blood   of the   Creek   Nation; that a male   child was born to me on 15 day of   Aug   , 1*(blank)* , that said child has been named   Wilson Bigpond , and is now living.

Daniel Bigpond

Witnesses To Mark:

{

Subscribed and sworn to before me this 14" day of   March   ,   1905.

Edw C Griesel
Notary Public.

BIRTH AFFIDAVIT.

DEPARTMENT OF THE INTERIOR.
COMMISSION TO THE FIVE CIVILIZED TRIBES.

IN RE APPLICATION FOR ENROLLMENT, as a citizen of the Creek Nation, of Wilson Bigpond , born on the 15 day of Aug , 1902

Name of Father:	Daniel Bigpond	a citizen of the	Creek	Nation.
(Euchee)				
Name of Mother:	Nancy "	a citizen of the	Creek	Nation.
(Euchee)				

Postoffice   Mounds

250

Applications for Enrollment of Creek Newborn
Act of 1905   Volume I

Child Present

UNITED STATES OF AMERICA, Indian Territory, ⎱
    Western   DISTRICT. ⎰

    I, Nancy Bigpond , on oath state that I am 36 years of age and a citizen by blood, of the Creek Nation; that I am the lawful wife of Daniel Bigpond , who is a citizen, by blood of the Creek Nation; that a male child was born to me on 15 day of Aug , 1902 , that said child has been named Wilson Bigpond , and was living March 4, 1905.

Nancy Bigpond

Witnesses To Mark:

{

    Subscribed and sworn to before me this 26 day of April , 1905.

(Seal)   Edw C Griesel
                                 Notary Public.

Father

UNITED STATES OF AMERICA, Indian Territory, ⎱
    Western   DISTRICT. ⎰

    I, Daniel Bigpond, ~~a~~ ----- on oath state that I attended on Mrs. Nancy Bigpond, my wife ~~of~~ *(blank)* on the 15 day of Aug , 1902 ; that there was born to her on said date a male child; that said child was living March 4, 1905, and is said to have been named Wilson Bigpond.

Daniel Bigpond

Witnesses To Mark:

{

    Subscribed and sworn to before me this 26 day of April, 1905.

(Seal)   Edw C Griesel
                                 Notary Public.

BA 95 B.

Muskogee, Indian Territory, May 15, 1905.

Cheasquah Harris,
        Muskogee, Indian Territory.

Applications for Enrollment of Creek Newborn
Act of 1905   Volume I

Dear Sir:

There is on file with the Commission an affidavit executed by you relative to the birth of your minor child, Winnie Davis.
The affidavit of the midwife or physician in attendance at the birth of said child is required.

There is herewith enclosed a blank form of birth affidavit, and in executing same care should be exercised to see that all blanks are properly filled, all names written in full and in the event that either of the persons signing the affidavit is unable to write, signature by mark must be attested by two witnesses. Each affidavit must be executed before a Notary Public and the notarial seal and signature of the officer must be attached to each separate affidavit.

Respectfully,

BC.   Chairman.

DEPARTMENT OF THE INTERIOR, **COMMISSIONER TO THE FIVE CIVILIZED TRIBES.**	REFER IN REPLY TO THE FOLLOWING: ——————— **N.C. 54.**

Muskogee, Indian Territory, August 4, 1905.

Cheasquah Harris,
> **Muskogee, Indian Territory.**

Dear Sir:

You are hereby advised that on **July 28, 1905** , the Secretary of the Interior approved the enrollment of your minor child, **Winnie Davis Harris** , as a citizen by blood of the **Creek** Nation, and that the name of said child appears upon the roll of new born citizens of the **Creek** Nation as Number 34 .

The child is now entitled to an allotment, and application therefor should be made without delay at the Land Office for the Nation in which the prospective allotment is located.

An entire allotment for said child must be selected at the time of the original application.

Respectively,

Commissioner.

Applications for Enrollment of Creek Newborn
Act of 1905   Volume I

BIRTH AFFIDAVIT.

DEPARTMENT OF THE INTERIOR.
COMMISSION TO THE FIVE CIVILIZED TRIBES.

IN RE APPLICATION FOR ENROLLMENT, as a citizen of the Creek Nation, of Winnie Davis Harris , born on the 18th day of June , 1901

Name of Father: Cheasquah B. Harris	a citizen of the Creek	Nation.
Name of Mother: Nellie A Harris	a citizen of the Creek	Nation.

Postoffice   Muskogee Ind Ty

AFFIDAVIT OF MOTHER.

UNITED STATES OF AMERICA, Indian Territory, ⎤
    Western   DISTRICT. ⎦

I, Nellie A Harris, on oath state that I am 28 years of age and a citizen by Adoption , of the Creek Nation; that I am the lawful wife of Chesquah[sic] B. Harris, who is a citizen, by Birth of the Creek   Nation; that a female   child was born to me on 18th   day of June , 1901 , that said child has been named Winnie Davis Harris , and was living March 4, 1905.

Nellie A Harris

Witnesses To Mark:

{

Subscribed and sworn to before me this 16th day of May , 1905.

My Commission Expires March 24, 1907   WE Abney
                       Notary Public.

AFFIDAVIT OF ATTENDING PHYSICIAN OR MID-WIFE.

UNITED STATES OF AMERICA, Indian Territory, ⎤
    Western   DISTRICT. ⎦

I, Lela C Harris, a Midwife, on oath state that I attended on Mrs. Nellie Harris , wife of Chesquah[sic] Harris on the 18th day of June , 1901 ; that there was born to her on said date a female child; that said child was living March 4, 1905, and is said to have been named Winnie Davis Harris.

Lela C Harris

Witnesses To Mark:

{

Subscribed and sworn to before me this 16th day of May, 1905.

My Commission Expires March 24, 1907 WE Abney
Notary Public.

BIRTH AFFIDAVIT.

DEPARTMENT OF THE INTERIOR.

COMMISSION TO THE FIVE CIVILIZED TRIBES.

IN RE APPLICATION FOR ENROLLMENT, as a citizen of the Creek Nation, of Winnie Davis Harris , born on the 18 day of June , 1901

Name of Father: Cheasquah Harris a citizen of the Creek Nation.
Name of Mother: Nellie " a citizen of the U.S. Nation.

Postoffice Muskogee

AFFIDAVIT OF MOTHER.

(Child Present)
UNITED STATES OF AMERICA, Indian Territory, }
Western DISTRICT. }

I, Nellie A Harris, on oath state that I am 29 years of age and a citizen by ----- of the U.S. Nation; that I am the lawful wife of Cheasquah Harris, who is a citizen, by blood of the Creek Nation; that a female child was born to me on 18 day of June , 1901 , that said child has been named Winnie Davis Harris , and is now living.

Nellie Harris

Witnesses To Mark:
{

Subscribed and sworn to before me this 7 day of March , 1905.

Edw C Griesel
Notary Public.

BIRTH AFFIDAVIT.

DEPARTMENT OF THE INTERIOR.

COMMISSION TO THE FIVE CIVILIZED TRIBES.

IN RE APPLICATION FOR ENROLLMENT, as a citizen of the Creek Nation, of Winnie Davis Harris , born on the 18 day of June , 1901

Applications for Enrollment of Creek Newborn
Act of 1905   Volume I

Name of Father: Cheasquah Harris   a citizen of the   Creek   Nation.
Name of Mother: Nellie   "   a citizen of the   U.S.   Nation.

Postoffice   Muskogee, I.T.

(Child Present – ECG)

AFFIDAVIT OF ~~MOTHER~~. Father

UNITED STATES OF AMERICA, Indian Territory, ⎫
    Western   **DISTRICT.** ⎭

     I, Cheasquah Harris, on oath state that I am 32 years of age and a citizen by adoption   , of the   Creek   Nation; that I am the lawful wife of Nellie Harris, who is a citizen, ~~by~~ U.S. of the ----- Nation; that a Female child was born to me on 18 day of June , 1901 , that said child has been named Winnie Davis Harris , and is now living.

Cheasquah Harris

Witnesses To Mark:

{

Subscribed and sworn to before me this 7 day of March, 1905.

Edw C Griesel
Notary Public.

BA 313 B.

Muskogee, Indian Territory, May 13, 1905.

Sam Richard,
     Checotah, Indian Territory.

Dear Sir:

     There is on file with the Commission an affidavit executed by you relative to the birth of your minor child, Albert Richard.
The affidavit of the mother of said child must be furnished.

     There is herewith enclosed a blank form of birth affidavit, and in executing same care should be exercised to see that all blanks are properly filled, all names written in full and in the event that either of the persons signing the affidavit is unable to write, signature by mark must be attested by two witnesses. Each affidavit must be executed before a Notary Public and the notarial seal and signature of the officer must be attached to each separate affidavit.

Respectfully,

BC.   Chairman.

_____

DEPARTMENT OF THE INTERIOR,
COMMISSIONER TO THE FIVE CIVILIZED TRIBES.

REFER IN REPLY TO THE FOLLOWING:
N.C. 55.

Muskogee, Indian Territory, **August 4, 1905.**

Sam Richard,
    Checotah, Indian Territory.

Dear Sir:

You are hereby advised that on **July 28, 1905** , the Secretary of the Interior approved the enrollment of your minor child, **Albert Richard** , as a citizen by blood of the **Creek** Nation, and that the name of said child appears upon the roll of new born citizens of the **Creek** Nation as Number **35** .

The child is now entitled to an allotment, and application therefor should be made without delay at the Land Office for the Nation in which the prospective allotment is located.

An entire allotment for said child must be selected at the time of the original application.

Respectively,

Commissioner.

_____

AFFIDAVIT.

United States of America,)
Western District,   ) ss.
Indian Territory.   )

Demascus M. Pate being first duly sworn on his oath deposes and says: My name is Demascus M. Pate, my age is 39 years, my residence is Checotah, Western District of the Indian Territory; during the year 1903 and the 10 years prior to this year I was engaged at Checotah, I.T. in the practice of medicine. I was in the year 1903 the family physician of the family of Sam Richard, who resided about 4 miles south of the Town of Checotah, in the Creek Nation; Sam Richard is a Creek Indian, his wife is a white woman; her name is Lula Richard; I have known both Sam Richard and his wife for a number of years. On the 17th day of September 1903 there was born to said Sam Richard by Lula Richard, his wife, a male child; I attended the wife of Sam Richard for some time before the child was born, was present as family physician at the birth of this

Applications for Enrollment of Creek Newborn
Act of 1905   Volume I

child and attended the mother for some time after the birth of this child. I know the child; he has been given the name of Albert and is now about one and one half years old.

Demascus M. Pate

Subscribed and sworn to before me this 8th day of March, A.D. 1905.

Charles Buford

My commission expires July 3rd 1906.   Notary Public.

BIRTH AFFIDAVIT.

DEPARTMENT OF THE INTERIOR.

COMMISSION TO THE FIVE CIVILIZED TRIBES.

IN RE APPLICATION FOR ENROLLMENT, as a citizen of the Creek Nation, of Albert Richard, born on the 17 day of Sept , 1903

Name of Father: Sam Richards[sic]	a citizen of the	Creek	Nation.
Name of Mother: Lula "	a citizen of the	U.S.	Nation.

Postoffice   Checotah

AFFIDAVIT OF MOTHER.

UNITED STATES OF AMERICA, Indian Territory, ⎫
      Western   **DISTRICT.** ⎭

I, Sam Richard , on oath state that I am 57 years of age and a citizen by blood , of the Creek   Nation; that I am the lawful ~~wife~~ hus of Lula Richard   , who is a citizen, by ----- of the U.S.   Nation; that a male   child was born to me on 17   day of Sept , 1903 , that said child has been named Albert Richard   , and is now living.

Sam Richard

Witnesses To Mark:

    {

Subscribed and sworn to before me this 17 day of March , 1905.

Edw C Griesel
Notary Public.

257

BIRTH AFFIDAVIT.

DEPARTMENT OF THE INTERIOR.
COMMISSION TO THE FIVE CIVILIZED TRIBES.

IN RE APPLICATION FOR ENROLLMENT, as a citizen of the Creek Nation, of Albert Richard, born on the 17th day of September , 1903

Name of Father: Sam Richard   a citizen of the   Creek   Nation.
Name of Mother: Lula Richard   a citizen of the United States Nation.

Postoffice   Checotah, Ind. Terr.

AFFIDAVIT OF MOTHER.

UNITED STATES OF AMERICA, Indian Territory, ⎫
     Western   DISTRICT. ⎭

I, Lula Richard, on oath state that I am 23 years of age and a citizen by ----- of the United States ~~Nation~~; that I am the lawful wife of Sam Richard , who is a citizen, by blood of the Creek Nation; that a male child was born to me on 17th day of September , 1903 , that said child has been named Albert Richard , and was living March 4, 1905.

                         Lula Richard
Witnesses To Mark:

{

Subscribed and sworn to before me this 20th day of May , 1905.

My commission expires July 3rd 1906.   Charles Buford
                                Notary Public.

AFFIDAVIT OF ATTENDING PHYSICIAN OR MID-WIFE.

UNITED STATES OF AMERICA, Indian Territory, ⎫
     Western   DISTRICT. ⎭

I, D. M. Pate, a physician, on oath state that I attended on Mrs. Lula Richard , wife of Sam Richard on the 17th day of September , 1903 ; that there was born to her on said date a male child; that said child was living March 4, 1905, and is said to have been named Albert Richard.

                     D.M. Pate M.D.
Witnesses To Mark:

{

Subscribed and sworn to before me this 20th day of May, 1905.

Applications for Enrollment of Creek Newborn
Act of 1905   Volume I

My commission expires July 3rd 1906.   Charles Buford
Notary Public.

BA 96 B.

Muskogee, Indian Territory, May 15, 1905.

W. Pierce Hays,
Gibson Station, Indian Territory.

Dear Sir:

There is on file with the Commission an affidavit relative to the birth of your minor child, Sallie Willison Hays. The Commission requires the affidavits of the mother and midwife or physician in attendance at the birth of said child.

There is herewith enclosed a blank form of birth affidavit, and in executing same care should be exercised to see that all blanks are properly filled, all names written in full and in the event that either of the persons signing the affidavit is unable to write, signatures by mark must be attested by two witnesses. Each affidavit must be executed before a Notary Public and the notarial seal and signature of the officer must be attached to each separate affidavit.

Respectfully,

BC.

Chairman.

DEPARTMENT OF THE INTERIOR,
COMMISSIONER TO THE FIVE CIVILIZED TRIBES.

REFER IN REPLY TO THE FOLLOWING:
_____

N.C. 56.

Muskogee, Indian Territory, **August 4, 1905.**

Sallie H. Hays,
Care of W. Pierce Hays,
Gibson Station, Indian Territory.

Dear Madam:

You are hereby advised that on **July 28, 1905** , the Secretary of the Interior approved the enrollment of your minor child, **Sallie Willison Hays** , as a citizen by blood of the **Creek** Nation, and that the name of said child appears upon the roll of new born citizens of the **Creek** Nation as Number **36.**

Applications for Enrollment of Creek Newborn
Act of 1905 Volume I

The child is now entitled to an allotment, and application therefor should be made without delay at the Land Office for the Nation in which the prospective allotment is located.

An entire allotment for said child must be selected at the time of the original application.

Respectively,

Commissioner.

BIRTH AFFIDAVIT.

DEPARTMENT OF THE INTERIOR.
COMMISSION TO THE FIVE CIVILIZED TRIBES.

IN RE APPLICATION FOR ENROLLMENT, as a citizen of the Creek Nation, of Sallie Willison Hays , born on the 27 day of Sept , 1902

Name of Father: W. Pierce Hays	a citizen of the U.S.	Nation.
Name of Mother: Sally H. Hays	a citizen of the Creek	Nation.

Postoffice   Gibson Station, IT

AFFIDAVIT OF ~~MOTHER~~. father

UNITED STATES OF AMERICA, Indian Territory, ⎫
    Western   DISTRICT. ⎰

I, W. Pierce Hays , on oath state that I am 29 years of age and a citizen by -----
of the U.S. Nation; that I am the lawful ~~wife~~ hus of Sally H. Hays , who is a citizen, by blood   of the Creek Nation; that a girl   child was born to me on 27   day of Sept , 1902 , that said child has been named Sallie Willison Hays , and is now living.

W Pierce Hays

Witnesses To Mark:

{

Subscribed and sworn to before me this 7 day of March, 1905.

Edw C Griesel
Notary Public.

260

Applications for Enrollment of Creek Newborn
Act of 1905   Volume I

DEPARTMENT OF THE INTERIOR.
COMMISSION TO THE FIVE CIVILIZED TRIBES.

IN RE APPLICATION FOR ENROLLMENT, as a citizen of the Creek Nation, of Sallie Willison Hays , born on the 27 day of Sept , 1902

Name of Father: W. Pierce Hays	a citizen of the U.S.	Nation.
Name of Mother: Sally H. Hays	a citizen of the Creek	Nation.

Postoffice   Gibson Station

(Child Present)

AFFIDAVIT OF MOTHER.

UNITED STATES OF AMERICA, Indian Territory, ⎤
    Western   **DISTRICT.** ⎦

    I, Sally H. Hays , on oath state that I am 21 years of age and a citizen by blood , of the Creek   Nation; that I am the lawful wife of W. Pierce Hays   , who is a citizen, by ----- of the U.S.   Nation; that a female   child was born to me on 27   day of Sept. , 1902 , that said child has been named Sallie Willison Hays , and is now living.

Sallie H. Hays

Witnesses To Mark:

{

Subscribed and sworn to before me this 15 day of March, 1905.

(No Signature)
Notary Public.

AFFIDAVIT OF ATTENDING PHYSICIAN ~~OR MID-WIFE~~.

UNITED STATES OF AMERICA, Indian Territory, ⎤
    Western   **DISTRICT.** ⎦

    I, G.W. Jobe, M.D. , a Physician, on oath state that I attended on Mrs. Sally H. Hays , wife of W. Pierce Hays on the 27 day of Sept , 1902 ; that there was born to her on said date a female child; that said child is now living, and is said to have been named Sallie Willison Hays.

G.W. Jobe, M.D.

Witnesses To Mark:

{

Subscribed and sworn to before me this 15 day of March, 1905.

Edw C Griesel
Notary Public.

BIRTH AFFIDAVIT.
DEPARTMENT OF THE INTERIOR.
COMMISSION TO THE FIVE CIVILIZED TRIBES.

IN RE APPLICATION FOR ENROLLMENT, as a citizen of the Creek Nation, of John Wilcox ,
born on the 28 day of Dec , 1901

Name of Father: H.H. Wilcox	a citizen of the U.S.	Nation.
Name of Mother: Ella Wilcox	a citizen of the Creek	Nation.

Postoffice   Muskogee, I.T.

(Child Present)

AFFIDAVIT OF ~~MOTHER~~. father

UNITED STATES OF AMERICA, Indian Territory, ⎱
      Western   DISTRICT. ⎰

I, H. H. Wilcox , on oath state that I am 39   years of age and a citizen by ----- of
the   U.S. Nation; that I am the lawful ~~wife~~ husb of Ella Wilcox   , who is a citizen, by
blood   of the Creek   Nation; that a male   child was born to me on 28   day of Dec.,
1901 , that said child has been named John Wilcox   , and is now living.

H H Wilcox

Witnesses To Mark:

⎰

Subscribed and sworn to before me this 7 day of March, 1905.

Edw C Griesel
Notary Public.

BIRTH AFFIDAVIT.
DEPARTMENT OF THE INTERIOR.
COMMISSION TO THE FIVE CIVILIZED TRIBES.

IN RE APPLICATION FOR ENROLLMENT, as a citizen of the Creek Nation, of John Harvison
Wilcox , born on the 28 day of December , 1901

262

Applications for Enrollment of Creek Newborn
Act of 1905   Volume I

Name of Father: Hiram H. Wilcox   a citizen of the   U.S.   Nation.
Name of Mother: Ella Wilcox   a citizen of the   Creek   Nation.

Postoffice   Muskogee, Ind. Ter.

AFFIDAVIT OF MOTHER.

UNITED STATES OF AMERICA, Indian Territory, ⎫
    Western   DISTRICT. ⎰

I, Ella Wilcox , on oath state that I am twenty-eight years of age and a citizen by blood , of the Creek Nation; that I am the lawful wife of ~~John Har~~ Hiram H. Wilcox , who is a citizen, by *(blank)* of the U.S. Nation; that a male child was born to me on 28th day of December , 1901, that said child has been named John Harvison Wilcox , and was living March 4, 1905.

Ella Wilcox

Witnesses To Mark:

{

Subscribed and sworn to before me this 23rd day of May , 1905.

Cecil M. Haines
Notary Public.

AFFIDAVIT OF ATTENDING PHYSICIAN OR MID-WIFE.

UNITED STATES OF AMERICA, Indian Territory, ⎫
    Western   DISTRICT. ⎰

I, Isabel Cobb, M.D.   , a physician , on oath state that I attended on Mrs. Ella Wilcox , wife of Hiram H Wilcox on the 28th day of December , 1901 ; that there was born to her on said date a male child; that said child was living March 4, 1905, and is said to have been named John .

Isabel Cobb, M.D.

Witnesses To Mark:

{

Subscribed and sworn to before me this 22nd day of May, 1905.

My com. expires May 7, 1908   *(Name Illegible)*
Notary Public.

Applications for Enrollment of Creek Newborn
Act of 1905   Volume I

BIRTH AFFIDAVIT.

DEPARTMENT OF THE INTERIOR.
COMMISSION TO THE FIVE CIVILIZED TRIBES.

IN RE APPLICATION FOR ENROLLMENT, as a citizen of the Creek Nation, of John Wilcox , born on the 28 day of Dec , 1901

Name of Father: H H. Wilcox	a citizen of the U.S.	Nation.
Name of Mother: Ella Wilcox	a citizen of the Creek	Nation.

Postoffice   Muskogee, I.T.

(Child Present)

AFFIDAVIT OF MOTHER.

UNITED STATES OF AMERICA, Indian Territory, ⎫
      Western   DISTRICT. ⎬

I, Ella Wilcox , on oath state that I am 29 years of age and a citizen by   blood , of the Creek   Nation; that I am the lawful wife of H H. Wilcox   , who is a citizen, by -- --- of the U.S.   Nation; that a   male   child was born to me on   28 day of Dec , 1901, that said child has been named John Wilcox , and is now living.

Ella Wilcox

Witnesses To Mark:

{

Subscribed and sworn to before me this 7 day of March , 1905.

Edw C Griesel
Notary Public.

BA 97 B.

Muskogee, Indian Territory, May 15, 1905.

H. H. Wilcox,
     Muskogee, Indian Territory.

Dear Sir:

The Commission is in receipt of affidavits by yourself and wife relative to the birth of your minor child, John Wilcox. You are advised that the Commission requires the affidavit of the midwife or physician in attendance at the birth of said child.

264

Applications for Enrollment of Creek Newborn
Act of 1905 Volume I

There is herewith enclosed a blank form of birth affidavit, and in executing same care should be exercised to see that all blanks are properly filled, all names written in full and in the event that either of the persons signing the affidavit is unable to write, signature by mark must be attested by two witnesses. Each affidavit must be executed before a Notary Public and the notarial seal and signature of the officer must be attached to each separate affidavit.

Respectfully,

BC.   Chairman.

DEPARTMENT OF THE INTERIOR,
COMMISSIONER TO THE FIVE CIVILIZED TRIBES.

REFER IN REPLY TO THE FOLLOWING:
N.C. 57.

Muskogee, Indian Territory, **August 4, 1905.**

Ella Wilcox,
    Care of H. H. Wilcox,
        Muskogee, Indian Territory.

Dear Madam:

You are hereby advised that on **July 28, 1905** , the Secretary of the Interior approved the enrollment of your minor child, **John Wilcox** , as a citizen by blood of the **Creek** Nation, and that the name of said child appears upon the roll of new born citizens of the **Creek** Nation as Number **37** .

The child is now entitled to an allotment, and application therefor should be made without delay at the Land Office for the Nation in which the prospective allotment is located.

An entire allotment for said child must be selected at the time of the original application.

Respectively,

Commissioner.

DEPARTMENT OF THE INTERIOR,
COMMISSIONER TO THE FIVE CIVILIZED TRIBES.

REFER IN REPLY TO THE FOLLOWING:
N.C. 58.

Muskogee, Indian Territory, **August 4, 1905.**

Myrtle L. Webb,
    Care of George W. Webb,
        Muskogee, Indian Territory.

Applications for Enrollment of Creek Newborn
Act of 1905 Volume I

Dear Madam:

You are hereby advised that on **July 28, 1905** , the Secretary of the Interior approved the enrollment of your minor child, **Ethel Samantha Webb** , as a citizen by blood of the **Creek** Nation, and that the name of said child appears upon the roll of new born citizens of the **Creek** Nation as Number **38** .

The child is now entitled to an allotment, and application therefor should be made without delay at the Land Office for the Nation in which the prospective allotment is located.

An entire allotment for said child must be selected at the time of the original application.

Respectively,

Commissioner.

DEPARTMENT OF THE INTERIOR,	REFER IN REPLY TO THE FOLLOWING:
COMMISSIONER TO THE FIVE CIVILIZED TRIBES.	**N.C. 58.**

Muskogee, Indian Territory, **August 4, 1905.**

Myrtle L. Webb,
> **Care of George W. Webb,**
> **Muskogee, Indian Territory.**

Dear Madam:

You are hereby advised that on **July 28, 1905** , the Secretary of the Interior approved the enrollment of your minor child, **Ettie Jane Webb** , as a citizen by blood of the **Creek** Nation, and that the name of said child appears upon the roll of new born citizens of the **Creek** Nation as Number **39** .

The child is now entitled to an allotment, and application therefor should be made without delay at the Land Office for the Nation in which the prospective allotment is located.

An entire allotment for said child must be selected at the time of the original application.

Respectively,

Commissioner.

BIRTH AFFIDAVIT.

DEPARTMENT OF THE INTERIOR.
COMMISSION TO THE FIVE CIVILIZED TRIBES.

IN RE APPLICATION FOR ENROLLMENT, as a citizen of the Creek Nation, of Ettie Jane Webb, born on the 17 day of February , 1905

Name of Father: George W. Webb	a citizen of the U. S.	Nation.
Name of Mother: Myrtle Luella Webb	a citizen of the Creek	Nation.

Postoffice   Muskogee

Child Present ECG

AFFIDAVIT OF MOTHER.

UNITED STATES OF AMERICA, Indian Territory, ⎫
    Western   DISTRICT. ⎰

I, Myrtle Luella Webb , on oath state that I am 15 years of age and a citizen by blood   , of the Creek   Nation; that I am the lawful wife of George W. Webb   , who is a citizen, by *(blank)*   of the U. S.   Nation; that a female   child was born to me on 17 day of February   , 1905 , that said child has been named Ettie Jane Webb   , and is now living.

Myrtle L Webb

Witnesses To Mark:

{

Subscribed and sworn to before me this 9 day of March , 1905.

Edw C Griesel
Notary Public.

AFFIDAVIT OF ATTENDING PHYSICIAN OR MID-WIFE.

UNITED STATES OF AMERICA, Indian Territory, ⎫
    Western   DISTRICT. ⎰

I, Samantha Depew   , a midwife   , on oath state that I attended on Mrs. Myrtle Luella Webb   , wife of George W Webb   on the 17   day of February   , 1905 ; that there was born to her on said date a female child; that said child was living March 4, 1905, and is said to have been named Ettie Jane Webb .

Samantha Depew

Witnesses To Mark:

{

Subscribed and sworn to before me this 9 day of March, 1905.

Applications for Enrollment of Creek Newborn
Act of 1905 Volume I

Edw C Griesel
Notary Public.

_____

BIRTH AFFIDAVIT.

DEPARTMENT OF THE INTERIOR.
COMMISSION TO THE FIVE CIVILIZED TRIBES.

_____

IN RE APPLICATION FOR ENROLLMENT, as a citizen of the Creek Nation, of Etta Jane Webb, born on the 17 day of Feb , 1905

Name of Father: George W. Webb	a citizen of the U. S.	Nation.
Name of Mother: Myrtle L "	a citizen of the Creek	Nation.

Postoffice   Muskogee

_____

AFFIDAVIT OF ~~MOTHER.~~ father

UNITED STATES OF AMERICA, Indian Territory, ⎫
    Western   **DISTRICT.** ⎭

I, George W Webb , on oath state that I am 26 years of age and a citizen by ----- of the U.S.   Nation; that I am the lawful ~~wife~~ husb of Myrtle L Webb , who is a citizen, by blood   of the Creek   Nation; that a female   child was born to me on 17 day of Feb. 1905   , 1*(blank)* , that said child has been named Etta Jane Webb , and is now living.

George W. Webb

Witnesses To Mark:

⎰
⎱

Subscribed and sworn to before me this 7 day of March, 1905.

Edw C Griesel
Notary Public.

_____

BIRTH AFFIDAVIT.

DEPARTMENT OF THE INTERIOR.
COMMISSION TO THE FIVE CIVILIZED TRIBES.

_____

IN RE APPLICATION FOR ENROLLMENT, as a citizen of the Creek Nation, of Ethel Samantha Webb , born on the 15 day of August , 1903

Applications for Enrollment of Creek Newborn
Act of 1905   Volume I

Name of Father: George W. Webb   a citizen of the   U. S.   Nation.
Name of Mother: Myrtle Luella Webb   a citizen of the   Creek   Nation.

Postoffice   Muskogee

Child Present P.D.

AFFIDAVIT OF MOTHER.

UNITED STATES OF AMERICA, Indian Territory, ⎱
    Western   DISTRICT. ⎰

      I, Myrtle Luella Webb, on oath state that I am 15 years of age and a citizen by blood , of the Creek   Nation; that I am the lawful wife of George W. Webb , who is a citizen, by blood of the Creek   Nation; that a female   child was born to me on 15 day of August , 1903 , that said child has been named Ethel Samantha Webb   , and is now living.

Myrtle L Webb

Witnesses To Mark:
{

    Subscribed and sworn to before me this 9 day of March , 1905.

Edw C Griesel
Notary Public.

AFFIDAVIT OF ATTENDING PHYSICIAN OR MID-WIFE.

UNITED STATES OF AMERICA, Indian Territory, ⎱
    Western   DISTRICT. ⎰

      I, Samantha Depew   , a midwife   , on oath state that I attended on Mrs. Myrtle Luella Webb   , wife of George W. Webb on the 15   day of August , 1903 ; that there was born to her on said date a female child; that said child is now living, and is said to have been named Ethel Samantha Webb .

Samantha Depew

Witnesses To Mark:
{

    Subscribed and sworn to before me this 9 day of March, 1905.

Edw C Griesel
Notary Public.

269

BIRTH AFFIDAVIT.

DEPARTMENT OF THE INTERIOR.
COMMISSION TO THE FIVE CIVILIZED TRIBES.

IN RE APPLICATION FOR ENROLLMENT, as a citizen of the Creek Nation, of Ethel Samantha Webb, born on the 15 day of Aug , 1903

Name of Father: George W. Webb   a citizen of the   U. S.   Nation.
Name of Mother: Myrtle L   "   a citizen of the   Creek   Nation.

Postoffice   Muskogee, I.T.

AFFIDAVIT OF ~~MOTHER~~. father

UNITED STATES OF AMERICA, Indian Territory, ⎱
     Western   DISTRICT. ⎰

    I, George W. Webb , on oath state that I am 26 years of age and a citizen by ----- of the U.S.   Nation; that I am the lawful ~~wife~~ husb of Myrtle L Webb , who is a citizen, by blood   of the Creek   Nation; that a female   child was born to me on 15 day of Aug. , 1903 , that said child has been named Ethel Samantha Webb , and is now living.
                               George W. Webb

Witnesses To Mark:
    {

    Subscribed and sworn to before me this 7 day of March, 1905.

                        Edw C Griesel
                          Notary Public.

BA-101-B.

DEPARTMENT OF THE INTERIOR,
COMMISSION TO THE FIVE CIVILIZED TRIBES,
MUSKOGEE, INDIAN TERRITORY, APRIL 11, 1905.

-ooOoo-

    In the matter of the application for the enrollment of Clarence Jones, as a citizen by blood of the Creek Nation.

HARRISON JONES, being duly sworn, testified as follows:

Applications for Enrollment of Creek Newborn
Act of 1905   Volume I

EXAMINATION BY COMMISSION:

Q What is your name? A Harrison Jones.

Q How old are you? A About twenty-eight years of age.

Q What is your postoffice address? A Muskogee, I.T.

Q Are you a citizen of the Creek Nation? A No, citizen by marriage.

Q Have you a child named Clarence Jones? A Yes.

Q Is that child living? A No, he is dead.

Q What is the name of the mother of that child? A Lelia Hodge Jones.

Q Is she a citizen of the Creek Nation? A Yes.

Q Is she living? A Yes.

Q Where is she? She is right here North of town; I forget the name of the place.

Q Why did she not come up here with you? A She is in bed sick. She has been sick three years.

Q Where was Clarence Jones born? A On Fourth Street in this town.

Q Did he live there from the time of his birth until he died? A No, I moved on the next Street------Iola Street.

Q But you did not move very far from the place where he was born? A No, just on the next Street.

Q You always lived pretty close to the same neighborhood during his lifetime? A Yes.

Q The records of the Commission show that on March 7, 1905 an affidavit was executed by you relative to the birth of your child, Clarence Jones, whom you stated was born on the 30th day of July, 1904. At that time you stated that this child, Clarence Jones, was living. Do you remember that affidavit? A Yes.

Q Do you now positively swear that when you made out that affidavit your child was living? A Yes.

Q Were you not told at that time that the Commission required the affidavit of the mother of the child? A Yes.

Q Why have you not supplied that? A She has been sick and could not get here.

Q The Commission did not tell you to bring her in did it? A Yes.

You are now advised that the Commission desires the affidavit of the mother and mid-wife, and you are not told at this time to bring them in person, but you are required to bring in an affidavit executed by them.

Q What did Clarence die of? A He had Whooping Cough and the Bold Hives.

Q Did you try to do anything for the child? A Yes, I had Mrs. Lyons, an old mid-wife, doctor on it.

Q Didn't you have any other doctor? A No, he was young and we did not want to have a doctor; we had one with out other and it did no good so we thought that she could raise Clarence.

Q Is Mrs. Lyons colored? A She is part colored and Indian.

Q Did she live in the neighborhood? A Yes.

Q When did that child die? A Sunday.

Q Last Sunday? A Yes.

Q Did you see a notice of it in the paper? A I just went over there and got the burial outfit last Sunday morning. It died on Saturday night.

Q And you had a funeral on Sunday? A We buried him out here at Mr. Lieber's place.

Applications for Enrollment of Creek Newborn
Act of 1905 Volume I

Q Then he knew about it? A Yes, he was out there and surveyed off the lot.

Q From whom did you purchase that burial outfit? A On the East side of here.

Q Do you know the name of the place from where you purchased it? A Yes, I have the picture of the man and the name of the place at home.

Q Did you pay him for that burial outfit? a No, for I did not have the money I wished I had the money, but I didn't.

Q Was he the undertaker? A Yes.

Q How old was the child when he died? A He would have been nine months old.

Q Was he a healthy child or sickly? A He was a healthy looking child. His trouble was Whooping Caugh[sic] and Bold Hives.

Q Who was present when this child died? A Mars.[sic] Lyons and two more colored ladies.

Q What is their names? A Mrs. Hodge and Birdie something—I forget the other part.

Q Was there any white people present? A There was one white lady came there Sunday morning and stayed awhile but I forget her name.

Q Did you put anykind[sic] of a mark on Clarence Jones' grave? No, we did not put any head board to the grave; we forgot it.

Q Didn't you have any kind of a mark on the grave at all? A No.

Q Do you think that you could go there and find the grave and distinguish it from others? A Yes.

Q Can you read? A No, not to amount to anything; I wish I could.

Q Have you hear any talk about this new law for enrolling babies? A Yes.

Q Do you know the requirements of that new law---do you know when a child would have to die and be born in order to be entitled to enrollment? A No.

Q Do you know that if a child died before March 4, 1905, it could not get any land in the Creek Nation---do you know that? A I can not read and I took no paper; I wish I could read---I am might sorry I can't read, sir.

Zera Ellen Parrish, on her oath states that as stenographer to the Commission to the Five Civilized Tribes she reported the above case and that this is a full, true and correct transcript of her stenographic notes in same.

Zera Ellen Parrish

Subscribed and sworn to
before me this 25 day of
April, 1905.

Edward Merrick
Notary Public.

N.C. 59.

DEPARTMENT OF THE INTERIOR,
COMMISSIONER TO THE FIVE CIVILIZED TRIBES.
Muskogee, I. T., July 31, 1905.

In the matter of the application for the enrollment of Clarence Jones as a citizen by blood of the Creek Nation.

HARRISON JONES, being duly sworn, testified as follows:

272

Applications for Enrollment of Creek Newborn
Act of 1905   Volume I

BY COMMISSIONER:

Q What is your name? A Harrison Jones.

Q You have made application for the enrollment of your child, Clarence Jones have you? A Yes, sir.

Q What is the name of the mother of that child? A Lela Jones.

Q Was she enrolled as Lela Jones? A As Lela Hodge.

Q Is she living? A No, sir.

Q When did she die? A She died the 4th of June.

Q The 4th of this last June? A Yes, sir.

Q She never executed an affidavit about this child did she? A Yes, sir, she came up here.

Q Did she have a mid-wife in attendance upon her when Clarence was born? A Yes, sir, Rhoda Harnage was the mid-wife.

Q When did Clarence die? A The 9th of April, 1904.

Q Are you sure of that? A Yes, sir.

Q What year? A 1904.

Q Are you certain of that? A Yes, sir.

ROBERT TOOMER, being duly sworn, testified as follows:

BY COMMISSIONER:

Q What is your name? A Robert Toomer.

Q How old are you? A Fifty-four.

Q What is your post office address? A Muskogee.

Q Do you know Harrison Jones? A Yes, sir.

Q Is he a citizen of the Creek Nation? A He says he is not.

Q Do you know a child of his named Clarence? A I knew it when it was living.

Q What is the name of its mother? A Lela Jones, formerly Lela Hodge.

Q Were you present when that child was born? A No, sir.

Q Do you live near them? A No, sir, not in the same neighborhood.

Q How long after the birth of the child until you heard of it? A Lela Jones was a consumptive and was in advanced stages of consumption she wanted my legal services and I went to the house, in March, this year. I could give the exact date if I could get from Mr. Schumeyer the acknowledgement of a deed which was taken by him that day. I came by his office but he was not in. I am pretty certain it was in March. I was there and saw the child and it was living on that date. It appeared to be a child about a year old or less.

Q How did you know that was his child? A I know the mother and the child was nursing with her at that time.

Q Do you know its name? A Clarence.

Q Did they tell you at the time? A Yes, sir. They were talking about getting another child enrolled that was dead and wanted me to look after it and from inquiry I found that the child had died too soon.

Q You found that out the time you were at their house? A Yes, sir, they told me about circumstances. That is all I know about it. I know that this child, Clarence, was living in March, this year. I could give you the exact date if it is required. The father and mother and this child was all that was there.

273

Applications for Enrollment of Creek Newborn
Act of 1905   Volume I

RHODA HARNAGE, being duly sworn, testified as follows:

BY COMMISSIONER:
Q What is your name? A Rhoda Harnage.
Q How old are you? A I don't know. My mother was 130 before she died.

Witness appears to be about sixty years of age.

Q What is your post office addres[sic]? A Muskogee.
Q Do you live here in town? A Yes, sir.
Q Do you know Harrison Jones? A Yes, sir. He came after me to wait on his wife.
Q Came after you to wait on his wife when a baby was born? A Yes, sir.
Q What is the name of that Baby? A I don't know they had not named it.
Q Is that child living? A No, sir.
Q When did they come after you? A In August.
Q What year? A I don't know.
Q Last year? A Yes, sir.
Q Did you ever see that child any more after that? A Yes, sir, I seen it after that.
Q When did it die? A I aint[sic] been home but three days.
Q You don't know when it died? A No, sir.
Q You were there when it was born? A Yes, sir, the Doctor who was there had to go off.
Q What doctor was that? A Doctor Simms.

I, D. C. Skaggs, on oath state that the above and foregoing is a full and true transcript of my stenographic notes as taken in said cause on said date.

D. C. Skaggs

Subscribed and sworn to before me this 1st day of August, 1905.

Edw C Griesel
Notary Public.

NC-59.

DEPARTMENT OF THE INTERIOR,
COMMISSIONER TO THE FIVE CIVILIZED TRIBES.
MUSKOGEE, INDIAN TERRITORY, NOV 14, 1905.

In the matter of the application for the enrollment of Clarence Jones as a citizen by blood of the Creek Nation.

Masterson Peyton appears as attorney for applicant.
Harrison Jones being first duly sworn testifies as follows:

274

Applications for Enrollment of Creek Newborn
Act of 1905 Volume I

EXAMINATION BY COMMISSIONER:

Qh[sic] What is your name? A Harrison Jones.
Q What is your age? A Twenty-eight.
Q What is your post office address? A Muskogee.
Q Did you have a child named Clarence Jones? A Yes, sir.
Q Is Clarence living? A No, sir.
Q When was he born? A He was born July 24 or 25th.
Q What year? A 1904.
Q How old was he when he died? A He was just about nine months old.
Q When did he die? A He died April 9, 1905.
Q You are sure he died in April this year, 1905? A Yes, sir.
Q Died last spring? A Yes, sir.
Q It wasn't 1904? A No, sir.
Q If the stenographer in your testimony got it down 1904 of was a mistake was it? A Yes, sir.

EXAMINATION BY ATTORNEY PEYTON:

Q You have there a certificate from the undertaker? A Yes, sir.
Q The Muskogee Furniture Company? A Yes, sir.
Q State whether that company attended at the funeral of your child and furnished a coffin? A Yes, sir.
Q Do you want to file that certificate? A Yes, sir.

The paper referred to is marked exhibit "A" and filed with the record in this case.

Witness excused.

Chas. T. Difendafer being first duly sworn states that the above and foregoing is a full, true and correct transcript of his stenographic notes taken in said cause on said date.

Chas T. Difendafer

Subscribed and sworn to before me this 15th day of November 1905.

Henry G. Hains
Notary Public.

Applications for Enrollment of Creek Newborn
Act of 1905   Volume I

BIRTH AFFIDAVIT.

DEPARTMENT OF THE INTERIOR.
COMMISSION TO THE FIVE CIVILIZED TRIBES.

IN RE APPLICATION FOR ENROLLMENT, as a citizen of the Creek Nation, of Clarence Jones, born on the 30 day of July , 1904

Name of Father: Harrison Jones	a citizen of the	U.S.	Nation.
Name of Mother: Lela "	a citizen of the	Creek	Nation.

Postoffice   Muskogee

AFFIDAVIT OF ~~MOTHER~~. father

UNITED STATES OF AMERICA, Indian Territory, ⎫
    Western   DISTRICT. ⎭

I, Harrison Jones , on oath state that I am 28 years of age and a citizen by ----- of the U. S.   Nation; that I am the lawful ~~wife~~ hus of Lela Jones , who is a citizen, by blood of the Creek   Nation; that a boy   child was born to me on 30 day of July   , 1904 , that said child has been named Clarence Jones , and is now living.

His
Harrison x Jones
mark

Witnesses To Mark:
  { J McDermott
  { ECGriesel

Subscribed and sworn to before me this 7 day of March, 1905.

Edw C Griesel
Notary Public.

BIRTH AFFIDAVIT.

DEPARTMENT OF THE INTERIOR.
COMMISSION TO THE FIVE CIVILIZED TRIBES.

IN RE APPLICATION FOR ENROLLMENT, as a citizen of the Creek Nation, of Clarence Jones, born on the (blank) day of (blank) , 1(blank)

Name of Father: Harrison Jones	a citizen of the	U.S.	Nation.
Name of Mother: Lela Jones (Deceased)	a citizen of the	Creek	Nation.

276

Applications for Enrollment of Creek Newborn
Act of 1905 Volume I

Postoffice   Muskogee, I.T.

UNITED STATES OF AMERICA, Indian Territory, ⎫
    Western   DISTRICT. ⎰

I, Rhoda Harnidge   , a midwife , on oath state that I attended on Mrs. Lela Jones, wife of Harrison Jones on the ------ day of July or August   , 1904 ; that there was born to her on said date a male child; that said child ~~was living March 4, 1905, and~~ is said to have been named Clarence Jones is now dead   her

Rhoda   x Harnidge

Witnesses To Mark: mark
  { H.G. Hains
  { Irwin Donovan

Subscribed and sworn to before me this 31 day of July, 1905.

Henry G Hains
Notary Public.

DEPARTMENT OF THE INTERIOR.
COMMISSION TO THE FIVE CIVILIZED TRIBES.

IN RE APPLICATION FOR ENROLLMENT, as a citizen of the Creek Nation, of Clarence Jones, born on the 24 day of July , 1904

Name of Father: Harrison Jones   a citizen of the   U.S.   Nation.
Name of Mother: Lela Hodge Jones   a citizen of the   Creek   Nation.

Postoffice   Muskogee

UNITED STATES OF AMERICA, Indian Territory, ⎫
    Western   DISTRICT. ⎰

I, Lela Hodge Jones , on oath state that I am 22 years of age and a citizen by blood , of the Creek   Nation; that I am the lawful wife of Harrison Jones   , who is a citizen, by ----- of the U.S. Nation; that a male   child was born to me on 24   day of July   , 1904 , that said child has been named Clarence Jones   , and ~~is now living~~. died April 9- 1905

Lela Jones

277

Applications for Enrollment of Creek Newborn
Act of 1905   Volume I

Witnesses To Mark:

{

Subscribed and sworn to before me this 11 day of April , 1905.

(Name Illegible)
Notary Public.

BIRTH AFFIDAVIT.

DEPARTMENT OF THE INTERIOR.
COMMISSION TO THE FIVE CIVILIZED TRIBES.

IN RE APPLICATION FOR ENROLLMENT, as a citizen of the Creek Nation, of Jency Jones ,
born on the 13 day of Aug , 1902

Name of Father: Harrison Jones	a citizen of the U. S.	Nation.
Name of Mother: Lela "	a citizen of the Creek	Nation.

Postoffice   Muskogee I.T.

AFFIDAVIT OF ~~MOTHER~~. father

UNITED STATES OF AMERICA, Indian Territory, ⎱
      Western   **DISTRICT.** ⎰

I, Harrison Jones , on oath state that I am 28 years of age and a citizen by ----- of
the U. S.   Nation; that I am the lawful ~~wife~~ husb of Lela Jones , who is a citizen, by
blood of the Creek   Nation; that a male   child was born to me on 13 day of Aug ,
1902 , that said child has been named Jency Jones , and ~~is now living~~. died Aug 20-1903

His
Harrison x Jones
mark

Witnesses To Mark:
{ J McDermott
  ECGriesel

Subscribed and sworn to before me this 7 day of March, 1905.

Edw C Griesel
Notary Public.

278

Applications for Enrollment of Creek Newborn
Act of 1905   Volume I

NC 59   JLD

DEPARTMENT OF THE INTERIOR,
COMMISSIONER TO THE FIVE CIVILIZED TRIBES.

. . . .

In the matter of the application for the enrollment of Jency Jones, deceased, as a citizen by blood of the Creek Nation.

. . . .

STATEMENT AND ORDER.

The record in this case shows that on March 7, 1905, application was made, in affidavit form, for the enrollment of Jency Jones, deceased, as a citizen by blood of the Creek Nation, under the provisions of the act of Congress approved March 3, 1905.

It appears that the affidavit filed in this matter that said Jency Jones, deceased, was born August 13, 1902, and died August 20, 1903.

The act of Congress approved March 3, 1905, (33 Stats., 1048), provides:

"That the Commission to the Five Civilized Tribes is authorized for sixty days after the date of the approval of this act to receive and consider applications for enrollment, of children, born subsequent to May twenty-fifth, nineteen hundred and one, and prior to March fourth, nineteen hundred and five, and living on said latter date, to citizens of the Creek tribe of Indians whose enrollment has been approved by the Secretary of the Interior prior to the approval of this act; and to enroll and make allotments to such children."

It is, therefore, ordered that the application for the enrollment of Jency Jones as a citizen by blood of the Creek Nation be, and the same is, hereby dismissed.

(Name Illegible) Commissioner.

Muskogee, Indian Territory.
    JAN 4 1907

————————

NC-59

Muskogee, Indian Territory, July 25, 1905.

Harrison Jones,
    Muskogee, Indian Territory.

Dear Sir:

In the matter of the application for the enrollment of your son Clarence Jones as a citizen by blood of the Creek Nation you are advised that it will be necessary, before the rights of said child can be finally determined, for you to furnish this office with the affidavit of the mother of the child and the attending physician or midwife at his birth as to the date of his birth and as to whether or not he was living on March 4, 1905.

Applications for Enrollment of Creek Newborn
Act of 1905   Volume I

For that purpose this is inclosed[sic] herewith a blank form for proof of birth which you are requested to have properly filled out, executed and return to this office. You should give this matter your immediate attention.

Respectfully,

Commissioner.

B C
Env.

NC 60.

Muskogee, Indian Territory, May 17, 1905.

George W. McGuire,
        Checotah, Indian Territory.

Dear Sir:

In the matter of the application for the enrollment of your minor child, Marcus Wilson McGuire, as a citizen of the Creek Nation, you are advised that the Commission requires the affidavit of the midwife or physician in attendance at the birth of said child.

There is herewith enclosed a blank form of birth affidavit, and in executing same care should be exercised to see that all blanks are properly filled, all names written in full and in the event that either of the persons signing the affidavit is unable to write, signature by mark must be attested by two witnesses. Each affidavit must be executed before a Notary Public and the notarial seal and signature of the officer must be attached to each separate affidavit.

Respectfully,

BC

Chairman.

DEPARTMENT OF THE INTERIOR,
COMMISSIONER TO THE FIVE CIVILIZED TRIBES.

REFER IN REPLY TO THE FOLLOWING:
_____
N.C. 60.

Muskogee, Indian Territory, **August 4, 1905.**

Sophia McGuire,
        Care of George W. McGuire,
                Checotah, Indian Territory.
Dear Sir:

Applications for Enrollment of Creek Newborn
Act of 1905   Volume I

You are hereby advised that on **July 28, 1905** , the Secretary of the Interior approved the enrollment of your minor child, **Marcus Wilson McGuire** , as a citizen by blood of the **Creek** Nation, and that the name of said child appears upon the roll of new born citizens of the **Creek** Nation as Number **40** .

The child is now entitled to an allotment, and application therefor should be made without delay at the Land Office for the Nation in which the prospective allotment is located.

An entire allotment for said child must be selected at the time of the original application.

Respectively,

Commissioner.

BIRTH AFFIDAVIT.

DEPARTMENT OF THE INTERIOR.
COMMISSION TO THE FIVE CIVILIZED TRIBES.

IN RE APPLICATION FOR ENROLLMENT, as a citizen of the Creek Nation, of Marcus Wilson McGuire , born on the 9th day of August , 1903

Name of Father: Geo W McGuire   a citizen of the   *(blank)*   Nation.
Name of Mother: Sophia McGuire (nee Johnson) a citizen of the   Creek   Nation.
Postoffice   Checotah Ind Ty

AFFIDAVIT OF ATTENDING PHYSICIAN OR MID-WIFE.

UNITED STATES OF AMERICA, Indian Territory, ⎫   N C 60
      Western   **DISTRICT.** ⎭

I, Geo. W. McGuire , a Physician   , on oath state that I attended on Mrs. Sophia McGuire , wife of Geo W McGuire on the 9th day of August   , 1903 ; that there was born to her on said date a male child; that said child was living March 4, 1905, and is said to have been named Marcus Wilson McGuire .

Geo. W. McGuire, MD.

Witnesses To Mark:

{

Subscribed and sworn to before me this 18th day of May, 1905.

JB Morrow
Notary Public.

Applications for Enrollment of Creek Newborn
Act of 1905 Volume I

BIRTH AFFIDAVIT.

DEPARTMENT OF THE INTERIOR.
COMMISSION TO THE FIVE CIVILIZED TRIBES.

———————

IN RE APPLICATION FOR ENROLLMENT, as a citizen of the Creek Nation, of Marcus Wilson McGuire , born on the 9 day of Aug , 1903

Name of Father: Geo W McGuire	a citizen of the U. S.	Nation.
Name of Mother: Sophia "	a citizen of the Creek	Nation.

Postoffice   Checotah I.T.

(Child Present) HGH

———————

AFFIDAVIT OF MOTHER.

UNITED STATES OF AMERICA, Indian Territory, ⎤
    Western   DISTRICT. ⎦

I, Sophia McGuire , on oath state that I am 29 years of age and a citizen by blood, of the Creek Nation; that I am the lawful wife of George McGuire , who is a citizen, by ------- of the U. S. Nation; that a male child was born to me on 9 day of Aug , 1903 , that said child has been named Marcus Wilson McGuire , and is now living.

Sophia McGuire

Witnesses To Mark:

{

Subscribed and sworn to before me this 7 day of March , 1905.

Edw C Griesel
Notary Public.

———————

BIRTH AFFIDAVIT.

DEPARTMENT OF THE INTERIOR.
COMMISSION TO THE FIVE CIVILIZED TRIBES.

———————

IN RE APPLICATION FOR ENROLLMENT, as a citizen of the Creek Nation, of Marcus Wilson McGuire , born on the 9 day of Aug , 1903

Name of Father: George W. McGuire	a citizen of the U. S.	Nation.
Name of Mother: Sophia "	a citizen of the Creek	Nation.

Postoffice   Checotah

———————

Child Present ECG

AFFIDAVIT OF ~~MOTHER~~. father

UNITED STATES OF AMERICA, Indian Territory, ⎱
   Western   DISTRICT. ⎰

    I, George McGuire , on oath state that I am 39   years of age and a citizen by -----
of the U. S.   Nation; that I am the lawful ~~wife~~ hus of Sophia McGuire , who is a
citizen, by blood of the Creek Nation; that a male   child was born to me on 9 day of
Aug, 1903 , that said child has been named Marcus Wilson McGuire , and is now living.

                     Geo. W. McGuire

Witnesses To Mark:
⎰

  Subscribed and sworn to before me this 7 day of March, 1905.

                     Edw C Griesel
                     Notary Public.

                     NC 61.
       Muskogee, Indian Territory, May 17, 1905.

Conny Murphy,
    Coweta, Indian Territory.

Dear Sir:

    In the matter of the application for the enrollment of your minor child, Blanche
Murphy, as a citizen of the Creek Nation, you are advised that the Commission requires
the affidavits of the mother and midwife or physician in attendance at its birth.

    There are[sic] herewith enclosed a blank form of birth affidavit, and in executing
same care should be exercised to see that all blanks are properly filled, all names written
in full and in the event that the persons signing the affidavits are unable to write,
signatures by mark must be attested by two witnesses. Each affidavit must be executed
before a Notary Public and the notarial seal and signature of the officer must be attached
to each separate affidavit.
                Respectfully,

BC.   Chairman.

NC.61.

Muskogee, Indian Territory, July 14, 1905.

Commissioner to the Five Civilized Tribes,
    Cherokee Enrollment Division,
        Muskogee, Indian Territory.

Gentlemen:

March 7, 1905, application was made to the Commission to the Five Civilized Tribes for the enrollment of John Murphy, born December 9, 1904, and Blanche Murphy, born May 23, 1903, as citizens by blood of the Creek Nation. It is stated in said application that the father of said children is Conny Murphy, a citizen of the Creek Nation, and that the mother is Sarah R. Murphy, a citizen of the Cherokee Nation.

You are requested to inform the Creek Enrollment Division as to whether application has been made for the enrollment of said children as citizens of the Cherokee Nation, and if so, what disposition has been made of the same.

Respectfully,

Commissioner.

REFER IN REPLY TO THE FOLLOWING:

DEPARTMENT OF THE INTERIOR,
COMMISSIONER TO THE FIVE CIVILIZED TRIBES.

Muskogee, Indian Territory, July 18, 1905.

Chief Clerk,
    Creek Enrollment Division,
        Muskogee, Indian Territory.

Dear Sir:

Replying to your letter of July 14, 1905, (NC. 61) asking to be advised whether or not any application has ever been made for the enrollment, as citizens of the Cherokee Nation, of John Murphy and Blanche Murphy, children of Conny Murphy, a citizen of the Creek Nation, and Sarah R. Murphy, a citizen of the Cherokee Nation, you are advised that from an examination of the records of the Cherokee Enrollment Division it does not appear that any application has ever been made for the enrollment of said children as citizens of that Nation.

Respectfully,

GHL   *(Name Illegible)* Commissioner.

Applications for Enrollment of Creek Newborn
Act of 1905   Volume I

DEPARTMENT OF THE INTERIOR.
COMMISSION TO THE FIVE CIVILIZED TRIBES.

IN RE APPLICATION FOR ENROLLMENT, as a citizen of the Creek Nation, of Blanche Murphy , born on the 23 day of May , 1903

Name of Father: Conny Murphy	a citizen of the	Creek	Nation.
Name of Mother: Sarah R Murphy	a citizen of the	Cherokee	Nation.

Postoffice   Coweta

AFFIDAVIT OF MOTHER.

UNITED STATES OF AMERICA, Indian Territory, ⎤
  Western   DISTRICT. ⎦

I, Sarah R. Murphy , on oath state that I am forty years of age and a citizen by blood , of the Cherokee Nation; that I am the lawful wife of Conny Murphy , who is a citizen, blood of the Creek Nation; that a female child was born to me on 23 day of May , 1903 , that said child has been named Blanche Murphy , and was living March 4, 1905.

Sarah R. Murphy

Witnesses To Mark:

{

Subscribed and sworn to before me this 20th day of May , 1905.

My commission expires   R W Lumpkin
      Jany 13th 1909   Notary Public.

AFFIDAVIT OF ATTENDING PHYSICIAN OR MID-WIFE.

UNITED STATES OF AMERICA, Indian Territory, ⎤
      Western   DISTRICT. ⎦

I, A E Carder   , a physician   , on oath state that I attended on Mrs. Conny Murphy , wife of Conny Murphy on the 23rd day of May , 1903 ; that there was born to her on said date a female child; that said child was living March 4, 1905, and is said to have been named Blanche Murphy .

A E Carder, MD

Witnesses To Mark:

{

285

Applications for Enrollment of Creek Newborn
Act of 1905   Volume I

Subscribed and sworn to before me this 28 day of March, 1905.

My commission expires   R W Lumpkin
    Jany 13th 1909   Notary Public.

BIRTH AFFIDAVIT.

DEPARTMENT OF THE INTERIOR.
COMMISSION TO THE FIVE CIVILIZED TRIBES.

IN RE APPLICATION FOR ENROLLMENT, as a citizen of the Creek Nation, of Blanche
Murphy , born on the 23 day of May , 1903

Name of Father: Conny Murphy   a citizen of the   Creek   Nation.
Name of Mother: Sarah   "   a citizen of the   Cherokee   Nation.

                        Postoffice   Coweta, I.T.

Child Brought – Mar 14- 05 – Gr
 Mother or *(illegible)* also present.
                    AFFIDAVIT OF ~~MOTHER~~. father

UNITED STATES OF AMERICA, Indian Territory, ⎤
        Western   DISTRICT. ⎦

I, Conny Murphy , on oath state that I am 42 years of age and a citizen by blood ,
of the Creek   Nation; that I am the lawful ~~wife~~ hus of Sarah Murphy , who is a citizen,
by blood   of the Cherokee   Nation; that a girl   child was born to me on 23 day of
May , 1903 , that said child has been named Blanche Murphy   , and is now living.

                                Conny Murphy
Witnesses To Mark:
  {
        Subscribed and sworn to before me this 7 day of March, 1905.

                                Edw C Griesel
                                   Notary Public.

286

BIRTH AFFIDAVIT.

DEPARTMENT OF THE INTERIOR.
COMMISSION TO THE FIVE CIVILIZED TRIBES.

IN RE APPLICATION FOR ENROLLMENT, as a citizen of the Creek Nation, of John Murphy ,
born on the 9 day of Dec , 1904

Name of Father: Conny Murphy	a citizen of the Creek Nation.
Name of Mother: Sarah "	a citizen of the Cherokee Nation.

Postoffice   Coweta, I.T.

AFFIDAVIT OF ~~MOTHER~~. father

UNITED STATES OF AMERICA, Indian Territory, ⎫
      Western   DISTRICT. ⎬
                                  ⎭

I, Conny Murphy , on oath state that I am 42 years of age and a citizen by blood ,
of the Creek   Nation; that I am the lawful ~~wife~~ hus of Sarah Murphy , who is a citizen,
by blood   of the Cherokee   Nation; that a male   child was born to me on 9 day of
Dec , 1904 , that said child has been named John Murphy   , and ~~is now living~~. died one
day after birth.

Conny Murphy

Witnesses To Mark:
  {

Subscribed and sworn to before me this 7 day of March, 1905.

Edw C Griesel
Notary Public.

NC 61   JLD
DEPARTMENT OF THE INTERIOR,
COMMISSIONER TO THE FIVE CIVILIZED TRIBES.
. . . .

In the matter of the application for the enrollment of John Murphy, deceased, as a
citizen by blood of the Creek Nation.
. . . .

STATEMENT AND ORDER.

The record in this case shows that on March 7, 1905, application was made, in

287

affidavit form, for the enrollment of John Murphy, deceased, as a citizen by blood of the Creek Nation, under the provisions of the act of Congress approved March 3, 1905.

It appears that the affidavit filed in this matter that said John Murphy, deceased, was born December 9, 1904, and died December 10, 1904.

The act of Congress approved March 3, 1905, (33 Stats., 1048), provides:

"That the Commission to the Five Civilized Tribes is authorized for sixty days after the date of the approval of this act to receive and consider applications for enrollment, of children, born subsequent to May twenty-fifth, nineteen hundred and one, and prior to March fourth, nineteen hundred and five, and living on said latter date, to citizens of the Creek tribe of Indians whose enrollment has been approved by the Secretary of the Interior prior to the approval of this act; and to enroll and make allotments to such children."

It is, therefore, ordered that the application for the enrollment of John Murphy. deceased, as a citizen by blood of the Creek Nation, be, and the same is, hereby dismissed.

(Name Illegible) Commissioner.

Muskogee, Indian Territory.
JAN 4 1907

DEPARTMENT OF THE INTERIOR,
COMMISSIONER TO THE FIVE CIVILIZED TRIBES.

REFER IN REPLY TO THE FOLLOWING:
_____
N.C. 62.

Muskogee, Indian Territory, August 4, 1905.

Florence A. Hart,
Care of Edward Hart,
Bald Hill, Indian Territory.

Dear Madam:

You are hereby advised that on **July 28, 1905** , the Secretary of the Interior approved the enrollment of your minor child, **Florence E. Hart** , as a citizen by blood of the **Creek** Nation, and that the name of said child appears upon the roll of new born citizens of the **Creek** Nation as Number **41** .

The child is now entitled to an allotment, and application therefor should be made without delay at the Land Office for the Nation in which the prospective allotment is located.

An entire allotment for said child must be selected at the time of the original application.

Respectively,

Commissioner.

BIRTH AFFIDAVIT.

DEPARTMENT OF THE INTERIOR.
COMMISSION TO THE FIVE CIVILIZED TRIBES.

IN RE APPLICATION FOR ENROLLMENT, as a citizen of the Creek Nation, of Florence E. Hart , born on the 25 day of Aug, 1904

Name of Father:	Edward Hart	a citizen of the U. S. Nation.
Name of Mother:	Florence Agnes "	a citizen of the Creek Nation.

Postoffice   Bald Hill

Child present

AFFIDAVIT OF MOTHER.

UNITED STATES OF AMERICA, Indian Territory, ⎫
    Western   DISTRICT. ⎭

     I, Florence Agnes Hart , on oath state that I am 24 years of age and a citizen by blood, of the Creek Nation; that I am the lawful wife of Edward Hart , who is a citizen, by ----- of the U. S. Nation; that a Female   child was born to me on 25 day of Aug. , 1904 , that said child has been named Florence E. Hart , and is now living.

                                  Florence A. Hart.

Witnesses To Mark:

    {

     Subscribed and sworn to before me this 14 day of March , 1905.

                              Edw C Griesel
                                  Notary Public.

AFFIDAVIT OF ATTENDING PHYSICIAN OR MID-WIFE.

UNITED STATES OF AMERICA, Indian Territory, ⎫
    Western   DISTRICT. ⎭

     I, Lizzie A Miller , a midwife   , on oath state that I attended on Mrs. Florence Agnes Hart , wife of Edward Hart on the 25   day of Aug , 1904 ; that there was born to her on said date a female child; that said child is now living, and is said to have been named Florence E. Hart .

                            Lizzie A Miller

Witnesses To Mark:

    {

Subscribed and sworn to before me this 14 day of March, 1905.

Edw C Griesel
Notary Public.

DEPARTMENT OF THE INTERIOR,	REFER IN REPLY TO THE FOLLOWING:
COMMISSIONER TO THE FIVE CIVILIZED TRIBES.	**N.C. 1.**

Muskogee, Indian Territory, **August 4, 1905.**

Martha Wilson,
Care of Jason Wilson,
Naudack, Indian Territory.

Dear Madam:

You are hereby advised that on **July 28, 1905** , the Secretary of the Interior approved the enrollment of your minor child, **Ida Wilson** , as a citizen by blood of the **Creek** Nation, and that the name of said child appears upon the roll of new born citizens of the **Creek** Nation as Number **42** .

The child is now entitled to an allotment, and application therefor should be made without delay at the Land Office for the Nation in which the prospective allotment is located.

An entire allotment for said child must be selected at the time of the original application.

Respectively,

Commissioner.

DEPARTMENT OF THE INTERIOR,	REFER IN REPLY TO THE FOLLOWING:
COMMISSIONER TO THE FIVE CIVILIZED TRIBES.	**N.C. 1.**

Muskogee, Indian Territory, **August 4, 1905.**

Martha Wilson,
Care of Jason Wilson,
Naudack, Indian Territory.

Dear Madam:

Applications for Enrollment of Creek Newborn
Act of 1905   Volume I

You are hereby advised that on **July 28, 1905** , the Secretary of the Interior approved the enrollment of your minor child, **Otto Wilson** , as a citizen by blood of the **Creek** Nation, and that the name of said child appears upon the roll of new born citizens of the **Creek** Nation as Number **43** .

The child is now entitled to an allotment, and application therefor should be made without delay at the Land Office for the Nation in which the prospective allotment is located.

An entire allotment for said child must be selected at the time of the original application.

Respectively,

Tams Bixby

Commissioner.

BIRTH AFFIDAVIT.

DEPARTMENT OF THE INTERIOR.
COMMISSION TO THE FIVE CIVILIZED TRIBES.

IN RE APPLICATION FOR ENROLLMENT, as a citizen of the Creek Nation, of Ida Wilson , born on the 17 day of Jan , 1902

Name of Father:	Jason Wilson	a citizen of the	U. S.	Nation.
Name of Mother:	Martha "	a citizen of the	Creek	Nation.

Postoffice   Naudack

(Child Present)

AFFIDAVIT OF MOTHER.

UNITED STATES OF AMERICA, Indian Territory, ⎞
         Western   DISTRICT. ⎠

I, Martha Wilson , on oath state that I am 27 years of age and a citizen by blood , of the Creek   Nation; that I am the lawful wife of Jason Wilson , who is a citizen, by ---- - of the U.S.   Nation; that a female   child was born to me on 17 day of Jan. , 1902 , that said child has been named Ida Wilson , and was living March 4, 1905.

Martha Wilson

Witnesses To Mark:
{

Subscribed and sworn to before me this 14 day of March , 1905.

291

Applications for Enrollment of Creek Newborn
Act of 1905   Volume I

Edw C Griesel
Notary Public.

DEPARTMENT OF THE INTERIOR.
COMMISSION TO THE FIVE CIVILIZED TRIBES.

IN RE APPLICATION FOR ENROLLMENT, as a citizen of the Creek Nation, of Otto Wilson , born on the 13 day of Feb , 1905

		non		
Name of Father:	Jason Wilson	a citizen of the	*(blank)*	Nation.
Name of Mother:	Martha Wilson	a citizen of the	Creek	Nation.

Postoffice   Naudack

AFFIDAVIT OF MOTHER.

UNITED STATES OF AMERICA, Indian Territory, ⎫
    Western   DISTRICT. ⎰

I, Martha Wilson , on oath state that I am 27 years of age and a citizen by Blood ,
                                                                            non
of the Creek   Nation; that I am the lawful wife of Jason Wilson , who is a citizen, by
(blank) of the *(blank)* Nation; that a male   child was born to me on 13 day of Feb ,
1902[sic] , that said child has been named Otto Wilson , and was living March 4, 1905.

Martha Wilson

Witnesses To Mark:
{

Subscribed and sworn to before me this 22 day of Mar , 1905.

My commission expires 11/17/06.   W.H. Harrison
                                                        Notary Public.

AFFIDAVIT OF ATTENDING PHYSICIAN OR MID-WIFE.

UNITED STATES OF AMERICA, Indian Territory, ⎫
    Western   DISTRICT. ⎰

I, Sintha Middleton   , a midwife , on oath state that I attended on Mrs. Martha Wilson , wife of Jason Wilson on the 13   day of Feb , 1905 ; that there was born to her on said date a male child; that said child was living March 4, 1905, and is said to have been named Otto Wilson .

292

Applications for Enrollment of Creek Newborn
Act of 1905   Volume I

Sintha Middleton

Witnesses To Mark:

{

Subscribed and sworn to before me this 22 day of Mar, 1905.

My commission expires 11/17/06.

W.H. Harrison
Notary Public.

BIRTH AFFIDAVIT.

DEPARTMENT OF THE INTERIOR.
COMMISSION TO THE FIVE CIVILIZED TRIBES.

IN RE APPLICATION FOR ENROLLMENT, as a citizen of the Creek Nation, of Otto Wilson , born on the 13 day of Feb , 1905

Name of Father:	Jason Wilson	a citizen of the	U S	Nation.
Name of Mother:	Martha "	a citizen of the	Creek	Nation.

Postoffice   Naudack

(Child Present)

AFFIDAVIT OF MOTHER.

UNITED STATES OF AMERICA, Indian Territory, ⎫
      Western   **DISTRICT.** ⎭

I, Martha Wilson , on oath state that I am 27 years of age and a citizen by blood , of the Creek   Nation; that I am the lawful wife of Jason Wilson , who is a citizen, by ----- of the U. S.   Nation; that a male   child was born to me on 13 day of Feb ,1905 , that said child has been named Otto Wilson , and was living March 4, 1905.

Martha Wilson

Witnesses To Mark:

{

Subscribed and sworn to before me this 14 day of March , 1905.

Edw C Griesel
Notary Public.

BIRTH AFFIDAVIT.

DEPARTMENT OF THE INTERIOR.
COMMISSION TO THE FIVE CIVILIZED TRIBES.

—————

IN RE APPLICATION FOR ENROLLMENT, as a citizen of the Creek Nation, of Ida Wilson , born on the 17 day of Jan , 1902

		non		
Name of Father:	Jason Wilson	a citizen of the	*(blank)*	Nation.
Name of Mother:	Martha Wilson	a citizen of the	Creek	Nation.

Postoffice   Naudack I.T.

—————

AFFIDAVIT OF MOTHER.

UNITED STATES OF AMERICA, Indian Territory,
    Western   **DISTRICT.**

I, Martha Wilson , on oath state that I am 27 years of age and a citizen by Blood ,
                                          non
of the Creek   Nation; that I am the lawful wife of Jason Wilson , who is a citizen, by *(blank)* of the *(blank)* Nation; that a female   child was born to me on 17 day of Jan., 1902 , that said child has been named Ida Wilson , and was living March 4, 1905.

                                          Martha Wilson
Witnesses To Mark:
{

Subscribed and sworn to before me this 22 day of Mar , 1905.

My commission expires 11/17/06.   W.H. Harrison
                                                Notary Public.

—————

AFFIDAVIT OF ATTENDING PHYSICIAN OR MID-WIFE.

UNITED STATES OF AMERICA, Indian Territory,
    Western   **DISTRICT.**

I, Emeline Lucus , a midwife , on oath state that I attended on Mrs. Martha Wilson , wife of Jason Wilson on the 17 day of Jan , 1902 ; that there was born to her on said date a Female child; that said child was living March 4, 1905, and is said to have been named Ida Wilson .   her
                                          Emeline x Lucus
Witnesses To Mark: mark
{ Henry Hill
  Alfred Nelson

294

Subscribed and sworn to before me this 22 day of Mar, 1905.

My commission expires 11/17/06.   W. H. Harrison
                                                              Notary Public.

NC 64.

Muskogee, Indian Territory, May 17, 1905.

Joseph McCalvey,
        Eufaula, Indian Territory.

Dear Sir:

In the matter of the application for the enrollment of your minor child, Joseph Hiram McCalvey, as a citizen of the Creek Nation, you are advised that the Commission requires your affidavit as to the birth of said child.

There is herewith enclosed a blank form of birth affidavit, and in executing same care should be exercised to see that all blanks are properly filled, all names written in full and in the event that you are unable to write, signature by mark must be attested by two witnesses. Each affidavit must be executed before a Notary Public and the notarial seal and signature of the officer must be attached to each separate affidavit.

Respectfully,

BC.   Chairman.

DEPARTMENT OF THE INTERIOR,
COMMISSIONER TO THE FIVE CIVILIZED TRIBES.

NC 64.

Muskogee, Indian Territory, July 7, 1905.

Ella McCalvey,
        Eufaula, Indian Territory.

Dear Madam:

In the matter of the application for the enrollment of your minor child, Joseph Hiram McCalvey, as a citizen of the Creek Nation, you are advised that proof of your marriage to Joseph McCalvey the father of said child, is required.

Applications for Enrollment of Creek Newborn
Act of 1905   Volume I

A certified copy of your marriage license or other satisfactory proof of your marriage to said Joseph McCalvey, should be forwarded to the office of the Commissioner to the Five Civilized Tribes at once.

Respectfully,

(Name Illegible) Commissioner.

C.E. Foley President   No. 5902   J.T. Crane Cashier
Phillip Brown Vice President   E.G. Bailey Asst. Cashier

Copy.   The First National Bank

Eufaula, Ind. Ter. July 15th, 1905

Dawes Commission,
        Muskogee, I.T.

Dear Sirs:

In reply to your letter of July 7th, I herewith hand you a certified copy of marriage certificate or license.

Yours respectfully,

Mrs. Ella McCalvey

Muskogee, Indian Territory, July 19, 1905.

Mrs. Ella McCalvey,
        Eufaula, Indian Territory.

Dear Madam:

Receipt is acknowledged of your letter of July 15, 1905, enclosing a certified copy of your marriage license.

Respectfully,

Commissioner.

NC-64.

Muskogee, Indian Territory, July 25, 1905.

Ella McCalvey,
Eufaula, Indian Territory.

Dear Madam:

In the matter of the application for the enrollment of your son Joseph Hiram McCalvey as a citizen by blood of the Creek Nation it appears from the evidence on file that the father of said child is Joseph McCalvey and from your affidavit that you are the lawful wife of said Joseph McCalvey.

Under date of July 7, 1905 this office requester you to furnish, in the matter of the enrollment of your said son, evidence of your marriage to Joseph McCalvey the father of said child. In response to said request you filed with this office what purports to be a certified copy of the marriage license and certificate between "Mr. James McCalvery" and Miss Ella Mannon.

You are requested to furnish this office with an affidavit showing whether or not the "Mr. James McCalvery" mentioned in said marriage license and certificate and your husband Joseph McCalvey are one and the same person and also setting forth whether or not the Miss Ella Mannon mentioned in said marriage license and certificate is identical with yourself.

Please give this matter prompt attention.

Respectfully,

Commissioner.

Certificate of Record.

United States of America,   x
Indian Territory,   x
Northern District. x
xxxxxxxxxxxxxxxxxxxxxxxxxxxxxx

I/, Charles A. Davidson, Clerk of the United States Court in the Northern District, Indian Territory, do hereby certify that the instrument hereto attached was filed for record in my office the 2nd day of May, 1902, at 8 A.M. and duly recorded in Book M, Marriage Record, Page 420.

Witness my hand and seal of said court at Kuskogee[sic], in said Territory., this 2nd day of May, A. D., 1902.

Chas. A. Davidson, Clerk.

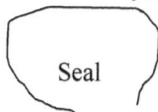

Seal

Eufaula, IT

July 15 – 1905.

United States of America,
Indian Territory,
Western District.

I. E. G. Bailey, a Notary Public, duly commissioned, within and for said Territory and District, do hereby certify that the attached copy of Marriage License issued to Mr. James McCalvery, April 21st, 1902, is a true and correct copy of said license.

E.G. Bailey
Notary Public.

My Commission Expires Sept. 22, 1906.

Copy of

MARRIAGE LICENSE.

United States of America,   x
Indian Territory,   x
Northern District.   x
xxxxxxxxxxxxxxxxxxxxxxxxxxxxxx

To any person authorized by law to solemnice[sic] marriage-Greeting:

You are hereby commanded to solemenize[sic] the rite and publish the Banns of Matrimony between Mr. James McCalvey of Eufaula, in the Indian Territory, aged 22 years, and Miss Ella Mannon of Eufaula, in the Indian Territory, aged 22 years, according to law, and do you officially sign and return this license to the parties therein named.

Witness my hand and official seal at Muskogee, Indian Territory, this 21st day of Aprilm[sic] A. D. 1902.

Chas. A. Davidson,

Clerk of the U. S. C o u r t.

By Wm. R. Shackelford, Deputy.

Applications for Enrollment of Creek Newborn
Act of 1905   Volume I

xxxxxxxxxxxxxxxxxxxxxxxxxxxxxxxxxxxxxxxxxxxxxxxxxxxxxxxxxxxxxxxxxx

Certificate of Marriage.

United States of America,   x
    Indian Territory,   x
       Northern District. x
xxxxxxxxxxxxxxxxxxxxxxxxxxxxxx

I, Chas. S. Leonard, a Minister of the Gospel, do hereby certify that on the 24th day of April, A. D., 1902, I did duly and according to law a commanded in the foregoing License, solemenize[sic] the Rite and publish the Banns of Matrimony between the parties therein named. Witness my hand this 24th day of April, A. D., 1902.

My credentials are recorded in the office of the Clerk of the United States Court, Indian Territory, Northern District, Book C., Page 75.

Chas. S. Leonard,
A Minister of the Gospel.

xxxxxxxxxxxxxxxxxxxxxxxxxxxxxxxxxxxxxxxxxxxxxxxxxxxxxxxxxxxxxxx

———————

United States of America ⎤
    Indian Territory   ⎬ SS.
Western Judicial Dist. ⎦

On this the 29th day of July A.D. 1905, before me, a Notary Public within and for the Western District of the Ind. Tery. personally appeared Ella McCalvey of Eufaula, Ind. Tery. who being first sworn according to law, states, that the "Mr. James McCalvery" mentioned in the certified copy of the marriage license and certificate of her marriage to her late husband, now on file with The Dawes Commission, is one and the same with her late husband Joseph McCalvey, now deceased. That her own name before her marriage to said Joseph McCalvey was Mannon, and the name "Miss Ella Mannon" mentioned in said marriage license and certificate and her present name are one and the same person.

Mrs. Ella McCalvey

Sworn to and subscribed before me, this July 29th, 1905.

My Commission Expires Sept. 22, 1906   EG Bailey

———————

299

Applications for Enrollment of Creek Newborn
Act of 1905   Volume I

BIRTH AFFIDAVIT.

DEPARTMENT OF THE INTERIOR.
COMMISSION TO THE FIVE CIVILIZED TRIBES.

IN RE APPLICATION FOR ENROLLMENT, as a citizen of the Creek Nation, of Joseph Hiram McCalvey , born on the 20 day of Jan. , 1903

Name of Father:	Joseph McCalvey	a citizen of the	Creek	Nation.
Name of Mother:	Ella McCalvey	a citizen of the	U.S.	Nation.

Postoffice   Eufaula I.T.

AFFIDAVIT OF MOTHER.

UNITED STATES OF AMERICA, Indian Territory, ⎫
    Western   DISTRICT. ⎭

I, Ella McCalvey , on oath state that I am 24 years of age and a citizen by ----- , of the U. S. Nation; that I am the lawful wife of Joseph McCalvey , who is a citizen, by blood of the Creek Nation; that a boy child was born to me on 20 day of January , 1903 , that said child has been named Joseph Hiram McCalvey , and is now living.

Mrs. Ella McCalvey

Witnesses To Mark:

{

Subscribed and sworn to before me this 7 day of March , 1905.

Edw C Griesel
Notary Public.

BIRTH AFFIDAVIT.

DEPARTMENT OF THE INTERIOR.
COMMISSION TO THE FIVE CIVILIZED TRIBES.

IN RE APPLICATION FOR ENROLLMENT, as a citizen of the Creek Nation, of Joseph Hiram McCalvey , born on the 20th day of Jan , 1903

Name of Father:	Joseph McCalvey	a citizen of the	Creek	Nation.
Name of Mother:	Ella McCalvey	a citizen of the	----------	Nation.

Postoffice   Eufaula I.T.

300

Applications for Enrollment of Creek Newborn
Act of 1905   Volume I

Uncle

AFFIDAVIT OF <s>MOTHER</s>.

UNITED STATES OF AMERICA, Indian Territory, ⎫
    Western   DISTRICT. ⎭

I, Everett McCalvey , on oath state that I am 27 years of age and a citizen by
uncle
birth , of the Creek Nation; that I am the <s>lawful wife of</s> of Joseph Hiram McCalvey ,
<s>who is a citizen, by birth of the Creek</s> Nation; that a male child was born to me on
20th day of Jan , 1903 , that said child has been named Joseph Hiram McCalvey , and is
now living.

Everett McCalvey

Witnesses To Mark:
{

Subscribed and sworn to before me this 10th day of March , 1905.

My Commission   EG Bailey
     expires Sept 22, 1906.   Notary Public.

AFFIDAVIT OF ATTENDING PHYSICIAN OR MID-WIFE.

UNITED STATES OF AMERICA, Indian Territory, ⎫
    Western   DISTRICT. ⎭

I, W. A. Tollison , a physician , on oath state that I attended on Mrs. Ella
McCalvey , wife of Joseph McCalvey on the 20th day of January , 1903 ; that there
was born to her on said date a male child; that said child is now living, and is said to have
been named Joseph Hiram McCalvey .

W.A. Tollison

Witnesses To Mark:
{

Subscribed and sworn to before me this 8th day of March, 1905.

My Commission   EG Bailey
     expires Sept 22, 1906.   Notary Public.

Applications for Enrollment of Creek Newborn
Act of 1905   Volume I

BIRTH AFFIDAVIT.

DEPARTMENT OF THE INTERIOR.
COMMISSION TO THE FIVE CIVILIZED TRIBES.

IN RE APPLICATION FOR ENROLLMENT, as a citizen of the Creek Nation, of Joseph Hiram McCalvey , born on the 20th day of Jan , 1903

Name of Father: Joseph McCalvey   a citizen of the   Creek   Nation.
Name of Mother: Ella McCalvey   a citizen of the   *(blank)*   Nation.

Postoffice   Eufaula I.T.

AFFIDAVIT OF MOTHER.

UNITED STATES OF AMERICA, Indian Territory, ⎱
       Western   DISTRICT. ⎰

I,   Ella McCalvey , on oath state that I am 25 years of age and a citizen by adoption , of the Creek   Nation; that I am the lawful wife of Joseph McCalvey , who is a citizen, by birth of the Creek   Nation; that a male   child was born to me on 20th day of Jan , 1903 , that said child has been named Joseph Hiram McCalvey , and was living March 4, 1905.

Mrs. Ella McCalvey

Witnesses To Mark:

{

Subscribed and sworn to before me this 20th day of May , 1905.

EG Bailey
Notary Public.

AFFIDAVIT OF ATTENDING PHYSICIAN OR MID-WIFE.

UNITED STATES OF AMERICA, Indian Territory, ⎱
       Western   DISTRICT. ⎰

I, W. A. Tollison , a physician , on oath state that I attended on Mrs. Ella McCalvey , wife of Joseph McCalvey on the 20th   day of Jan , 1903 ; that there was born to her on said date a male child; that said child was living March 4, 1905, and is said to have been named Joseph Hiram McCalvey .

W.A. Tollison

Witnesses To Mark:

{

302

Subscribed and sworn to before me this 20 day of May, 1905.

EG Bailey
Notary Public.

NC 65.

Muskogee, Indian Territory, May 17, 1905.

Unah Daniel,
Okmulgee, Indian Territory.

Dear Sir:

In the matter of the application for the enrollment of your minor child, Unah Daniel, Jr. , as a citizen of the Creek Nation, you are advised that the Commission requires the affidavits of the mother of said child and of the midwife or physician in attendance at its birth.

There is herewith enclosed a blank form of birth affidavit, and in executing same care should be exercised to see that all blanks are properly filled, all names written in full and in the event that either of the persons signing the affidavit is unable to write, signatures by mark must be attested by two witnesses. Each affidavit must be executed before a Notary Public and the notarial seal and signature of the officer must be attached to each separate affidavit.

Respectfully,

BC.   Chairman.

	REFER IN REPLY TO THE FOLLOWING:
DEPARTMENT OF THE INTERIOR,	
COMMISSIONER TO THE FIVE CIVILIZED TRIBES.	**N.C. 65.**

Muskogee, Indian Territory, **August 4, 1905.**

Unah Daniel, Sr.
Okmulgee, Indian Territory.

Dear Sir:

You are hereby advised that on **July 28, 1905** , the Secretary of the Interior approved the enrollment of your minor child, **Unah Daniel, Jr.** , as a citizen by blood of the **Creek** Nation, and that the name of said child appears upon the roll of new born citizens of the **Creek** Nation as Number **44** .

Applications for Enrollment of Creek Newborn
Act of 1905   Volume I

The child is now entitled to an allotment, and application therefor should be made without delay at the Land Office for the Nation in which the prospective allotment is located.

An entire allotment for said child must be selected at the time of the original application.

Respectively,

Commissioner.

BIRTH AFFIDAVIT.

DEPARTMENT OF THE INTERIOR.
COMMISSION TO THE FIVE CIVILIZED TRIBES.

IN RE APPLICATION FOR ENROLLMENT, as a citizen of the Creek Nation, of Unah Daniel Jr., born on the 10 day of Nov. , 1903

Name of Father: Unah Daniel   a citizen of the   Creek   Nation.
Name of Mother: Mary   "   a citizen of the   "   Nation.

Postoffice   Okmulgee, I.T.

AFFIDAVIT OF ~~MOTHER.~~ father

UNITED STATES OF AMERICA, Indian Territory, ⎤
     Western   DISTRICT. ⎦

I, Unah Daniel , on oath state that I am 33 years of age and a citizen by blood , of the Creek   Nation; that I am the lawful ~~wife~~ hus of Mary Daniel   , who is a citizen, by blood of the Creek   Nation; that a boy   child was born to me on 10 day of Nov. , 1903 , that said child has been named Unah Daniel Jr. , and is now living.

Unah Daniel

Witnesses To Mark:
{

Subscribed and sworn to before me this 8" day of March, 1905.

Edw C Griesel
Notary Public.

304

Department of the Interior,
COMMISSION TO THE FIVE CIVILIZED TRIBES.

IN RE *Application for Enrollment,* as a citizen of the Creek Nation, of
Uneh[sic] Daniel Jr , born on the 10 day of Nov. , 1903

Name of Father: Unah Daniel   a citizen of the   Creek   Nation.
Name of Mother: Mary Daniel   a citizen of the   Creek   Nation.

Postoffice,   Okmulgee, Ind. Ter.

AFFIDAVIT OF MOTHER.

UNITED STATES OF AMERICA,
    Indian Territory.
Western   District.

I, Mary Daniel , on oath state that I am 33 years of age and a citizen by
blood , of the Creek Nation; that I am the lawful wife of Unah Daniel , who is a
citizen, by blood of the Creek Nation; that a male child was born to me on 10
day of Nov , 1903 , that said child has been named Uneh Daniel , and is now
living.   her
                                    Mary Daniel   x
WITNESSES TO MARK: mark
    { JHW Dorsey
     E E Riley

Subscribed and sworn to before me this 16 *day of* March, *1905.*

My Commission expire   E E Riley
              June 18-1908   *NOTARY PUBLIC.*

AFFIDAVIT OF ATTENDING PHYSICIAN OR MID-WIFE.

UNITED STATES OF AMERICA,
    Indian Territory.
Western   District.

I, Nicey Scott , a midwife   , on oath state that I attended on Mrs. Mary
Daniels[sic] , wife of Unah Daniels[sic] on the 10   day of Nov   , 1903 ; that there
was born to her on said date a male child; that said child is now living, and is said
to have been named Unah Daniel Jr.

Applications for Enrollment of Creek Newborn
Act of 1905   Volume I

her
Nancy[sic] Scott x
mark

WITNESSES TO MARK:
{ JHW Dorsey
{ E E Riley

Subscribed and sworn to before me this 15 *day of* March, 1905.

My Commission Expires June 18-1908   E E Riley
NOTARY PUBLIC.

BIRTH AFFIDAVIT.

DEPARTMENT OF THE INTERIOR.
COMMISSION TO THE FIVE CIVILIZED TRIBES.

IN RE APPLICATION FOR ENROLLMENT, as a citizen of the Creek Nation, of Unah Daniel
Jr., born on the 10 day of November , 1903

Name of Father: Unah Daniel	a citizen of the	Creek	Nation.
Name of Mother: Mary "	a citizen of the	"	Nation.

Postoffice   Okmulgee, I.T.

AFFIDAVIT OF MOTHER.

UNITED STATES OF AMERICA, Indian Territory, ⎤
      Western   DISTRICT. ⎦

I, Mary Daniels , on oath state that I am 33 years of age and a citizen by Birth   ,
of the Creek   Nation; that I am the lawful wife of Unah Daniels   , who is a citizen, by
Birth of the Creek   Nation; that a male   child was born to me on 10 day of November,
1903 , that said child has been named Unah Daniels   , and was living March 4, 1905.

her
Mary Daniels x
mark

Witnesses To Mark:
{ John Schad
{ James D Cooper

Subscribed and sworn to before me this 19 day of June , 1905.

My commission expires   E E Riley
June 18-1908   Notary Public.

306

Applications for Enrollment of Creek Newborn
Act of 1905 Volume I

AFFIDAVIT OF ATTENDING PHYSICIAN OR MID-WIFE.

UNITED STATES OF AMERICA, Indian Territory,
Western   DISTRICT. }

I, Mattie Scott , a midwife , on oath state that I attended on Mrs. Mary Daniels , wife of Una[sic] Daniels on the 10 day of November , 1903 ; that there was born to her on said date a male child; that said child was living March 4, 1905, and is said to have been named Una Daniels.

her

Mattie Scott   x

Witnesses To Mark: mark
{ John Schad
{ John D Cooper

Subscribed and sworn to before me this 19 day of June, 1905.

My commission expires   E E Riley
June 18-1908   Notary Public.

NC 66.

Muskogee, Indian Territory, May 17, 1905.

John C. Smock,
      Eufaula, Indian Territory.

Dear Sir:

In the matter of the application for the enrollment of your minor child, Annie Louise Smock , as a citizen of the Creek Nation, you are advised that the Commission requires the affidavit of the midwife or physician in attendance at the birth of said child.

There is herewith enclosed a blank form of birth affidavit, and in executing same care should be exercised to see that all blanks are properly filled, all names written in full and in the event that either of the persons signing the affidavit is unable to write, signature by mark must be attested by two witnesses. Each affidavit must be executed before a Notary Public and the notarial seal and signature of the officer must be attached to each separate affidavit.

Respectfully,

BC.   Chairman.

Applications for Enrollment of Creek Newborn
Act of 1905 Volume I

DEPARTMENT OF THE INTERIOR,
COMMISSIONER TO THE FIVE CIVILIZED TRIBES.

REFER IN REPLY TO THE FOLLOWING:

N.C. 66.

Muskogee, Indian Territory, **August 4, 1905.**

Eloise Grayson Smock,
    Care of John C. Smock,
      Eufaula, Indian Territory.

Dear Madam:

You are hereby advised that on **July 28, 1905** , the Secretary of the Interior approved the enrollment of your minor child, **Anna Louise Smock** , as a citizen by blood of the **Creek** Nation, and that the name of said child appears upon the roll of new born citizens of the **Creek** Nation as Number **45** .

The child is now entitled to an allotment, and application therefor should be made without delay at the Land Office for the Nation in which the prospective allotment is located.

An entire allotment for said child must be selected at the time of the original application.

Respectively,

Commissioner.

COMMISSION TO THE FIVE CIVILIZED TRIBES.

In Re Application for enrollment of Anna Louise Smock, born Sept. 30th, 1901. Name of Father John C. Smock. Name of Mother Eloise Grayson Smock a citizen by Blood of the Creek Nation. Post Office Eufaula, I.T.

AFFIDAVIT OF MOTHER

Indian Territory
Western District.

Eloise Grayson Smock, being duly sworn, on oath states that I am 25 years of age, a citizen by Blood of the Creek Nation; that I am the lawful wife of John C. Smock; that on the 30th day of September 1901 there was born unto me a female child; that the said child is now living and has been named Anna Louise Smock.

Eloise Grayson Smock

Subscribed and sworn to before me this 7th day of March 1905.

B A Jennings
Notary Public.

308

Applications for Enrollment of Creek Newborn
Act of 1905   Volume I

AFFIDAVIT OF GEORGE W. GRAYSON AND ANNIE GRAYSON.

Indian Territory
Western District.

Grayson

We George W. Grayson and Annie ^ being duly sworn on oath state that we are
the parents of Eloise Grayson Smock; that we were present on 30th day of September

her

1901; that there was born unto ^ on said date a female child; that the said child is now
living and has been named Anna Louise Smock.

George W. Grayson
Annie Grayson

Subscribed and sworn yo[sic] before me this 7th day of March, 1905.

B A Jennings
Notary Public.

BIRTH AFFIDAVIT.

DEPARTMENT OF THE INTERIOR.
COMMISSION TO THE FIVE CIVILIZED TRIBES.

IN RE APPLICATION FOR ENROLLMENT, as a citizen of the Creek Nation, of Anna Louise
Smock , born on the 30th day of September , 1901

Name of Father: John C. Smock   a citizen of the   *(blank)*   Nation.
Name of Mother: Eloise Grayson Smock   a citizen of the   Creek   Nation.

Postoffice   Eufaula, I. T.

AFFIDAVIT OF MOTHER.

UNITED STATES OF AMERICA, Indian Territory, ⎫
       Western   DISTRICT. ⎰

I, Eloise Grayson Smock , on oath state that I am 25 years of age and a citizen by
Birth   , of the Creek   Nation; that I am the lawful wife of John C. Smock   , who is a
citizen, by Marriage of the Creek   Nation; that a Female child was born to me on
30th   day of September , 1901 , that said child has been named Anna Louise Smock,
and was living March 4, 1905.

Eloise Grayson Smock

Witnesses To Mark:
{

309

Subscribed and sworn to before me this   18th day of May , 1905.

(Illegible) Washington
Notary Public.

AFFIDAVIT OF ATTENDING PHYSICIAN OR MID-WIFE.

UNITED STATES OF AMERICA, Indian Territory,
    Western   **DISTRICT.**

I, R. M. Counterman , a Physician , on oath state that I attended on Mrs. Eloise Grayson Smock , wife of John C. Smock on the 30th day of September , 1901 ; that there was born to her on said date a Female child; that said child was living March 4, 1905, and is said to have been named Anna Louise Smock .

R.M. Counterman MD

Witnesses To Mark:

{

Subscribed and sworn to before me this 18th day of May, 1905.

(Illegible) Washington
Notary Public.

COMMISSION TO THE FIVE CIVILIZED TRIBES.

In Re application for enrollment of Dorothy Smock, born Dec. 18th, 1903. Name of Father John C. Smock. Name of Mother Eloise Grayson Smock a citizen by blood of the Creek Nation. Post Office Eufaula, I.T.

AFFIDAVIT OF MOTHER

Indian Territory
Western District.

Eloise Grayson Smock, being duly sworn, on oath states that I am 25 years of age, a citizen by blood of the Creek Nation; that I am the lawful wife of John C. Smock; that on the 18th day of December 1903 there was born unto me a female child; that the said child died Jan. 5th, 1904; that said child was named Dorothy Smock.

Eloise Grayson Smock

Subscribed and sworn to before me this 7th day of March 1905.

B A Jennings
Notary Public.

310

AFFIDAVIT OF GEORGE W. GRAYSON AND ANNIE GRAYSON.

Indian Territory
Western District.

We George W. Grayson and Annie Grayson being duly sworn on oath state that we are the parents of Eloise Grayson Smock; that we were present on 18 day of December 1903; that there was born unto said Eloise Grayson Smock a female child; that said child died Jan. 5th 1904; that said child was named Dorothy Smock.

George W. Grayson
Annie Grayson

Subscribed and sworn to before me this 7th day of March, 1905.

B A Jennings
Notary Public.

NC 66   JLD

DEPARTMENT OF THE INTERIOR,
COMMISSIONER TO THE FIVE CIVILIZED TRIBES.

. . . .

In the matter of the application for the enrollment of Dorothy Smock, deceased, as a citizen by blood of the Creek Nation.

. . . .

STATEMENT AND ORDER.

The record in this case shows that on March 8, 1905, application was made, in affidavit form, for the enrollment of Dorothy Smock, deceased, as a citizen by blood of the Creek Nation, under the provisions of the act of Congress approved March 3, 1905.

It appears that the affidavit filed in this matter that said Dorothy Smock, deceased, was born December 18, 1903, and died January 5, 1904.

The act of Congress approved March 3, 1905, (33 Stats., 1048), provides:

"That the Commission to the Five Civilized Tribes is authorized for sixty days after the date of the approval of this act to receive and consider applications for enrollment, of children, born subsequent to May twenty-fifth, nineteen hundred and one, and prior to March fourth, nineteen hundred and five, and living on said latter date, to citizens of the Creek tribe of Indians whose enrollment has been approved by the Secretary of the Interior prior to the approval of this act; and to enroll and make allotments to such children."

It is, therefore, ordered that the application for the enrollment of said Dorothy Smock, as a citizen by blood of the Creek Nation be, and the same is, hereby dismissed.

(Name Illegible) Commissioner.

Muskogee, Indian Territory.
JAN 4 1907

NC 67

Muskogee, Indian Territory, May 17, 1905.

Charles Aubrey,
Sapulpa, Indian Territory.

Dear Sir:

In the matter of the application for the enrollment of your minor child, Alice Hiawatha Aubrey, as a citizen of the Creek Nation, you are advised that the Commission requires the affidavit of the midwife or physician in attendance at the birth of said child.

There is herewith enclosed a blank form of birth affidavit, and in executing same care should be exercised to see that all blanks are properly filled, all names written in full and in the event that either of the persons signing the affidavit is unable to write, signature by mark must be attested by two witnesses. Each affidavit must be executed before a Notary Public and the notarial seal and signature of the officer must be attached to each separate affidavit.

Respectfully,

BC.   Chairman.

DEPARTMENT OF THE INTERIOR,
COMMISSIONER TO THE FIVE CIVILIZED TRIBES.

REFER IN REPLY TO THE FOLLOWING:
_____
N.C. 67.

Muskogee, Indian Territory, **August 4, 1905.**

Millie Aubrey,
       Are[sic] of Charles Aubrey,
              Sapulpa, Indian Territory.

Dear Sir:

You are hereby advised that on **July 28, 1905** , the Secretary of the Interior approved the enrollment of your minor child, **Alice Hiawatha Aubrey** , as a citizen by blood of the **Creek** Nation, and that the name of said child appears upon the roll of new born citizens of the **Creek** Nation as Number **46** .

312

Applications for Enrollment of Creek Newborn
Act of 1905   Volume I

The child is now entitled to an allotment, and application therefor should be made without delay at the Land Office for the Nation in which the prospective allotment is located.

An entire allotment for said child must be selected at the time of the original application.

Respectively,

Commissioner.

BIRTH AFFIDAVIT.

DEPARTMENT OF THE INTERIOR.
COMMISSION TO THE FIVE CIVILIZED TRIBES.

IN RE APPLICATION FOR ENROLLMENT, as a citizen of the Creek Nation, of Alice Hiawatha Aubrey , born on the 6 day of June , 1903

Name of Father: Charles Aubrey   a citizen of the   U. S.   Nation.
Name of Mother: Millie   "   a citizen of the   Creek   Nation.

Postoffice   Sapulpa, I.T.

(Child present)HGH

AFFIDAVIT OF MOTHER.

UNITED STATES OF AMERICA, Indian Territory, ⎫
     Western   **DISTRICT.** ⎭

I, Millie Aubrey , on oath state that I am 35 years of age and a citizen by blood , of the Creek   Nation; that I am the lawful wife of Charles Aubrey   , who is a citizen, by ----- of the U. S.   Nation; that a girl   child was born to me on 6 day of June , 1903 , that said child has been named Alice Hiawatha Aubrey   , and is now living.

Millie Aubrey

Witnesses To Mark:

{

Subscribed and sworn to before me this 8" day of March , 1905.

Edw C Griesel
Notary Public.

313

Applications for Enrollment of Creek Newborn
Act of 1905   Volume I

BIRTH AFFIDAVIT.

DEPARTMENT OF THE INTERIOR.
COMMISSION TO THE FIVE CIVILIZED TRIBES.

IN RE APPLICATION FOR ENROLLMENT, as a citizen of the Creek Nation, of Alice Hiawatha Aubrey , born on the 6 day of June , 1903

Name of Father: Charles Aubrey   a citizen of the   not   Nation.
Name of Mother: Millie Aubrey   a citizen of the   Creek   Nation.

Postoffice   Sapulpa

AFFIDAVIT OF ATTENDING PHYSICIAN OR MID-WIFE.

UNITED STATES OF AMERICA, Indian Territory, ⎫
        Western   DISTRICT. ⎭

I, H O *(Illegible)*   , a Physician   , on oath state that I attended on Mrs. Millie Aubrey , wife of Charles B. Aubrey on the 6th day of June , 1903 ; that there was born to her on said date a Female child; that said child was living March 4, 1905, and is said to have been named Alice Hiawatha .

H. O *(Illegible)*

Witnesses To Mark:

{

Subscribed and sworn to before me this 18 day of May, 1905.

Joseph Brewer
My commission expires 10/20-1906   Notary Public.

BIRTH AFFIDAVIT.

DEPARTMENT OF THE INTERIOR.
COMMISSION TO THE FIVE CIVILIZED TRIBES.

IN RE APPLICATION FOR ENROLLMENT, as a citizen of the Creek Nation, of Lena May Marshall , born on the 13 day of July , 1904

Name of Father: Thomas J. Marshall   a citizen of the ~~U.S.~~. Creek Nation.
Name of Mother: Belle   "   a citizen of the ~~Creek~~ U.S. Nation.

Postoffice   Coweta

314

Applications for Enrollment of Creek Newborn
Act of 1905   Volume I

(Child Present)

AFFIDAVIT OF MOTHER.

UNITED STATES OF AMERICA, Indian Territory, ⎫
　　Western　　　　**DISTRICT.** ⎰

　　　　Belle

　　I, ~~Lena May~~ Marshall, on oath state that I am 26 years of age and a citizen by ----, of the U. S. Nation; that I am the lawful wife of Thomas J. Marshall   , who is a citizen, by blood of the Creek Nation; that a female   child was born to me on 13 day of July, 1904 , that said child has been named Lena May Marshall, and was living March 4, 1905.　　　　　　　　　　　　　　　　Her

　　　　　　　　　　　　　　　Belle x Marshall

Witnesses To Mark:　　　　　　　　　mark
　　⎰ Benj. Marshall
　　⎱ ECGriesel

　　Subscribed and sworn to before me this 14 day of March , 1905.

　　　　　　　　　　　Edw C Griesel
　　　　　　　　　　　　　Notary Public.

AFFIDAVIT OF ATTENDING PHYSICIAN OR MID-WIFE.

UNITED STATES OF AMERICA, Indian Territory, ⎫
　　Western　　　　**DISTRICT.** ⎰

　　I, Sophy Luther　　, a Assistant Midwife , on oath state that I attended on Mrs. Belle Marshall , wife of Thos. J. Marshall on the 13 day of July , 1904 ; that there was born to her on said date a female child; that said child was living March 4, 1905, and is said to have been named Lena May Marshall .

　　　　　　　　　　Sopa[sic] Luther

Witnesses To Mark:

　　⎰

　　Subscribed and sworn to before me this 14 day of March, 1905.

　　　　　　　　　　Edw C Griesel
　　　　　　　　　　　Notary Public.

315

BIRTH AFFIDAVIT.

DEPARTMENT OF THE INTERIOR.
COMMISSION TO THE FIVE CIVILIZED TRIBES.

————————

IN RE APPLICATION FOR ENROLLMENT, as a citizen of the Creek Nation, of Lena May Marshall , born on the 13" day of July , 1904

Name of Father: Thos. J. Marshall   decd.   a citizen of the   Creek   Nation.
Name of Mother: Bell Marshall   a citizen of the non citizen   Nation.

Postoffice   Coweta Ind. Ter.

————————

AFFIDAVIT OF MOTHER.

UNITED STATES OF AMERICA, Indian Territory, ⎱
    Western Judicial   DISTRICT. ⎰

I, Bell Marshall, on oath state that I am 25 years of age and a citizen by -----, of the non citizen of Creek Nation; that I am the lawful wife of Thos. J. Marshall deceased, who is was a citizen, by blood of the Creek   Nation; that a female   child was born to me on 13" day of July, 1904 , that said child has been named Lena May Marshall, and was living March 4, 1905.   her
                                                        Bell x Marshall
Witnesses To Mark: mark
    ⎰ A E Carder
    ⎱ J F Darr

Subscribed and sworn to before me this 18" day of May , 1905.

My term expires   W.A. Brigham
    Oct. 28" 1906   Notary Public.

————————

AFFIDAVIT OF ATTENDING PHYSICIAN OR MID-WIFE.

UNITED STATES OF AMERICA, Indian Territory, ⎱
    Western Judicial   DISTRICT. ⎰

I, Archie E Carder   , a Physician   , on oath state that I attended on Mrs. Bell Marshall , wife of Thos. J. Marshall decd. on the 13" day of July   , 1904 ; that there was born to her on said date a female child; that said child was living March 4, 1905, and is said to have been named Lena May Marshall .
                                   Archie E Carder MD.
Witnesses To Mark:
    ⎰

316

Applications for Enrollment of Creek Newborn
Act of 1905   Volume I

Subscribed and sworn to before me this 14 day of March, 1905.

My term expires
    Oct. 28" 1906

W.A. Brigham
    Notary Public.

CERTIFICATE OF TRUE COPY.

United States of America.
Indian Territory,   ⎱ ss.
Western District.

I, **R. P. HARRISON**, *Clerk of the United States Court in the Western District, Indian Territory, do hereby certify that the instrument hereto attached is a full, true and correct copy of* a Marriage License *as the same appears from the records of my office.*

WITNESS my hand and seal of said Court at Muskogee, *in said Territory, this* 13" *day of* July *A. D. 19*05

By   John Harlan
          Deputy Clerk.

R.P. Harrison
    Clerk and Ex-Officio Recorder.
Book O page 305

United States of America.
Western Judicial District
of Indian Territory.

A. E. Carder, M.D. after being duly sworn says that he is a regular practicing physician, having practiced his profession at Coweta, I.T. for the three years last past; That he was in attendance at the birth of Thomas and Belle Marshall's child; which occurred on the 13th day of July A.D. 1904. That said child is a girl and is named Lena Belle[sic] Marshall.

A E Carder M.D.

Sworn to and subscribed before me this 13th day of March 1905.

)))) W.S. Vernon
       Notary Public.

My commission expires JAug[sic] 9 1908

MARRIAGE LICENSE

UNITED STATES OF AMERICA ⎤
    Indian Territory   ⎬ ss.   No.   156
    Western District ⎦

To Any Person Authorized by Law to Solemnize Marriage – Greeting:

You are Hereby Commanded to Solemnize the Rite and Publish the Banns of Matrimony between Mr. T. E. Marshall *of* Wagoner, *in the Indian Territory, aged* 28 *years, and* Mrs. Belle Bryant *of* Wagoner, *in the Indian Territory, aged* 21 *years, according to law, and do you officially sign and return this License to the parties therein named.*

(Seal

WITNESS my hand and official seal at Muskogee, Indian Territory, this 1st *day of* April, *A.D. 19*03.

                      R.P. Harrison
                      Clerk of the U.S. Court.

By A.J. Byrum Deputy.

CERTIFICATE OF MARRIAGE

UNITED STATES OF AMERICA ⎤
    Indian Territory   ⎬ ss.
    Western District ⎦

I, H. H. Lane Mayor of Coweta, *a ~~Minister of the Gospel~~, DO HEREBY CERTIFY, that on the* 19 *day of* Apr. , *A.D. 19*03 *did duly and according to law as commanded in the foregoing License, solemnize the Rite and Publish the Banns of Matrimony between the parties therein named.*

WITNESS my hand this 19 *day of* Apr. *A.D. 19*03.

My credentials are recorded in the office of the Clerk of the United States Court, Indian Territory, Western District, Book 1 , Page 1

                    H. H. Lane, Mayor
                    ~~A Minister of the Gospel~~

Filed and duly recorded, this 23 day of April 1903
By John Harlan Deputy   Book O page 305   R.P. Harrison Clerk U.S. Courts

---

Applications for Enrollment of Creek Newborn
Act of 1905   Volume I

NC 68.

Muskogee, Indian Territory, May 17, 1905.

Thomas J. Marshall,
    Coweta, Indian Territory.

Dear Sir:

In the matter of the application for the enrollment of your minor child, Lena May Marshall, as a citizen of the Creek Nation, you are advised that the Commission requires your affidavit as to the birth of said child.

There is herewith enclosed a blank form of birth affidavit, and in executing same care should be exercised to see that all blanks are properly filled, all names written in full and in the event that you are unable to write, signature by mark must be attested by two witnesses. Each affidavit must be executed before a Notary Public and the notarial seal and signature of the officer must be attached to each separate affidavit.

Respectfully,

BC.   Chairman.

NC 68.

Muskogee, Indian Territory, July 5, 1905.

Belle Marshall,
    Coweta, Indian Territory.

Dear Madam:

In the matter of the application for the enrollment of your minor child, Lena May Marshall, as a citizen of the Creek Nation, you are advised that there is no proof at this office of your marriage to the father of said child, Thomas J. Marshall, a citizen of the Creek Nation.

A certified copy of your marriage license or other satisfactory proof of your marriage to said Thomas J. Marshall should be forwarded at once to this office.

Respectfully,

Commissioner.

Applications for Enrollment of Creek Newborn
Act of 1905 Volume I

Copy

U.G. Phippen, President.   J.L. Dabbs, V.Prest.   W.S. Vernon, Cashier.

THE FIRST NATIONAL BANK,
Coweta, Ind. Ter. July 15, 1905.

Commissioner to the Five Civilized Tribes,
Muskogee, I.T.

Sir:

Herewith certificate of copy of marriage license—refer to your letter of the 5, inst., to Bell Marshall of Coweta--kindly return this to bank when you are through with this copy.

Yours truly,

Signed   W.G. Phippe[sic],

Pres.

Muskogee, Indian Territory, July 19, 1905.

U.G. Phippen,
Coweta, Indian Territory.

Dear Sir,

Receipt is acknowledged of your letter of July 15, 1905, enclosing copy of marriage license of Bell Marshall of Coweta.

Respectfully,

Commissioner.

N.C. 69.

DEPARTMENT OF THE INTERIOR,
COMMISSIONER TO THE FIVE CIVILIZED TRIBES.
Senora, I.T., March 15, 1906.

In the matter of the application for the enrollment of Nathanial McIntosh as a citizen by blood of the Creek Nation.

ROSA McINTOSH, being duly sworn, testified as follows:

320

Through Alex Posey official interpreter:

BY THE COMMISSIONER:
Q What is your name? A Rosa McIntosh.
Q How old are you? A Thirty to thirty-one.
Q What is your post office address? A Senora.
Q Are you a citizen of the Creek Nation? A Yes, sir.
Q To what town do you belong? A Tuckabatche.
Q What was your maiden name? A Rosa Beaver.
Q Who were your parents? A Sandy and Nicey Beaver.
Q To what town did your father belong? A Broken Arrow and my mother belonged to Tuckabatchee[sic].
Q Have you a child named Nathanial McIntosh? A Yes, sir.
Q What is the name of the child's father? A Dick McIntosh, who is also known as Greely McIntosh.
Q Do you know under what name he is enrolled? A I do not know.
Q to what town does he belong? A Hillabee.
Q Do you know whohis[sic] parents are? A Rosanna Herred was his mother but I do not know the name of his father.
Q Are you and Dick McIntosh now living together? A No, sir, we have separated and he has again married.

---oooOOOooo---

I, D. C. Skaggs, on oath state that the above and foregoing is a full and true transcript of my stenographic notes as taken in said cause on said date.

D.C. Skaggs

Subscribed and sworn to before me this 21st day of March, 1906.

(Name Illegible)
Notary Public.

N.C.69.   F.H.W.
DEPARTMENT OF THE INTERIOR,
COMMISSIONER TO THE FIVE CIVILIZED TRIBES.

In the matter of the application for the enrollment of Nathaniel McIntosh, as a citizen by blood of the Creek Nation.

D E C I S I O N.

The record in this case shows that on March 14, 1905, application was made, in affidavit form, for the enrollment of Nathaniel McIntosh as a citizen by blood of the Creek Nation. Supplemental affidavits as to the birth of the said applicant filed on June 19, 1905 and March 23, 1906, are attached to and made part of the record herein. Further

Applications for Enrollment of Creek Newborn
Act of 1905   Volume I

proceedings were had at Senora, Indian Territory, March 15, 1906, before a Creek enrollment field party.

The evidence shows that Nathaniel McIntosh is the child of Dick and Rosa McIntosh. Said Dick McIntosh is identified as Greely McIntosh, whose name appears on a partial schedule of citizens by blood of the Creek Nation approved by the Secretary of the Interior March 28, 1902, opposite No. 7253. Said Rosa McIntosh is identified as Rosa Beaver whose name appears on a partial schedule of citizens by blood of the Creek Nation approved by the Secretary of the Interior March 13, 1902, opposite No. 1493.

The evidence further shows that the said Nathaniel McIntosh was born on August 28, 1904 and was living March 15, 1906.

The act of Congress approved March 3, 1905, (33 Stats., 1048) provides in part as follows:

> "That the Commission to the Five Civilized Tribes is authorized for sixty days after the date of the approval of this Act to receive and consider applications for enrollments of children born subsequent to May twenty five, nineteen hundred and one, and prior to March fourth, nineteen hundred and five, and living on said latter date, to citizens of the Creek tribe of Indians whose enrollment has been approved by the Secretary of the Interior prior to the date of approval of this act; and to enroll and make allotments to such children."

It is therefore, ordered and adjudged that the said Nathaniel McIntosh is entitled to be enrolled as a citizen by blood of the Creek Nation, in accordance with the provisions of law above quoted, and the application for his enrollment as such is accordingly granted.

(Name Illegible) Commissioner.

Muskogee, Indian Territory,
January 16, 1907.

BIRTH AFFIDAVIT.

DEPARTMENT OF THE INTERIOR.
COMMISSION TO THE FIVE CIVILIZED TRIBES.

IN RE APPLICATION FOR ENROLLMENT, as a citizen of the Creek Nation, of Nathanial McIntosh , born on the 28 day of August , 1904

Name of Father: Dick McIntosh   a citizen of the Creek   Nation.
Name of Mother: Rosa McIntosh   a citizen of the   Creek   Nation.

Postoffice   Senora, I.T.

Applications for Enrollment of Creek Newborn
Act of 1905 Volume I

AFFIDAVIT OF MOTHER.

UNITED STATES OF AMERICA, Indian Territory, ⎱
    Western   DISTRICT. ⎰

    I, Rosa McIntosh, on oath state that I am 31 years of age and a citizen by blood , of the Creek Nation; that I am the lawful wife of Dick McIntosh , who is a citizen, by blood of the Creek Nation; that a male child was born to me on 28 day of August , 1904 , that said child has been named Nathanial McIntosh, and was living March 4, 1905.

Rosa McIntosh

Witnesses To Mark:

{

    Subscribed and sworn to before me this 15 day of March , 1906.

Drennan C. Skaggs
Notary Public.

AFFIDAVIT OF ATTENDING PHYSICIAN OR MID-WIFE.

UNITED STATES OF AMERICA, Indian Territory, ⎱
    Western   DISTRICT. ⎰

    I, Fannie Hawkins , a mid-wife   , on oath state that I attended on Mrs. Rosa McIntosh , former wife of Dick McIntosh on the 28 day of August , 1904 ; that there was born to her on said date a male child; that said child was living March 4, 1905, and is said to have been named Nathanial McIntosh .

her
Fannie x Hawkins
mark

Witnesses To Mark:
{ Alex Posey
  DC Skaggs

    Subscribed and sworn to before me this 15 day of March, 1906.

Drennan C Skaggs
Notary Public.

323

Applications for Enrollment of Creek Newborn
Act of 1905   Volume I

BIRTH AFFIDAVIT.

DEPARTMENT OF THE INTERIOR.
COMMISSION TO THE FIVE CIVILIZED TRIBES.

IN RE APPLICATION FOR ENROLLMENT, as a citizen of the Creek Nation, of Nathanial McIntosh , born on the 28 day of August , 1904

Name of Father: Dick McIntosh	a citizen of the Creek	Nation.
Name of Mother: Rosa McIntosh	a citizen of the Creek	Nation.

Postoffice   Senora, I.T.

AFFIDAVIT OF MOTHER.

UNITED STATES OF AMERICA, Indian Territory, ⎫
    Sixth   DISTRICT. ⎭

I, Rosa McIntosh, on oath state that I am 30 years of age and a citizen by Blood , of the Creek   Nation; that I am the lawful wife of Dick McIntosh   , who is a citizen, by Blood of the Creek   Nation; that a Male   child was born to me on 28 day of August , 1904 , that said child has been named Nathanil[sic] McIntosh, and was living March 4, 1905.

Rosa McIntosh

Witnesses To Mark:

{   My Commission Expires April 22, 1908.

Subscribed and sworn to before me this 13th day of June , 1905.

William B Morgan
Notary Public.

AFFIDAVIT OF ATTENDING PHYSICIAN OR MID-WIFE.

UNITED STATES OF AMERICA, Indian Territory, ⎫
    Western   DISTRICT. ⎭

I, Fannie Hawkins , a Midwife , on oath state that I attended on Mrs. Rosa McIntosh , wife of Dick McIntosh on the 28 day of August , 1904 ; that there was born to her on said date a Male child; that said child was living March 4, 1905, and is said to have been named Nathanil[sic] McIntosh .

her
Fannie x Hawkins
mark

Witnesses To Mark:
{ Joe S. Eaton
  John *(Illegible)*

324

Applications for Enrollment of Creek Newborn
Act of 1905   Volume I

Subscribed and sworn to before me this 13 day of June, 1905.

William B Morgan
Notary Public.
My Commission Expires April 22, 1908.

BIRTH AFFIDAVIT.

DEPARTMENT OF THE INTERIOR.
COMMISSION TO THE FIVE CIVILIZED TRIBES.

IN RE APPLICATION FOR ENROLLMENT, as a citizen of the Creek Nation, of Nathaniel McIntosh , born on the 28 day of Aug. , 1904

Name of Father: Dick McIntosh	a citizen of the Creek	Nation.
Name of Mother: Rosa "	a citizen of the "	Nation.

Postoffice   Senora

(Child Present)

AFFIDAVIT OF MOTHER.

UNITED STATES OF AMERICA, Indian Territory, ⎫
    Western   DISTRICT. ⎭

    I, Rosa McIntosh, on oath state that I am 30 years of age and a citizen by blood , of the Creek   Nation; that I am the lawful wife of Dick McIntosh   , who is a citizen, by blood   of the Creek   Nation; that a male   child was born to me on 28 day of Aug , 1904 , that said child has been named Nathaniel McIntosh, and was living March 4, 1905.

Rosa McIntosh

Witnesses To Mark:

    { -

Subscribed and sworn to before me this 14 day of March , 1905.

Edw C Griesel
Notary Public.

NC 69.

Muskogee, Indian Territory, May 17, 1905.

Dick McIntosh,
Senora, Indian Territory.

Dear Sir:

In the matter of the application for the enrollment of your minor child, Nathan McIntosh , as a citizen of the Creek Nation, you are advised that the affidavit of the midwife or physician in attendance at the birth of said child is required by the Commission.

There is herewith enclosed a blank form of birth affidavit, and in executing same care should be exercised to see that all blanks are properly filled, all names written in full and in the event that the person signing the affidavit is unable to write, signature by mark must be attested by two witnesses. Each affidavit must be executed before a Notary Public and the notarial seal and signature of the officer must be attached to each separate affidavit.

Respectfully,

BC.   Chairman.

NC 69.

Muskogee, Indian Territory, June 22, 1905.

Rosa McIntosh,
Senora, Indian Territory.

Dear Madam:

In the matter of the application for the enrollment of your minor child, Nathaniel McIntosh , as a citizen of the Creek Nation, you are advised that the Commission cannot identify Dick McIntosh, the father of said child, on any of the rolls as a citizen of the Creek Nation.

You are requested to inform the Commission as to the names of his parents, the Creek Indian Town to which he belongs, and if possible the numbers which appear on his deeds to land in the Creek Nation.

You are further advised that the name of your said child appears a Nathaniel and Nathanil McIntosh. You are requested to advise the Commission as to the correct name of said child.

326

Applications for Enrollment of Creek Newborn
Act of 1905 Volume I

Respectfully,

Chairman.

_____

NC-69

Muskogee, Indian Territory, December 11, 1905.

Rosa McIntosh,
  Care of Dick McIntosh,
    Senora, Indian Territory.

Dear Madam:

In the matter of the application for the enrollment of your minor child, Nathaniel McIntosh , as a citizen of the Creek Nation, you are advised that this Office cannot identify Dick McIntosh, the father of said child, on its rolls of citizens of the Creek Nation.

You are requested to inform this Office as to the names of his parents and other members of his family, the Creek Indian Town to which he belongs and, if possible, his name and roll number as same appear on his deeds to land in the Creek Nation.

You are further advised that the name of said child appears in the records of this Office as Nathaniel and "Nathanil." You are requested to ad vise this Office as to the correct name of said child.

This matter should receive your immediate attention.

Respectfully,

Acting Commissioner

_____

N.C. 69

Henryetta, Indian Territory, March 21, 1906.

Commissioner to the Five Civilized Tribes,
  Muskogee, Indian Territory.
Sir:
In the matter of the application for the enrollment of Nathaniel McIntosh as a citizen by blood of the Creek Nation, there is enclosed herewith the testimony and affidavits of the mother and midwife, taken March 15, 1906, in said case.

Respectfully,

Alex Posey
In Charge Creek Field Party.

N.C.69

Muskogee, Indian Territory, July 3, 1906.

Rosa McIntosh,
> Care Greeley McIntosh,
> > Senora, Indian Territory.

Dear Madam:

In the matter of the application for the enrollment of your minor child, born August 28, 1904, you are advised that the name of said child appears on affidavits in the possession of this office as Nathanial, Nathaniel and Nathinal.

You are again requested to advise this office as to which, if any, of the above is the correct name of said child.

This matter should receive your prompt attention.

Respectfully,

Commissioner.

NC 69.

EK.

Muskogee, Indian Territory, March 1, 1907.

Rosa McIntosh,
> c/o Dick McIntosh,
> > Senora, Indian Territory.

Dear Madam:

You are hereby advised that on February 15, 1907, the Secretary of the Interior approved the enrollment of your minor child, Nathaniel McIntosh, as a citizen by blood of the Nation, and that the name of said child appears upon the roll of New Born citizens by blood of the Creek Nation, enrolled under the act of Congress approved march 3rd, 1905, as number 1131.

The child is now entitled to allotment, and application therefor should be made without delay at the Creek Land Office, Muskogee, Indian Territory.

Respectfully,

Commissioner.

www.ingramcontent.com/pod-product-compliance
Lightning Source LLC
Chambersburg PA
CBHW020244030426
42336CB00010B/604